SMALL WONDERS

CHRISTY KENNEALLY

SMALL WONDERS

To Pat.
With our best
wishes – a speedy
recovery. We will
miss you in P.C.B
ENJOY
God Bless

Bernie & Brenda

MERCIER PRESS

Mercier Press
Douglas Village, Cork
www.mercierpress.ie

Trade enquiries to Columba Mercier Distribution,
55a Spruce Avenue, Stillorgan Industrial Park,
Blackrock, Dublin

© Christy Kenneally, 2005

Parts of this book were first published in
Maura's Boy in 1996 and *The New Curate* in 1997

1 85635 482 2

10 9 8 7 6 5 4 3 2 1

Mercier Press receives financial assistance from
the Arts Council/An Chomhairle Ealaíon

Printed and Bound by J. H. Haynes & Co. Ltd, Sparkford

CONTENTS

INTRODUCTION

The stories we loved as children in Cork's northside were stories about the childhood of our elders. The fire spat, the terrier twitched and we sat entranced on any available lap. These stories were a glimpse of the past and a setting for the present. They also gave us access to the loves, laughs and tears that shaped their lives.

My mother Maura died when I was five years old.

In the vacuum that followed, the stories of our kin assured me that I belonged to a 'long-tailed' loving tribe who would protect me from the dark.

The first section of the book, *Maura's Boy*, deals with the first ten years of my life. It is made up of the memories I have carried from that time into adulthood. It is not a history of that decade but rather a history of the heart and so the facts are always less important than the feelings.

The second section, *The New Curate*, deals with my time spent as a fledgling curate in the cathedral and as chaplain to St Patrick's Hospital, now renamed Marymount Hospice. It was known to generations of Cork people as 'The Incurable'.

In my youth, St Patrick's was a place spoken of in whispers. Behind its forbidding walls and reputation, I discovered an oasis of love, humour and heroism. I owe an enormous debt of gratitude to the patients, relatives and staff of St Patrick's who were my mentors and friends.

I couldn't have prepared this edition without the love and support of my immediate and extended family and the encouragement of my friends in the Vale of Clara. Memories, converted into stories, can become a monument of sorts to the remembered.

This is my intention and my hope.

Christy Kenneally

I

BEGINNINGS

Cork is a sharp bark of a word. It has none of the long-vowelled music of Galway or the rapid nasal cuteness of Kerry. It hits you a clip on the ear and stands there defying you to do something about it. The old joke goes that only Cork people can be homesick at home and, like many an old joke, it homes to the heart of the truth. Many an exiled Corkman, living abroad in Dublin or Boston, has incurred the wrath of his spouse by suggesting, 'We'll go home to Cork next summer.'

Cork is a place, a state of mind, a life-long passion for those born within the boundaries of its embrace.

My childhood city was as clearly defined as the red sandstone face of the North Chapel in crisp September sunlight. At that time it was laced into a corset of hills. In later years, it would run to fat toward Blarney, blurring into suburbs on the way to Kinsale. My world was bounded by the skyline at the rim of this nest that cupped the shiny domes of Cork. Beyond that rim was Ireland, a place we studied with no great interest at school. Kerry had the highest mountain, and the longest river drained out of the flat midlands at Limerick but that big red wedge at the bottom of the map was ours. My world was smaller still, because a river bisected my city.

The Lee trickled out of the lake at Gougane Barra and moved at a donkey-trot to Cork. At the edge of the city, opposite the Mental Hospital, it fell over a weir and in the confusion of white water split in two. The narrow south channel moved self-consciously through the college, stepping down another weir to bow under the Southgate bridge. At high tide, in high summer, it loitered green and stagnant outside the labour exchange before joining its sister beyond the City Hall.

The north channel moved broad and purposeful under the Shaky bridge, flanked by the Park and the cliff of Sunday's Well. It banked left at the Mercy hospital and threw up a spume of swans on the far bank before sailing under more bridges to the opera house. Looming over its left bank, the anaemic stalagmite of Shandon poked above the humble jumble of black-slated roofs, that balanced on the marble shoulders of St Mary's.

This was our river. It marked the boundaries between the high hills of the northside and the flat of the island at the city centre. Despite dire threats of grievous bodily harm and shouts of 'Come home here to me drowned and I'll kill ya,' we were lured, as children, down Shandon Street to the North Gate bridge. There we would climb the iron rails to marvel at the black mass of mullet or the skill of the 'strawkhaulers' as they whipped one for their supper in a frenzy of blood and small boys. Every morning, the northside workers would walk or freewheel across this bridge to shop and factory. And every evening, they would pull it up behind them like a drawbridge as they hunched into the hills for home.

The northside itself was honeycombed with neighbourhoods. These were clustered around the main arteries of Shandon Street and Blarney Street, Gurranebraher and Gerald Griffin Street, Roman Street, Fair Hill and Blackpool.

My mothers' parents, Christy and Bridget Hartnett, lived in a warren of lanes and tenements and crowded houses with half doors. This world within a world could be accessed from Gerald Griffin Street by a single arch, and so, appropriately enough, was called the 'Arch'. The Arch was not a place you passed through to anywhere. If you entered you belonged or you were observed until you absolved yourself by leaving. The high side was bordered by the wall of St Mary's Road. In the background, St Vincent's convent loomed behind its own wall. Christy and Bridget were part of a clan living with, around and above each other. Two of my grand-uncles and a grandaunt also reared families in the Arch. Years later, when my mother tugged me reluctantly to school through the Arch, we had to leave home early to give her 'talking time'.

'Is that the second fella, Maura? He's the spit of Christy Hartnett. Here's a lop for a candy apple, good boy.'

As I fidgeted behind her skirt, I was convinced that the whole world knew my Mam, and in that world, they did.

At some stage, my grandparents migrated to number four Convent Place. If you threw a stone (and I did) from the end of their lane, you could land it on the slates or on a cousin in the Arch. The Lane was off St Mary's Road, which ran by the sedate convent, past the unruly gate of the North Mon, on by the bishop's palace to Farna, where the country boys went to school. We basked in the boast that we had the most religious address in Ireland. My brother tried to spell it out one day for a fella in a Bronx bar. 'Convent Place, St Mary's Road, down from St Anne's Terrace, near Redemption Road.'

'Don't tell me,' interrupted the American. 'Jesus Avenue, right?'

At the main gate of the convent, a side road ran, skirting the wall to Wolfe Tone Street. Convent Place was a narrow cobbled lane, tucked into the left. On one side the houses stood cheek by jowl until they were blocked by the garden walls of the 'new houses' on Cathedral Road. Our side ended abruptly at number four. Then there was a rise of open ground which spread to a square behind the houses. This was mysteriously called the Quarry. At the high end of the Quarry was St Anne's Terrace. It was in a two up-two down house with an outside toilet, at the top of the lane, in No. 4 Convent Place, that my grandparents came to live with their four sons and two daughters. My mother Maura was the eldest.

My parents had a mixed marriage; my father was from the southside. His street, Wycherley Terrace, had the distinction of being entered through two arches. He was the only son of Katie Barrett, who buried her husband Michael, when my father was just a boy. Katie worked as a cook at the Penny Dinner to rear Dave and his three sisters. The times and circumstances being what they were, he left school early and went to work in the Hanover shoe factory. As with many of his generation, this gave him an enormous respect for education and a firm resolution that his children would have the chances he missed.

By some quirk of fortune, Dave got friendly with my mother's cousin Delia who lived in the Arch. The story goes that on his way up Shandon Street one evening, he met Maura as she came out of Ormond and Ahern's bakery carrying a bag of flour. The flour bag hit the footpath and Maura started to cry. The more romantic sources say he replaced the flour bag from his wages and Maura replaced Delia in his affections. It can't have been too serious between himself and Delia to start with as she became their bridesmaid.

Maura and Dave started a line that drew him into the home of the Hartnett's and his conversion to a northsider. She was a gregarious, impulsive girl, with a northsider's relish for 'ballhopping' (teasing) and a withering turn of phrase when she was crossed. He was shy and angular, and had a slight impediment in his speech when excited. Courting at that stage meant going for walks and going to matches. The household gods were the players in the local club and names like Jack Lynch and Jim Young could conjure thousands swathed in red and white, the blood and bandages, to Kent Station for the All-Ireland Final pilgrimage. Once Dave and Maura swayed along with the rest of them out the tunnel, waving flags at the children on the Blackpool embankment, as they rattled off to Dublin for the big game. Heady from the excitement of a great victory, he decided to splash out and brought Maura for her tea to a restaurant on O'Connell Street. Later they strolled at their ease beside the river to Heuston Station to catch the last train home. They were in time to see the last carriage leave the empty platform. ' The breath was knocked outta me,' he said, years later. 'In them days, there was no stayin' out. You had to bring the girl home.' Needless to mention, there was no phone in number four Convent Place or at any of the other numbers for that matter. In desperation, they phoned the garda barracks in Watercourse Road and explained their predicament. 'That guard was a man among men, boy. He saved our lives.' In an act of great sensitivity, often cited by my father in his honour, the guard changed out of his uniform when his shift was over and climbed the hill to Convent Place, knowing, only too well that a uniform at the door would alarm my Nan and alert the neighbours. 'They'll be down on the mail train in the morning, ma'am,' he said quietly.

Maura and Dave kept their cold vigil in Heuston Station and boarded the train at half past five the following morning, 'the longest journey of our lives.' Dave should have gone straight to work but insisted on going home with Maura to see her mother. My Nan was so taken by his thoughtfulness that she forgot any lecture she'd prepared, sitting distracted by the fire all night. All was forgiven and no barriers were placed in his way when he asked to marry her.

They went to Glengarriff for their honeymoon and returned to a flat over a shop on the southside. Leaving her beloved northside was the greatest test to her marriage vows. She lasted four days. When he arrived home from work on the fifth day, she was gone. My uncle Paddy was the nervous messenger.

'Hello Dave.'

'Hello Paddy. Where is she, boy?'

'She's gone home to Convent Place, Dave. She said you're to follow her up.'

He did. Shortly after that, they got the key to number six, just two doors down from my grandparents. It was as far away as she would ever voluntarily move and that became my home.

2

HOME

God turned the dark into light, and so did I. 'You turned night into day,' my father said. 'We'd be walking the floor at all hours of the night trying to pacify you and then you'd be out to the world for the day. We were jaded from you. I remember coming home from work one day and your mother stopped me on the step. "He's inside asleep in the front room,," she said. "I beseech you, in the name of all that's good and holy, don't wake him." I swear before God, I only put me eye to the crack in the door and you were off. 'Twasn't wishin' for me.'

Well, who could blame me? I had come from the glow of paradise to this half-light, peopled with monsters who leered into my pram making loud noises.

Most of my early memories are woven of light and water and Maura, my mother. Somehow it is always summer in these recollections and I am sitting on the step outside the front door. From this high throne, close to the sanctuary and safe from harm, I could oversee the doings of the day. There was a regular and comforting rhythm to the cycle of life about us. The women woke early, usually to the crying of a child. They rattled the range awake and set the porridge burping on the stove. Then the men were called for work. One of the jokes we loved as children was about the small boy at catechism class who was asked: 'Where did the Holy Family live?'

'In Blarney Street Miss.'

'How do you know that?'

'Well, when I was coming down to school this morning with

me Mam, I heard a woman shoutin', "Jesus, Mary and Joseph, get outta dat bed."'

My father always hit the floor running, maybe because the lino was so cold or, more likely, because he hated to be late for work. In later years, he would go immediately and hammer on the bedroom wall. 'Right, Dave', Johnny Mul would answer sleepily from next door. Washing and shaving was done in the kitchen sink, his braces dangling down behind him. He said his morning prayers there as well: 'Oh sweet sufferin' God!' as he splashed cold water in his face.

Click-click-click, Bertie Barrett coasted past the door, side-pedalling to Murphy's Corner before he swung his leg over the bar, heading for the ESB. Peggy and Sheila were next, their arms wrapped around them from the cold, their faces stretched with sleep, followed by the heavy steady tread of Mr Barrett, a dark block-like man with lively eyes. All obeyed the unwritten code of quiet that respected sleeping children in the huddled houses. Mr O'Leary never kicked his motorbike to life until he reached St Mary's Road.

The children's breakfast was a mixture of porridge and whingin'. I remember the little eye-bubbles, winking from the top of the porridge and the way the sugar melted into dark lines before rich milk raised an island from the bottom of the bowl. This was my oasis of interest in the middle of chaos.

'Mam, where's me book?'

'What book?'

'Me reading book.'

''Tis wherever you left it. Wash behind your ears, you caffler.'

'Mam, we must bring a penny for the black babies.'

'Them nuns must think we're made of money. Go on, the other ear. I have me eye on you. Come here to me. Look up.'

She licked the corner of her apron and scrubbed the crumbs from Michael's face.

'Hold his hand and cross the road at Annie's.'

Then, at the door, a drenching of holy water from the font,

and they were off, ribboned and capped, to school. I remember she'd sit sideways on the kitchen chair, her legs crossed, holding herself with her left hand, a cup of tea in the other, half awake in the sudden quiet of the kitchen. At last, the house and day were all our own.

We had a small house, a tiny kingdom of special places. The glass in our back door let in a square of sunlight on the bottom steps of the stairs. The lino there was gloriously warm, seeping up through my pyjama pants. I could close my eyes and float in a world of honey gold, smelling the rich polish from the brushes stacked in the corner and feeling the wax and wane of warmth as the light dimmed or strengthened through the panes.

A locked front door was an affront to neighbours. The door was always 'on the push' for Auntie from next door (no relation) or Dotey Purcell from up the lane or Nan from number four.

'Maura, will you call to Billy's for me? Three chump chops and two centre loins, and ask him for a small bit of suet. The poppies in Annie's are like balls of flour. Have Mulcahy's any fresh bodice?'

In a time before fridges, shopping was a daily pilgrimage, a social occasion for the women of the parish, and a mixed blessing for their children. I was harnessed into the go-car and bumped headfirst out the door down to Annie's. There was the smell of clay from the potatoes piled in the corner and the clink of the weights as the scales balanced. The serious stuff started on Shandon Street. The fresh-meat shop was a shop of horrors. Crubeens were stacked like firewood on a plate, drisheen swam in a milky dish and a pig's head glared from the window. Billy the butcher's was just as bad. Lamb carcasses swung from hooks and dripped dark blood into the sawdust on the floor. Livers pulsed purple under glass, and the sounds were always of hacking and chopping and the awful sound of the electric saw through bone. Billy and Mike were a study of synchronous movement, swerving in and out to chop, cut, weigh. 'There, ma'am, a lovely piece of meat.' Then wrapped in white paper, trussed with twine.

'That's three and six.'

'Ye bloody robber.'

Ormond and Ahern's was a cathedral kind of shop, brown and aching with the smell of fresh bread.

'Hold that pan for me like a good boy. Eat the crust and I'll kill you.'

The moving was great but parking was a problem. Maura liked to talk and perform. She would have the shop in roars about the gasman or the milkman. Meanwhile, I was being mauled by her audience.

'Would you look at the white head on him. Hello, blondie, will you give us a birdie?'

Long noses jutted from black shawls and stubbly kisses raked my cheeks. The upside was the penny bar which always worked itself sideways in my mouth and stuck. Grinning hideously and drooling brown spit like an eejit, I was parked outside the post office or the snuff shop until the damned thing softened enough to be chewed. Many of the women heard mass read at ten o'clock and read their neighbours until eleven, time to put the meat in the oven. The poppies went on at twelve and the table was set for the first invasion when the other two bowled in from school. From one to two was Dave's dinnertime. He ate solidly and stoically in a whirlpool of voices.

'The nun said ...'

'A boy in my class swallowed the mala.'

'Drink up that milk; hush for the news.'

There was always solemn silence for the news, Then back to school and work for them and peace and quiet for the two of ourselves.

Nailed to the wall at the left of our front door, a porcelain angel held a scallop shell of holy water. It was always half full of dusty liquid. The dust was salt. I discovered this when Michael obligingly gave me a leg-up for a drink. The gasmeter hung on the other side. 'I'm robbed from that,' she said. It was an intruder, a lodger, something she barely tolerated in the house.

Every morning, the threshold and hall would be scrubbed and

I would step across the archipelago of the previous night's *Evening Echo* to and fro. 'Don't put a foot on me clean threshold!' The open-banister'd stairs led down into the kitchen and doubled as an observation post above the action or as a perilous slide because of the kink at the bottom. Under the stairs, we had a 'caboosh', a sort of enclosed space, concealed by a small door. Here, the coats were hung and everything was flung that couldn't perch on a nail or nest in a drawer. I loved it. Maura ran for the Nan more than once before she discovered my hidey-hole. Auntie Nelly opened it one day to put in her shawl and went straight to confession after I appeared Lazaruslike from the gloom.

The caboosh smelled of must and mildew. Every hanger groaned under four coats of different sizes and textures but the gold mine was the floor. Under a topsoil of curtains and collarless shirts, lay the real nugget: an iron, high-heeled shoes, a handbag with a challenging clasp and my father's metal last, which I found with my knee. I could sit there for hours, eyes closed, feeling around with my hands, guessing the garment from the Braille of its texture, smelling out the lair of a Russian boot or a pair of galoshes snuggled up together in the dark. Every now and again, I'd make a grand entrance to the kitchen, 'Da-raaan!' sweeping out of the caboosh dressed in Nan's funeral hat, one clip-on earring, a tripping skirt and odd football boots.

'He'll end up in the opera house.'

The front room had a closed door with stippled glass panels. The doorknob was loose and challenging. Inside, on the left, the brown radio squatted on a bamboo stand. The table was solid and square, crosshatched underneath with beams from leg to leg. This was my boat above a lino sea, where I would sway to my own sea-sounds under a canopy of white wood and a fringed tablecloth. The window-sill was painted white and hosted a dusty geranium. Geraniums always had a fly-spray smell. For years, I thought it did kill flies because there were always bluebottle bodies strewn across the white landscape. The chairs had a green leatherette top with an interesting hole in one which I mined for dry stuffing.

Above the cast-iron fireplace, a mantelpiece held vases, souvenirs, and geegaws of every shape and hue but the holy of holies was the glass case. Enshrined on three glass shelves was the 'good' ware. China teasets and elaborate teapots, slabs of icing from someone's wedding cake and a small silver horseshoe exhausted my admiration. This was the great untouchable, opened only by adults or my eldest sister, with smirking superiority, whenever we had visitors. My mother had a 'plank' there, a secret stash of cash in a yellow teapot. As years went by, school certificates, insurance policies and all the archival material of the family, crowded the glass case. Even now, I can remember with awful clarity, the day I smashed the glass.

Michael was doing what older brothers do, annoying me. He was a practised disturber. Why we were in there or how I came to have a hurley I'll never know. I do know I missed him and hit the glass case. There was no dramatic crash and shower of splinters like in the pictures. There was the barest tinkle as a large jagged piece of glass landed on a teapot. For all its understatement, that tinkle was my death knell. We were shocked into comradeship by the disaster. Michael knew there would be no selective surgical strike, no smart bomb that would swerve around him and level me. Dave would discover and we would die.

We took off like greyhounds for number four, trying to get in first with accusation and excuse. He won.

'Auntie Noreen, he smashed the glass case.' The shock saved me. She deflated into a chair.

'Oh my God, and all the years that stood there!'

My bladder threatened to burst. 'Oh my God.' She looked through the hole as I tried to block sight of the hurley. Then she sat us down and calmly concocted a story for Dave. I was shocked and elated, shocked that a grown-up could come up with such a terrific lie and elated at how terrific a lie it really was. He might actually believe it. To her eternal credit, she stayed to face him. She waited until he was safely behind the table and into his tea. He listened, nodded and reached for the jam. We were weak with joy. We were the chosen people, God's elect. The avenging angel had passed us by to shag the Egyptians but we were saved. But I could see he didn't believe it. Thirty years later, I almost told him but something about that sacred repository of memories and the awfulness of its violation held me back.

Upstairs I never wanted to go. The shadows pooled on the landing and overflowed into the bedrooms. The bedroom was a place for shape-shifting. When the light went out, the shaky chair in the corner could suddenly grow another leg and move. I swear I saw it flicker in the corner of my eye. The wardrobe loomed, massive and menacing. Somebody told me of a bold boy who climbed into the wardrobe and it fell on him. My chest tightened at the thought of the suffocating dark, the boy swallowed up and gone. My father one time hung his coat on the wardrobe door and in the morning I lay transfixed in a cooling pool of terror.

Our fifth room was the yard. Our yard had high whitewashed walls, an outdoor toilet and a tap. There was a coal shed tucked between the toilet and the house. The wash on the walls would come off on your hands and on to your face and you could look in Bernie's pram and go 'Aaagh!'

'You lightin' caffler, and it took me hours to settle her!'

The sting of the teatowel lasted for ages but, 'twas worth it. My father was obsessed with having a clean yard; this was linked, I believe, to his fear of rats. He thought a trace of dirt in the yard would lure them up the shore and into the house. The way he spoke of rats obliged us to kill them with hurley or dog at every opportunity.

'They'd bring a fit of sickness on us all.'

I remember sharing a bedroom with him once. We had an oil heater in the room which we hardly used for fear we'd smother.

During the night I could hardly sleep so I drummed my fingers on the top of the heater. Tippity tap, tippity tap.

'Christy!'

'Yes Dad?'

'D'ye hear that?'

'What?'

'That scratchin'?'

'Ah, that's only me on the heater.'

I had him in the horrors.

There were houses that weren't as clean as our yard. One of the fastest ways to his good books was to bless it with Dettol and scrub it with the yard brush. 'Doubt ya, boy, a great clean smell!'

'No r-a-t-s here,' I felt like saying, as if to comfort a child.

The outside world had two borders. The marker stones at the end of the Lane blocked my passage to the possibility of being trampled by a horde of homing children from the schools or a clip from a freewheeling bike. The other end, where the Quarry met the Lane, was the wide open prairie. Neilus was my pal. We surveyed the world and planned our day risking piles on the cold concrete step outside Barrett's. One special day, we stood at the foot of the Lane, our eyes closed, hands outstretched touching the wall, and traced the contours of the Lane all the way to number four: Cremin's gable end, dashed and prickly, a patch of smooth warm plaster marked the flue; Auntie's house next door to ours, the bubbles on her painted door you could burst with your fingers; our door and the window, reach up and spin the shutter clasp, then, Mul's and Hartnett's, Nan's window lower than the rest. Then round the wooden pole tingling with warnings of electrocution, the rising slope to the low backyard wall, and then, the Quarry.

Oh the wonders of waste ground! The grass was high and lush at our end, vivid with dandelions. Pluck them and their revenge was ire. Later, we learned to rub their milky sap on warts. Pull a sod and there were worms and small dried spiders. Sometimes, we surprised an earwig and ran. We'd heard the horror stories from the big ones.

'And d'ye know what happened: the earwig ate his way right through his head and out the other ear. On me soul.'

Butterflies were a real challenge. Catch the two wings and you have a butterfly, catch the one and you have a creepy crawly, legs all over your hand. We crouched like tiny Sumo wrestlers in the grass, thumb and forefinger extended, ready to grip them when they closed their wings and dance them to the jar.

The centre of the Quarry caught the run-off after rain into three expansive pools. Lollipop stick ships left a wake of smoky brown as they sailed from shore to shore, urged on by a bombardment of small stones. Sometimes, Neilus couldn't wait. He picked up a rocker and launched it two-handed into the water.

'Hey, watch out, boy. I'm soaked. They're me new anklets; me Mam will mombilise me.'

These were summers of sensations, lying on our backs, with a wary eye for earwigs, watching the small clouds sail across the skylight of our world. We fell in and out of being pals a hundred times a day. My father wisely observed, 'Parents should never get involved when children fight. The children are playing again in five minutes, the parents don't talk for years.'

There was something else about Neilus that I haven't mentioned up to now. Why? Because it wasn't of any consequence then, but it serves to show how children accept and adapt to difference. He had a speech defect, rectified in later life. I had no problem with it; I understood him perfectly and automatically translated for him. In a group when we were deciding on where to play, I'd fill in the subtitles.

'He said he can't play down the front Quarry, his Mam won't let him.'

I never heard anyone from around the place mock him for it and a stranger never did it twice. There was one story of our friendship that became part of the local lore. Neilus must have been very sick because the doctor was called. I was at my tea at home, my mouth full of bread, and watching Michael's slice, when his mother arrived in the kitchen. 'Christy boy, come down and tell the doctor what ails Neilus.' I stood by his bed and translated for a man in a suit, who thanked me for my diagnosis with a tap on the head and sent me home a hero.

Teatime always came too soon. The deep bass Angelus bell of

the North Chapel, rang a curfew to our play and we trailed reluctantly home. Now the early morning sounds rewound themselves as bikes clicked homeward past the door and heavy footsteps sounded up the evening Lane. Hot milk for bed, a frowning skin floating on the top, sweet with sugar and spiced with a shake of pepper. We climbed into pyjamas before the fire, then, 'Up them steps. G'night and God bless. Not a word now, mind ye, don't draw me up that stairs.' Head to toe or back to back in the bed butting hollows in the bolster, we carved a warm cocoon beneath the spread.

'Take your feet outa me face.'

'You're taking up all the room, move out outta that.'

'Why didn't you go before you came up?'

'Boys! What did I tell ye? G'night and God bless.'

There were definite rites of passage in our tribe. Graduating from the cloth nappy to the potty was a major one, to be announced and demonstrated.

'Nan, look what I did! I'm a big boy now.'

The outside toilet was the honours course. The bowl was set into a shelf. The first task was to climb up backwards, the pants around the ankles. To the left and right were stubs of candles, and scraps of the *Echo* were hung beside me on a handy nail. Was there ever a newspaper that played so many roles in the lives of its readers? Dave bought it every evening for tuppence from the jolly paperboy on Flaherty's corner. The paperboy was as old as Dave but titles were hard to change. He was a reserved man, who called out the name of the paper rarely and self-consciously. Some of the others could make an opera out of it: 'Six a'clock *Echo*'

With his elbows on the table, Dave would turn first to the death column.

'God help us, hah, poor ould Batna. God be good to him, he's going to the chapel tonight.'

There followed a long discussion of how old he was, where he had worked, ('Sure he was years in Dagenham') and most importantly, was he related to us in any way. If that was the way we'd have to send an ambassador to the wake. Mutt and Jeff were firm favourites, to be read out and laughed at and, of course, the sports page was always a bone of contention. 'That fella is all the bars. He had nothin' to say about the eight in a row we won.'

The *Echo* wrapped messages, covered books, lined cupboards, went up under wallpaper, was a bedding and a draughter for the fire, protected washed floors from muddy boots and, exhausted of all other uses, ended up in the outside toilet. Even there, at its lowest ebb, it could be twisted into a makeshift fag, sucked ablaze from the candle, then puffed into a steady glow. More than once, I reeled in from the yard, blue in the face.

'That boy is very chesty?'

'Sure his father is the same; it runs in his crowd.'

I loved to sit out there in a downpour. The rain rattled on the corrugated roof and gurgled noisily down the shore outside. Thin wooden walls gave it an air of fragility as if the merest membrane seperated me from the elements. The other great thing about the outside toilet was that they would forget you were there. I always had big ears. They stuck out from the side of my head like indicators on a Ford Prefect.

'Maura, you should glue back his ears.'

'Yerra, he'll be all right when his hair grows.'

For a time I worried that because of these lugs if a big wind came I'd be blown away. One dawdly sunny morning near summer's end, they picked up the first signals of impending doom. Maura and a neighbour were chatting in the kitchen, the back door open, 'for a breath of air'. I filtered out their small talk until school was mentioned.

'Isn't he a bit young yet?'

'Sure he was four last April, girl. I have his name down in the Pres.'

'I still thinks he's a bit young. Wouldn't you hold on to him 'til next year?'

'No, he'd miss a book, and, anyway, he's runnin' wild around the place.'

This was serious. School was where the big ones went. According to them, you sat in a desk all day and put up your hand to go to the toilet. Why anyone would sit in a desk when they had only recently escaped from the captivity of the high chair was a mystery to me. Even more puzzling to me, from my lofty perch on the outside toilet, was why you had to put up your hand to go! The big ones also talked dramatically about slaps and something fearsome called a 'bata' which the nun kept in a special cupboard. I didn't like the sound of that animal at all. School was something we small ones played in the Quarry. We made a square of loose stones, and brought pieces of slate and a sharp stone for paper and pen. A girl always bossed her way to being the teacher. She put on an adenoidal Montenotte accent which jarred with the optional 'th-s' of our area.

'Now chuldrun, show me yur nails. Oh, look at dat: yur nails is turrible. Dis is de way to keep dem clean.'

This was not encouraging for a boy with an aversion to the facecloth. The pressure began to build as the summer waned. Nan bought my new school sack and presents of pencils and a rubber appeared. I played along to humour them, fitting on the sack that fastened in the front, and parading in my new knitted pullover, short pants and kneesocks. But I resolved in my heart that I would not go, sure she couldn't make me. The dreadful day dawned and we were tumbled to the lino, filled with porridge and swiped with a face cloth. As she took me by the hand, I lay out flat on the floor, passive resistance. Maura was made of sterner stuff.

''Tis up to yourself now. You can lie like that and be dragged to school or get up, like a good boy, and walk, but down to school you're going.'

She was true to her word; halfway out the hall I got up and surfed behind her down the hill. We wheeled left at Hill's shop, another cousin, and plunged down the Lane to the brown door. I was caught up in a stampede of new sacks, red eyes and runny noses, and she was gone.

Actually, it wasn't so bad but I wouldn't give her 'the soot of it'. She had broken the bond and now, she would pay. I usually started whingin' at Keating's on my way home from school. By the time I turned the corner into the Lane, I had changed gear twice and had a tuct in my heart. Eily Leary, an adopted aunt, was soft-hearted to a fault.

'What happened you boy? Did you get a slap? I'll go down and soften her face for her.'

I was well into my agony by the time the door opened. I wouldn't tell her anything; just rubbed my nose in misery along my sleeve. I had her distracted.

Delia lived in the Arch and Maura brought me there one evening after school.

'I'm demented from him Delia. He has me disgraced every morning.'

Delia took me by the hand.

'Come out here boy 'til I show you something.'

Intrigued I trailed her to the spacious back garden. Chickens! They were everywhere, picking and clucking and scratching all over the place. She bent into a box and wiped something on her apron.

'Now, Christy, if you're a good boy and go to school for your mother, you can call to my door for one of them every day,' and she put a smooth brown still-warm egg into my hands. Oh, the wiles of women, my education had begun.

We had a lady teacher who wore thick brown stockings. Every morning, after the half-nine bell had sounded from the chapel, we lined up in the yard and filed into school singing, 'Half-past nine, plenty time, hang your britches on the line.' We sat in wooden desks with a groove along the top for pens and a hole for the inkwell. Religion was big on the agenda and we started the day with the Hail Mary. Wacker sat beside me. He was a 'wilder' and I was in awe of him. 'Hail Mary,' she'd intone in a loud voice. 'Full of grace,' we roared back. 'The Lord is a tree,' Wacker whispered. God, he was desperate. I loved him. When we went to the yard for our break, we got an aluminium 'ponny' of watery milk and a dry bun. Sometimes, Wacker produced a length of twine which he looped around my neck and under my arms as reins. Then horse and driver, we galloped around the yard scattering the girls. Later in the day, we had, 'Teir a chodladh' [go to sleep]. On that instruction, we folded our arms and laid our heads on the desks for a sleep. 'Hey Wacker?'

'Wha'?'

'What does she do while we're a chodladh?

'She changes her nylons!'

Neither of us slept much after that.

The Lane outside the school had a soft yellow-brick wall. We could scrape some of the dust into our palms, spit to make a mixture and polish a penny to pure gold. While we were starting the best days of our lives, the pigs in Denny's bacon factory were losing theirs and the air resounded to their squeals. The factory smell was all pervasive to the point that the locals ceased to notice. Across the road, in Gerald Griffin Street, the vegetable shop overflowed into crates along the path. Almost every day, I took a carrot from the stall and chewed it thoughtfully all the way home. In later life I was convinced that the combination of Delia's eggs and the stolen carrots gave me high cholesterol and terrific eyesight.

The really great days were when the priest called. 'God bless the work.' Fr O'Sullivan was bigger than Dave and he had wavy black hair over a red face. As soon as he walked in the door, all semblance of sanity and order flew out the window. Like all children, we recognised and responded to an adult who was a bigger child than ourselves. He drew us into occasions of sin, vying with each other to tell the tallest tale. Then he would put his fingers in his mouth and whistle long thrilling bird calls. Sometimes he got totally carried away and, to the teacher's confusion, declared a half-day. We boiled around him, tugging at his coat for notice.

'What's your name boy? Sure I know your Nan well and your uncle Josie.'

He did and would appear at home for the dues.

'No, no ma'am. I'm only up from the table. Well, if you're sure you have enough,' and he'd put his long legs under the table like the rest of us.

I found the lessons easy enough, rattling off the tables with the help of fast fingers but reading was my passion. A houseful of comics was a great incentive but I longed to do more than look at the pictures. The real story was in the balloons that came out of their mouths. Little did I know that cracking that code of letters and gaining access to the plot, would limit my imagination but it did, as television would do to a generation reared on the radio.

There was yet another ritual I had to experience before I could be classed a 'big boy', a haircut. Maura's skills as a stylist were limited to the 'bowl' cut. She simply combed it all down flat and snipped the fringe in a straight line all round. Now that I was a schoolboy, I could go on Saturday with Michael and Dave to Mr Regan's. His shop was a single room at the top of Gerald Griffin Street, beside Coleman's. It was no bigger than the front room at home but was magnified by the two large mirrors on the wall. Two enormous highbacked chairs squatted before the mirrors. These were covered with red leather and had arm rests. A plank across the arm rests was a seat for a child. Arrayed before the mirrors on a narrow shelf were all the tools of the trade. It was filled with bottles of hair oil, some of them two-toned, and cards of styptic pencils and combs. The lino always wore a soft drift of hair and a padded bench ran around the wall. But the glory of the shop was overhead. Cages of canaries, finches and linnets bordered the wall at ceiling height. We sat under their cages reading our comics waiting our turn, hoping that that small bump on the head was corn. Mr Regan was a small balding man, trim and tidy, with the erect bearing and direct clipped manner of an old soldier. The men would hang their caps behind the door and shuffle into the seat for a shave. Mr Regan swung the cloth around them like a conjuror and tucked the top inside their shirts. Then he sharpened the ivory-handled open razor on a leather strap. The ritual involved laying a hot white cloth over the face while he arranged a piece of paper on the victim's shoulder, so he could wipe the excess from the blade. The talk never faltered. Dogs, birds, matches, hunted, flew and played around the room in rapid-fire argument. Mr Regan was in the thick of it, varying the sweep of the razor to match the intensity of the debate. Speed had no place in his vocabulary nor was it expected by his patrons. As small boys, we preferred Finbarr, his son, a gentle smiling young man who was the soul of tact and good humour. When my turn came, I was hoisted on to the plank. Mr Regan pushed my head forward with his left hand and held the hand-worked clippers in his right, plying me with riddles along the lines of: 'If a man and a half dug a hole and a half for a day and a half ...' He was an original barber, committed to the simple concept of the haircut. You paid your shilling and that's what you got, right into the bone. 'There you are now, boy: that'll keep you going for another while.'

Head suddenly cold, I would rush home to wash my hair in the sink and soothe the prickling of small hairs inside my collar.

My worst day in school was the day I had 'a little accident'. The fact that I considered myself a 'big boy' made it all the more awful. I suppose the warning signs were evident. I was feeling frettish that morning and had a pain in my stomach, which Maura diagnosed as 'schoolitis', a regular condition that cleared up by being ignored. It didn't and halfway through the morning, the inevitable happened. Wacker was subtle as ever.

'Miss, I tink he's after doin' his number two.'

I remember she kept her distance, standing in the aisle of desks near the top.

'Why didn't you put up your hand? Go on, go straight home.' It was the longest journey of my life. I hobbled up Gerald Griffin Street, trying to keep to the dry front of my pants, my disgrace trickling disconsolately into my socks. Maura was out and the house was being minded by Mary Kate, a distant relative. Mary Kate hadn't chick nor child and was ill-equipped for this emergency.

'God, you're home very early. Your Mam won't be long. What's wrong? Oh Jesus Mary and Joseph, go out in the yard quick and take off that pants.'

I stood in the middle of the yard miserable and crying, my treacherous trousers pooled around my feet, as Mary Kate connected the hose to the cold tap and sprayed me. I remember thinking then that nothing worse could ever befall me but I was wrong. Already the clouds were gathering at the edges of my world and when the lightning struck, the world I knew would be no more and I would never be the same again.

3

MAURA

The year 1953 is a shattered mirror. There is no complete picture of events in my mind, only sharp and painful slivers. I remember Maura had a headache and I had to be a good boy and hush. We were standing in the limed backyard, pale with reflected sunlight. She took a drink of water from the outside tap.

'God, I think I've swallowed a spider.'

There was a song doing the rounds at the time about an old lady who swallowed a spider that 'wriggled and wriggled and tickled inside her'. The last line was: 'Perhaps she'll die.' I watched her very carefully but she managed to make it back to the sanctuary of the kitchen, moist and warm with the smell of ironing. Our Nan began to spend more time with us than she did in number four, to give Maura 'a bit of a break'. Neighbours, who would normally breeze into the house, came cautiously, wrapped in shawls, perching on the edges of kitchen chairs.

'How is she, ma'am?'

'The same, girl.'

'We're stormin' heaven for her.'

'Sure I know that.'

One of the visitors brought grapes in a damp paper bag and distractedly handed them to me. I went up the stairs to her bedroom, my hands and jaws moving very fast, my feet moving very slowly, and sat at the end of her bed.

'Oh grapes! Are they for me?'

'No,' I replied, 'they're mine,' and ate every single one. Being good was an awful strain and the games in the Quarry were a great escape into normality.

'She's gone up to Dublin, shifted. Sure 'tis all in the hands of God now.'

Dave and my grandfather disappeared and Auntie Nelly, my Nan's sister, became a fixture. Good news percolated from the kitchen through the lattice of the bannisters to the small group huddled in pyjamas on the stairs.

'Dave and Pop, are staying with the Donovan's in Dublin.' Paddy, Liz and their daughter, Hannah, our Dublin cousins, opened their hearts and their home to the two men who kept the vigil at her bed in St Vincent's on the Green.

'Wait 'til I tell you. When Dave and Pop went home for their tea, she was sitting up in the bed. "Here's Paddy," she told the nurse, and Paddy walked into the ward all the way from America.'

These were sparks of hope to be fanned in the telling and retelling as they waited.

There is a scene that is printed indelibly in my memory. Nan and Auntie Nelly sit flanking the fire in number four. They seem to be listening for something and this quells our talk. Kay, my eldest sister, is sitting upright on the green topped chair near Nan. She is wearing her school gymslip and sits very upright, her hands in her lap, her feet crossed. She too seems to be listening. Michael and I are sitting on the mat before the fire, giddy with uncertainty. Even Bernie, the baby, is hushed by the mood of the room. There are heavy footsteps outside the window and the front door opens. Pop, my grandfather, and my father loom large in their belted overcoats. My father's face is tight, a mask of high white cheekbones and shadows. Pop's powerful shoulders are lost in the big coat, his normally bright round faced is stretched into a puzzled expression. He looks at my grandmother and shakes his head. Nan and Nelly begin to cry, a terrible suffocating soundless crying that pulls their lips inwards and their eyes closed. Kay joins their crying from the chair. Michael and I are skitting with fright while Bernie looks from one to the other, lost.

We were farmed out to relatives for the funeral. It was the way at the time. There would be scenes they thought we shouldn't witness and perhaps our reactions would be too much for them to bear. Auntie Noreen's friend, Monica, spirited us away to a high house in Blarney Street where herself and her sisters tried to distract us with songs from the show in the opera house. At some stage, I was sent to a cousin in Spangle Hill, a woman about my mother's age who had a big girl and a boy almost as old as me. His name was Eddie. She fussed over me in a distracted kind of way. Once, she came out of the kitchen, her apron to her eyes.

'Are you cryin'?' I asked her.

'Ah no, boy,' she said quickly, 'I'm making chips.'

That made perfect sense. Chip shops were beginning to become popular on Fridays and my Dad disapproved of them. He said that chips weren't proper food at all and only lazy mothers got them for their children. She was ashamed of herself. Well she might cry! But, there was something wrong, something very wrong. I was getting too much attention and no correction. Eddie innocently added to my foreboding. Probably threatened into generosity by his mother, he produced a biscuit tin full of Dinky toys.

'You can play with them if you like.'

When five-year-olds play there is an understanding that: 'What's yours is mine and what's mine is me own.' There was something very wrong. We arrived home to find black crepe on the door. All the women looked pale and washed-out in black skirts and cardigans and my father wore a black tie and a black cloth diamond on his sleeve. I will never forget their eyes, red rimmed and haunted as if constantly on the verge of tears. None of them had an ounce of energy. Only Bernie asked the question that choked the rest of us.

'Where's me Mam?'

'She's up in Dublin in hospital love, sure you know that, out now and play.'

We were building a dam to block the narrow channel in the Lane when Bernie nudged me.

'C'mere, Mammy's dead you know.' She said it in her matter-of-fact ould woman's voice.

'Who told you that?'

There was always some scut who delighted in telling small ones things they didn't need to know.

'Sure they're all saying she's up in Dublin, in hospital,' she continued. 'She is in me eye.'

Dead was something we knew. Early on, we had discovered a second community living in the Lane. Under the eaves of every house, nested a large clan of sparrows. We called them 'spadgies'. These dusty, freckled birds mirrored the life below, chirping busily in the morning, foraging to and fro from bin to bin throughout the day in search of a crust, swapping contented small talk as the sunlight slanted in the evening and the shadows filled the Lane with silence. Every now and then, we'd find a young one dead on the Lane, a faller, all yellow beak and baldy body. We knew the rituals and went about our tasks. Someone borrowed a matchbox from Granda Sutton. He had a soft hat and enormous white whiskers. A gardener, he had never lost his country accent for all his years in the Lane. I took the good cloth from the table in the front room and this was wrapped around Neilus, as he was the biggest. Neilus held the matchbox in his two hands, out before him like an offering. Jim Mack and I were his two altar boys, holding up the corners of his cope on either side. We moved in procession up the Lane and into the Quarry, an unruly mob of mourners following behind. Then, we dug a sod and placed the matchbox in the hole stamping the sod flat again. 'Buzz, buzz, buzz,' Neilus intoned, because that's what the priest said in Latin every Sunday. But this dead was different: Maura had gone away, disappeared and not come back.

Signs of my new status were everywhere. I was bold at school one day and the teacher made a drive at me but she walloped Wacker instead. Wacker never minded a clatter on credit; he could always earn it later but I knew it marked me out of the ordinary. Dave and Pop took us walking as always on Sunday mornings after mass. Men would stop them on Nash's boreen to shake hands.

'I'm very sorry for your trouble.'

We came home with pockets of tanners and threepenny bits weighing on our hearts. Our consolation was the clan that spread wider and knit closer than we had ever known before. Our Nan just slept in number four, appearing at first light in our house to tackle the doings of the day. The freight of cut knees and tales from school and tears were laid in the print apron of her ample lap. I remember her as a big woman of temper and tenderness, her still black hair tied back behind her head, her hands always moist from washing and scrubbing. Auntie Nelly too became a regular, especially in the evenings. Where Nan was broad and bustling, her sister was a porcelain doll, a madonna in a black shawl. She had silky snow-white hair and milky short-sighted eyes.

'Would you thread that needle for me, alanna. That's right, lick the end of it. Are you done? Wisha God bless and spare your eyesight!'

These were the rocks who underpinned the rubble of our lives, and there were others.

Noreen and Eily, our aunts, brought life and laughter to our home. On Saturday nights, we were scrubbed in the aluminium bath and set in our pyjamas on the mat before the fire to dry our hair. Armed with forks and slices of bread, we toasted the night supper to the grate. The toast was always striped from the barred grate and flavoured with ash. My aunts would whirl around the house preparing for the 'Ark'. The Arcadia Ballroom on the Lower Road was the Mecca for northside dancers. Noreen and Eily raced around the house, half-dressed, a crown of curler thorns bubbled on their heads.

'Mam, is me hem straight?'

'You could tug it down a small bit.'

'Auntie Noreen you have a ladder.'

'Where? Go 'way, ye ballhopper. Hold up the mirror for me.'

They made the most amazing faces streaking on the lipstick that would then be blotted on the *Echo*; where else? Their friends, the 'girls', Monica and Eileen would arrive later and the four would flounce away, leaving the front room heady with talc and perfume.

'If you can't fascinate them, intoxicate them,' Bernie would remark dryly years later. We called all the women who came and went 'Auntie', though some were cousins and some were no relation in the world. Mamie was a real aunt, my father's sister from the southside. Mamie worked in the M Laundries in the Mallow Road and came every week to 'give a hand' and collect the washing from my Nan. We knew her step and bate each other to the door because she never came empty handed. Rolos, Crunchies and three-penny bars of chocolate came with teasing slowness from the bag.

'I dunno if I've anythin' for you.'

'Ah Mamie.'

Saturday was her big day in our house. An early riser, she'd walk from the southside and announce her presence in a haze of Woodbines.

'Are ye still in bed? My God, and half the day gone.'

She had no sense of smell, and that, combined with the ever-present fag was a lethal combination in a house that revolved around gas. Often enough, someone had to rush down the stairs to save us all from suffocation or explosion. 'Well, it got ye out of bed anyway,' she'd say philosophically. Auntie Nora Mack would also come from Grawn, and Mary Anne, who was no relation at all but treated like blood all the same. Mary Anne had a big nose. Some-one remarked, to censure from my Nan, that she could 'smoke a fag in a downpour'. I was fascinated by it but was kept in check by looks from Nan. Once I couldn't contain myself: 'Mary Anne, what happened your nose?'

Nelly got a fit of coughing and Nan rolled her eyes up to Heaven but Mary Anne took it in her stride.

'A slate came off a roof in a storm, love, and broke me nose.' When she left, I was crucified for being 'pass-remarkable'. These women were the heart of the house; the fresh tender skin that grew around the hurt in our hearts.

The men, my father and grandfather, were gone to work by the time we got up, and only came into our lives in the evening. We watched for Pop at half past five and took a running jump from the low wall in St Mary's Road, to ride his arms to Convent Place. We hovered at his elbows as the Nan heaped the poppies, bursting out of their jackets, on his plate. 'Ye're eyes are bigger than ye're bellies,' she'd say, swaddling a spud for each of us in greaseproof paper, and we'd race off with our prize, to eat it on the road and watch for Dave. At six o clock, he weathered the charge, striding up the path. We pecked like magpies at his tea and his attention. I remember, his clothes always smelled of leather and solution, the glue they used in the factory. The creases on his palm were lined with it and we would pick it out with our nails. He had hairless white forearms and a big lump above the wrist of his right hand. 'A bullet in the war,' he said and we believed him.

On Saturday afternoons, he took us two boys to bowling matches in Togher. I hated it. I remember the deadly stop-start boredom, as men with shirtsleeves rolled up to their elbows held the twenty-eight ounce bowl in white fists and tightened up to run. They started their run with the bowl outstretched, aiming where they wanted it to go, then swung with mighty force to fire the bowl explosively away, hanging in the air to watch the flight. Another man stood in the middle of the road chanting encouragement and advice. 'Lave her down here! Toss boy!' pointing at a spot on the crown of the road, that would kick with sparks as the bowl rode the camber right around the bend. Others boiled off the ditches, flapping their coats like matadors before the charging bowl, shouting in its wake, 'All the way, all the way, a bowl of odds.'

The barrier of bridge or sharp corner would be lofted, the bowl soaring up on an intake of breath to explode on the far side in whoops and cheers. I hated it. We dangled out of him, our hands in his pockets for warmth. Eventually, he'd take pity on us and walk the bordering ditches, foraging for nests. Like many another cityman Dave had a reverence for nature.

'Stand still now!'

He would slap the ditch with the flat of his hand and a robin shot out to chide us from afar.

'Don't lay a finger on them now lads, or she won't come back.'

The eggs were like blue marbles, in a cup of woven grass and feathers. Sometimes there was a mound of down that flowered into yellow beaks when we blew kisses. Trailing behind the bowlers, he taught that leaves had veins like us, and why the moss grew only on that flank of a tree.

In the spring, he took us under the Eight-Arched bridge to gather bluebells for the May altar in school, and sometimes, there was the bonus of a steam train overhead, hammering our ears with sound as we clung to his knees and screamed in terror and delight.

Wading happily through the purple haze, we were not to know that the lofty bridge that spanned above us or the humbler one across the valley nearby, marked a watershed in Dave's life. Many years later, he told us how after Maura's death he would go walking, always alone, always striding long and fast as if to stay ahead of his pain. One summer evening he walked to Whitechurch to visit her grave and made his way homeward by the lower bridge. The weight of his mind was more than his legs could carry, he swung them over the parapet and sat there on a cushion of moss.

'I had terrible thoughts in me head. How would I manage? Then a woman came along. I knew her to see and saluted her. She sat up on the wall beside me, just talking about children and the way things turn out. After a while, she wished me luck and went home. And d'ye know, I was in the better of it. I got down off that bridge and went home to me own house.'

Then he paused and asked with all the openness and wonder of a child 'I dunno was she my guardian angel?'

Murphy's Rock was at the top of the valley. We entered over a stile and passed the ruined mill to cross the stream for primroses. Murphy's Rock was the Riviera of the northside. Families left the lanes in summer to paddle or swim in the stream. The women sat on blankets, their legs tucked up under bright skirts watching the small ones at their play. The men were in their shirts and braces, reading the paper or, 'balmed out' under it. Dave's hanky doubled as a net as we swung it up under the weeds to catch the wriggling tawrneens for the jam jar. Always too soon we'd hear, 'Come on now, boys. 'Tis turning cold.' Jam jars swinging on twine loops, he urged us up the hill. One magic evening, he caught an owl. It was sitting on the sill of the mill window dazed, dazzled by the last of the light. He crept along the wall and grabbed it by the legs, then promptly turned it upside down as it pecked his fingers. After we had a good look from a safe distance, he let it go.

'Sure isn't it one of God's creatures like ourselves!'

Sundays, after mass, we were joined by Pop for a walk.

'Put away that book and come on. 'Twill put a bit of colour in your cheeks.'

We turned at the top of the green, passing Johnny Mahony's pub; the boundary wall of the convent and the little house where the two sisters taught piano was to our right. Michael and I picked up the pace there in case the men got any notions. Then on by Mullane's shop and into the slope of Fair Hill past the Mon gate on our right and Auntie Nelly's house up on a height on the left. We skirted Leary's field across the top of Churchfield. Below us the North Chapel and Shandon were tiny and the silver thread of the estuary wound down beyond Blackrock Castle. The North Mon field delayed us as they commented on a match. We saluted the Shea's, our cousins and Timmy Delaney the bowler, then turned at the reservoir to downhill past the Croppy Boy and add a 'rocker' to its mound of stones. Before us, the view ran clear to Blarney, the blue hummocks of the mountains a faint outline in the far distance.

'Would you look at that, Dave,' Pop would always say. 'The finest view in Ireland.'

Nash's boreen snapped with dogs of all makes and shapes; dopey hounds with small men surfing on their leather leads, and saucy, cocky terriers, worrying the ditches for rats and rabbits. We turned for home again at Mickey Sullivan's pub, a tether of dogs patient at the door. Our two non-drinkers never broke their stride except to let us slake our thirst and soak our shoes at the water pump. Then, over the brow of the Hill, coasting ever faster home for the dinner.

'I could ate the legs of the table.'

Sunday afternoons were 'down the Park', walking, of course, to the match. I remember the crush of the crowd and the clicking of the turnstile, pressed up against Pop's coat. 'Two adults please.' Our spot was behind the goal at the city end, under the scoreboard, where Jimmy Rourke flashed up the numbers and ran an unofficial commentary on the game. Our Uncle Joe played for the Glen. He shared the banded jersey with Ring and Young, Lyons, Twomey, Mul and Creedon, the northsider's household gods. Michael was infected early with the fever, swaying under his cap in perfect time with the two men to watch the flight of the ball. 'Get under it, get under it. Ah lovin' God, ref.' Sometimes the roar would soften to a hush and I'd come back from throwing stones into a trough of green water that bordered the ground. The small baldy man would stand squat above the sliotar, facing a massed line of blue jerseys in the goal.

'Put it over Christy! Take your point, boy.'

'Is it mad you are? Sure we're two points down. Shush!'

Alone in the sudden quiet in the eye of the hurricane he would bend. As if on cue before his baton, the bunched choirs on the hills about began a roar that mounted as he lifted, tossed and smashed the white blur into the net. The roar cracked and peaked to madness as caps flew, men danced with men and the green flag fluttered from beside the post. I saw a ship move majestically up the river behind the stand.

'Pop, look at the boat!'

'Where did we get him, Dave?'

'I don't know Pop. I don't know.'

Home by Ford's and Dunlop's, the sidecars clattering past with cheering men and women to Blackpool; then up the hill again to Swiss roll or fairy and queen cakes, droolingly hot out of the oven. The match was replayed over the oil cloth, Dave moving the milk jug and sugar bowl into strategic positions. The excitement of a goal was too much for him so he'd stand up to tell that bit. After tea, the coats were on again for the Miraculous Medal devotions in the North Chapel. We always sat on the left side of the main aisle, surrounded mostly by women, as we barrelled through the hymns, Pop's bass and Dave's baritone a palpable sound all about us. 'Oh purest of creatures, sweet mudder, sweet maid,' accompanied by Herr Fleischman, the organist. The rosary droned interminably on. We perked up at Benediction as the incense clouded up around the plaster saints. Then last of all, coped in gold, the priest raised the monstrance to jangling bells, and blessed another County for the Glen.

4

UNCLES

If the women healed our hearts, and Pop and Dave propped up our broken world, our uncles, Maura's brothers, were our heroes.

Uncle Paddy was our piece of exotica, our ace card in all besting arguments. We let the others up the ante about uncles in Liverpool and London before we trumped them with Paddy. 'Anyway our uncle lives in New York and flies aeroplanes.' They were shot down in flames. Actually, Paddy was a purser with TWA. For a long time, I thought he was like a bus conductor on an aeroplane, walking up and down the aisle with a leather sack and a ticket dispenser saying, 'Fares please.' The postcards came regularly from all parts of the world to be studied for news and steamed for the stamps. Even better were the long light blue envelopes he flighted home to our Nan, crinkly with dollars. Nan would get the first read and dab her eyes as it did the round of the table. Pop would hold it a foot from his glasses, head tilted back.

'He says he's off to Egypt next week, by Jove.'

'By Jove' was a souvenir Pop brought home from Dagenham. I tried it out a few times on the lads in the Quarry but no one took a blind bit of notice so I dropped it. We sailed up the Lane fluttering our dollars, up to our elbows in envy before changing them for seven and six in the Shandon Street post office.

'Maybe he'll be home,' Nan would say wistfully. 'Please God he won't,' we added silently, pockets heavy with silver from the States. Both houses were littered with souvenirs from his travels, a bone-handled wicked-looking letter opener in Pop's we fantasised into a dagger, and a German Stein in our glass case that played an unrecognisable tune when lifted from the shelf.

Nan's prayers were answered when Paddy came home. Cars were hired from O'Connors and all manner of bangers were pressed into service to convey the clan to Shannon. I was bundled into John Downey's station wagon and had a choice of laps. I woke occasionally to a soft thumping sound against the car. 'Rabbits,' said someone in the dark. 'Sure the country's crawlin' with them.' I dreamed of country roads, carpeted with furry rabbits, and two long tracks of squashed ones where our cars had passed.

He came through the gate in a shiny Yankee suit. I expected him to be in black and white like the pictures. He was smaller than I expected with jet black receding hair and a huge toothy smile. Wading from hugs to handshakes, he picked me up in his arms. 'Gee, will you look at this guy!' he said. I decided he was the genuine article. Paddy was a bundle of energy with a mad infectious laugh. The two houses crackled with life while he was home and we trailed after him like Murphy's pup.

'Can you give us a lift to the pictures?'

He had hired a car, a Zodiac, an enormous concoction of fins and chrome. 'Sure thing. Let's go!' Twelve children rushed the car. He pulled up outside the Coliseum cinema and we swaggered across the road, absolutely septic about ourselves. I remember the gawping of the queue and the embarrassment of finding we were threepence short and doing 'Eeny, meeny, miny, mo' to see who would beg the difference. Paddy never forgot a birthday and marked each one with a sensible educational present. At the time, we regarded them as just one step above a pullover or a new pair of shoes but I can remember a dictionary that served as judge and jury for years of Scrabble disputes and an encyclopaedia sent for me in 1959 that pushed the horizons of my imagination far beyond the limits of the Lane.

Trips in Paddy's humble Volkswagen to Fountainstown for a swim were a mixed blessing. Paddy and Michael loved the water and couldn't wait to be togged off and 'out of pain'. I was wary of that cold green world, contenting myself with foraging for shells and stones, watching uneasily as Paddy swam straight out through a reef of swimmers in the shallows to a frightening distance from the beach. If he drowned, how would we get home? To my relief, he'd come tiptoeing awkwardly over the stony beach and we would head for home. On the journey back, he often gave a gentle tutorial in elocution: this, that, these, and those. 'This, that, these and dem.' Michael would say to get a rise out of him but you couldn't provoke Paddy and we'd nod off on the back seat, sated with ice-cream, sleepy from the salty air. We came wideawake one day outside the city hall when a red-haired girl slipped into the front seat. Paddy was even more animated than usual and we were unusually quiet, X-raying this interloper from the back seat. Their wedding was our first and Michael and I sang 'De Minstrel Boy' and Bernie wondered what the dinner could be like after such a huge breakfast. Mary Carroll from Gardiner's Hill was to become as dear to us as our own.

Uncle Joe was our warrior sportsman, wholehearted and passionate in his pursuit of sliotar, terrier or hound. Nan always said he had been her salvation when Pop was in England, supplementing her purse and table with rabbits culled from the ditches around the Brake. To a child's eye, he loomed larger than life, his frame too big for the chair he sat on, his passion too broad for the confines of small houses and concrete. Some memories are crystal-clear. We were smuggled into the dressing-room under the stand one Sunday at half time. In the halflight, we watched our heroes from behind our father's coat. Ring checked his hurley in swift nervous movements, bright and shimmering with inner intensity, locked into the private contemplation of moves and counter moves. John Lyons sat as always, solid and still, his round face wet and blotchy with sweat. Joe was hunched over, steam rising from his broad shoulders. The air was heady with the smell of oranges and wintergreen. Donie, with the bad leg, limped from one to the other, checking the band of a hurley, replacing from his store or shaking resin on an upturned palm. Now Tom Reilly appears in the middle of the room and a hush falls. He starts to speak in a low intense voice that builds to a crescendo.

'Ye have 'em; ye have 'em; ye have 'em on the run. Take the points; the goals will come.'

Like a drum he pounds the hurley on the concrete floor; then in a roar they race the steps to batter on the blue-clad foe.

Joe had a longing for fields and streams. He chased the hounds on foot or ferreted the ditches or read calm water for trout in Waterloo, with the same sure grace as he could track the flighting ball and smash it in the net for club or county to avalanche the roars around the Park. The girl who won his heart was a gentle radiant girl from the Deasy's of the Commons Road, an open singing household that was Glen-mad like ourselves.

Uncle Christy inherited Pop's round face, blue eyes and soft-ness. A mild smiling man, blessed with a wry sense of humour, he was a storyteller in the best traditions of the northside. Around the fire, Noreen and Eily would prompt him into stories of 'long 'go' and he would weave a wonderful tapestry of a world that we had never known. Characters like Klondike, the Rancher, Dinny Daly and the Bowler ranged around the room as the women gasped for air. 'Oh stop, stop!' And, in the same breath, 'What about the Roman fejollica?' Then he was off into his favourite story of a classmate in Eason's Hill school who always had his hand up first waving at the teacher to answer the question, while pulling at Christy with the other hand for the answer. Christy got tired one day of being straight man to the star. 'Now, boys,' the teacher asked, 'who condemned Jesus to death?'

'Sir! Sir!' in a loud voice, 'Hartnett, Hartnett,' in a whisper.

'A Roman fejollica.'

'Sir, a Roman fejollica.'

He was bate good-lookin' around the room. Kathleen was the perfect match, a bright and jolly girl from Kerryhall road. She was a knitter of warm Christmas pullovers and a great favourite of Nan's who loved her for the love she gave her son.

Uncle Michael was the youngest, a tall rangy man with the dark good looks of my Nan's people, the McCarthys. His visits from England are laced with memories of threepenny bits slipped to us on the sly. He delighted in our school stories and listened with endless patience as we vied to top each other. He was the one who heard our tables, admired our essays and weaned me from my inability to pronounce the letter 'r' with 'The rippling river runs over the rugged rocks'. A deeply religious man, he told me years on how his faith had crumbled under the weight of my mother's death. His own mother sent him to live in our house for a while 'to give Dave a hand'. He watched every morning as Dave swung his knees to the floor before dressing for work and last thing at night after his day, and that simple faith restored his own.

We had a fifth uncle who was really our first cousin once removed. Val was Nelly's son, an only child, and the closeness of Nelly and Nan, made brothers of the boys. He was initiated into hounds, bowls and hurley at an early age and played with some distinction for the Glen. 'A great boy for the books,' the family said with pride, he got a job with the *Cork Examiner* after school. Val played a large part in our story when the polio hit Cork.

5

EVACUATION

The minor plagues of mumps and measles swept the Lane like seasonal rain. These were expected, unwelcome visitors and the families were geared to them. Money was scarce and Nan was more likely to summon Mrs Geoghegan to a sick child than the doctor. Mrs Geoghegan was referred to in the local language as a 'handsome woman'. This meant she was not pretty but she had strong good looks and a character to match them. I remember her as a big woman with gleaming white hair swept back in a bun. She had two lively foxy daughters at home who were great friends with my aunts and a son Paddy, who gave us 'spins' on the bar of his bike. Mrs Geoghegan had a cool head for a crisis and a cool hand for a hot forehead. We relaxed when she made an appearance at the bed, under the spell of her slow calming voice.

'You'll have to keep him in the bed Mrs Hartnett, and stop him scratchin' or he'll poison himself. He'll be out of school for a week or so. That's an awful affliction to the poor child,' she'd say roguishly. 'Twas no affliction at all, but I'd pretend to be disappointed to humour them. Being sick meant being enthroned on the big bed in the back room and having the satisfaction of watching a tide of children being chivvied down the hill by their mothers to beat the half-nine bell. The mothers retraced their steps in chatting pairs, only to reappear later on their way to Shandon Street 'for the messages'. The day unreeled before the back window like a filmstrip and there was always a plastic cowboy on a plastic horse to race around the arroyos in the blankets to while away the time.

'Heigho Silver! Away!'

'Are you playin' up in that bed?'

'No, Nan, I was coughin' and barkin'.'

'Don't let me hear you again.'

'Right Nan. Aisy on there, Silver, or she'll have us landed back to school.'

Occasionally, even Mrs Geoghegan was confounded.

'You'd better send for Youngy, ma'am.'

Dr Jim Young had been a great hurler on the Cork team and with our own club, Glen Rovers, and this qualified him as a member of the extended family: 'one of our own'. A small erect man, he'd breeze in the front door and march straight up the stairs. He was kindly in a brisk sort of way, pushing the cold stethoscope up under the pyjamas, arguing non-stop about the composition of the Cork team. 'Hmm,' meant you were sick. Silence meant you were doomed. He could be merciless if he thought you were playing the old soldier.

'Get out of that bed, ye caffler, and get down to school.'

The stories about him were legion. One day, a group of corporation workers were sent to cut off the water in Cook Street. Youngy had his surgery there on the top floor of a three-storey house. Tom, a heavy smoker, lost the toss and climbed the stairs to tell Youngy. He came out eventually with a slip of paper in his hand.

'Did'ya tell him?'

'No, boy. I couldn't get me breath at the top of the stairs and he came out and gave me a prescription.'

My father swore by him. He loved to tell the story of sending for Youngy when I had pneumonia. After the diagnosis, Dave trailed him out the hall trying to press payment on him; sometimes he'd take it and more times he wouldn't. Michael raced in the hall with a ball on a hurley. 'Put him up to bed straight away, Dave,' Youngy said, without breaking his stride. 'He has it as well.'

'And he had,' Dave would conclude in wonder.

Cuts were a different class of ailment altogether. We dreaded a fall in the Quarry and a dirty scrape on the knee. 'That'll go septic,' was the diagnosis that always prompted a good whinge because we knew what was coming. They boiled up a saucepan of water and dropped in a lump of bread. The steaming white mess was sieved off on a clean cloth and slapped on the cut. We were off, like greyhound pups on polished lino, skittering around the kitchen with the pain. 'Dat'll draw the poison,' they said with satisfaction. It gave third-degree burns as well; we'd have preferred the gangrene. Serious cuts were picked up playing hurling and were a great source of blood and excitement. Both teams escorted the wounded warrior to the casualty in the local hospital. The North Infirmary was at the bottom of Roman Street, a sprawling building with a glazed yellow-brick section that looked like an inside-out public toilet. The nuns had huge white butterfly veils and always put the plaster on the hairiest part of your leg.

'What happened him?'

'Sister, he got a puck in the poll and he was in his gores.'

The puzzled nun would throw her eyes to heaven and haul the victim inside the swinging doors. We sat importantly on the benches in the corridor, staring with genuine interest at the broken and blighted of the parish. A roar from inside meant he was 'gettin' the needle'. 'Das for lockjaw,' Jim Mack would say knowledgeably, as the whole bench rolled sideways to rub one buttock in sympathy. To pass the time, we mimed lockjaw, making terrible faces until some woman put manners on us. 'Will ye stop that in God's holy name! Ye have the heart driven crosswise in me poor child.'

At last the hero reappeared, usually in a huge unnecessary bandage, cadged from a soft-hearted nurse. 'Jay!' we chorused enviously; then helped him home by the longest possible route, basking in reflected attention.

Like all matters of adult interest, we overheard the word 'polio' from our perch on the stairs.

'A poor young fella from the southside went up the baths and came out of the water crippled.'

The southside was miles away. But this thing of winks and nods and hasty signs of the cross came closer to home. A small girl up the Lane showed symptoms and we were confined to playing ludo on the mat before the fire. Meanwhile, the house was scrubbed with Dettol and the Yard was milky white and pungent from liberal blessings with Jeyes fluid. Somehow, Bernie escaped the blockade, wandering off on 'walkabout' like the aborigines in the comics. This fateful day she strolled past the minders up the Lane and right into the bedroom of the sick child. 'D'you think you'll live?' she asked seriously before she was plucked bodily out of the house and planted back in our kitchen. That was it, we'd have to go. Like city people everywhere in the world, the adults believed the country was the cure for all ills. The country was Auntie Nelly's house in Fair Hill, about ten minutes walk from our house, but, it was away from the Lane and out in the fresh air. This was a shock to Nelly's system. She had reared her only child in the commune of the Arch, now she was landed with the four of us, one wilder than the other.

Nelly lived in a two-storey semi-detached house up on a height off Fair Hill. A high bulging wall fronted on to the slope of the hill. A narrow path ran down the inside of the wall to a dead end and Nelly's gate was second off the path. She was houseproud without being a martyr to a mop, and the lino shone. Inside the front door, to the right of the stairs, was the front room, shadowy and full of furniture. Bigger even that our glass case and dominating the room was a massive sideboard of dark wood with mother-of-pearl inlay. Apart from state visits by Nan, this room was out of bounds for us. The back kitchen was full of sunlight and had a small porch outside the back door cluttered with picks, rakes and shovels for the garden. We followed the flight of the sun in our play, starting in the front garden in the morning and moving to the back when the shadow of the house flooded down to the front hedge in the evening. The hedge was alive with invisible birds, grumbling bees and small spiders. This was my 'plank,' my hideaway when I tired of being outrun by Michael and Kay, and wasn't tired enough to make daisy chains with Bernie. I loved to lodge in a crook of branches, daydreaming in a sway of leaves and dappled light.

The back garden shamed the bare patches and sparse grass of the Quarry. Dave came at the weekends to tease the black earth into bubble-leaved cabbage, foxy carrots, onions and rhubarb. In that fertile jungle we hunted hairy caterpillars and searched for snails, bringing them as trophies to Nelly. Her sight was so bad that we had them up to her nose before she saw them. 'Oh Jesus' she'd say, and flap us out of the house with her print apron. The hedges at the back were heavy with loganberries, bees and 'wassies' (as we called wasps), fair game for a fast jamjar. But we were after bigger and more exotic game. Up to the time of our invasion, the back garden had been a sanctuary for wild birds. Our brown spadgies were drab compared to finches, linnetts, robins and thrushes. Our spadgies were also expert at escape, streetwise to the wiles of the stalking child. The blood of generations of bird-limers bubbled in our veins. These were country birds we thought smugly; they haven't a clue. The thrush was really provoking us, tantalising us out of the bed in the mornings with the knocking of a snail upon a stone, hopping and pecking beyond our reach. Naturally, the plan came straight from a comic. Lean a butter box on an upright stick at the top of the garden near the hedge. Tie a string to the stick and run it down the garden behind the barrow, leaving a trail of crumbs outside the box and a few crusts underneath and wait. The thrush must have read the comic too. He bobbed along the line of crumbs and right in under the box. Whip went the string, down came the box, we had him. We also had a problem. When the first mad elation wore off, the question was asked who was going to put a hand in there and catch the bird. I remembered trying to catch an injured swallow in Lyons' yard and he nearly took the top of my finger as a souvenir back to Capistrano. We were stumped. 'Dad!.' Dave lifted him out gently. 'Here ye are now. Put your finger there. D'ye feel his little heart thumpin'?'

We felt ashamed that we had somehow broken the code of innocence in the back garden and promised to play boats with the butterbox in future.

Freed from the rhythms of the schoolday we hopped from the

beds without persuasion in the early morning, taking our buttered bread from the table to soak our sandals in the diamond-dripping grass. The only forays beyond the gate were to mass on Sundays or to Mullane's for the messages. It was a special thrill to pass the gate of North Mon school and look in through the latticed bars at the buildings and playgrounds empty and aching for the sound of children's voices. Nan came every Saturday night, laden with sweets and fruit; it was better than being in hospital. Nelly had a real bath and the two women scrubbed us spotless for mass.

'Wash behind your ears. You could grow potatoes there!'

Around the fire, we regaled Nan with the adventures of the week.

'Are they driving you demented, Nelly?'

'Yerra no, girl! Sure they're no trouble.'

'Keep an eye on that caffler or he'll break your heart.'

We didn't break Nelly's heart but we broke her pledge.

'I have Yanks comin' today,' she told us one morning. 'So let ye be good, for the love of God!' She divided the dusting, polishing and sweeping jobs between us. 'And be sure to sweep under the beds.' What kind of people were Yanks, I wondered, that they went upstairs and looked under the beds? Our chores led us to explore the wardrobe in Nelly's room and we rescued a hat and topcoat that had belonged to her late husband. Michael climbed in to the hat and coat and Kay rigged herself in a hat and coat of Nelly's. They snuck out the front door and stood on the step. I ran around the back. 'Auntie Nelly, Auntie Nelly, the Yanks are here.'

In a panic, she whipped off her apron and opened the front door.

'How'ya doin' Auntie Nelly?' Michael said in a bad imitation of Uncle Paddy's twang. It was too much for her. She slumped on the last step of the stairs and started to cry. Silently we trailed her into the kitchen where she took a bottle from the back of the press and splashed a generous measure into a cup.

'I'm distracted from ye,' she said and emptied the cup. 'And now I'm after breakin' me pledge' she said and burst into fresh tears.

She could also be a thunderin' rogue when the notion took her. 'I must get that chimney cleaned,' she declared one evening as we toasted ourselves and bread to the fire. This statement was in answer to a down draught that nearly smothered the lot of us. We perked up straight away; this meant that John would be arriving from the Arch with his bike and brushes, the two white eyes staring out of his back face like Al Jolson in a perpetual state of amazement. Nelly had other plans and we were to be her accomplices.

'Kathleen, shove the *Echo* up the chimney like a good girl.'

Our mouths fell open.

'Will ye do what I tell ye! Roll it up in a ball and shove it up a good bit. That's the girl. Light it now with a match and mind your fingers.'

With a mixture of delight and dread we lit the paper. Whoosh! 'Auntie Nelly, the chimney is blazin',' we shouted. 'Go in next door and call Mr Barrett,' she said calmly. Mr Barrett went down on his hands and knees on the mat and craned his head sideways as smouldering balls of soot bombed all around him in the grate.

''Tis like a paper stuck up there, ma'am.'

'Well, sweet heart of Jesus protect us' Nelly said piously, 'but you couldn't watch children.' Poor Mr Barrett covered himself in soot as he lugged bucketfuls of the black avalanche out of the grate. After she had ushered him out the door dizzy with the bless-ings she showered on him, she turned to face our accusing eyes. 'Yerra, 'tis the least he might do,' she said in her defence, 'and me a poor widda.'

Bedtime was a series of pilgrimages up and down the stairs for 'a bate of bread' or 'a drop of milk.' No sooner would one be settled than another would be up an about. 'I'll tell yer father,' was the ultimate threat that glued us to the beds. The old house would settle into quiet, creaking its floorboards for comfort, the heavy dark furniture soaking up the last of the firelight, and then, Val would come home. He'd bound up the stairs and throw himself into the bed on top of us. 'Tell us a story.' To this day, I have never met a man who could weave word-spells like Val. He had us laughing and crying as a parade of fantastic figures played out their adventures between the two beds. We threw the eiderdown over our heads at the scary bits and screamed in advance to soften the shock. 'Val, Val, come down outa that; they'll wet the beds.'

'All right, mother.'

'Ah, one more, Val.'

'Tomorrow night I'll tell ye about the witch that grabbed Joe Twomey in Shandon Street.'

Her son safely home, Nelly went through the close of day rituals.

'Say yer prayers now and remember yer poor mother.' Sometimes she led us through the rosary, the northside lullaby, the repetition of well-worn words losing us one by one to sleep until she faced into the 'Hail, Holy Queen' on her own. If it was a stormy night she would add a ballast of trimmings to her prayers. 'For sailors abroad on the sea this night, Hail Mary …' I wondered what sailors our saintly grandaunt was so concerned about. Before she climbed the stairs she pushed in every trailing plug in the house, in the firm belief that if she didn't electricity would leak out of the sockets during the night and kill all of us in our beds. Last of all, she toured the bedrooms with a Lucozade bottle full of holy water, splashing it shortsightedly in all directions.

'Did ye get it?'

'We did,' we chorused, dry and unblessed under the blankets.

'Goodnight and God bless ye.'

'Goodnight, Auntie Nelly.'

6

ALLEY UP OU' DAT

The story goes that the Sunbeam workers poured out of the factory gates one summer and headed off in singing buses for the vast green silences of Gougane Barra. As they stepped from the bus one asked another suspiciously 'What's the funny smell?'
'Yerra, that's the fresh air, girl,' was the reply.

The wide-open spaces of Nelly's garden, eventually made us headachy and fretful for home. We grew lonesome for the sunny patch of wall and the small houses leaning like shawled women whispering secrets. We longed for the smells from open doors, the sounds of familiar footsteps, the kingdom of women whose consorts came home in the evening to spread the *Echo* on the oil-cloth. We were eager for the pals and hungry for the games.

It was a time before television when a free imagination could whirl a full 360 degrees. I can't remember being bored. If the day dawned bright, the Place was humming with possibilities. If we were washed indoors, then a paper ball, tied with twine was the only prop we needed to stage an epic contest complete with commentary in the front hall.

'Is that someone at the front door?'
'No Nan, I scored a goal.'

When that palled, I could kneel on the upstairs sill, under the shelter of the angled window and watch the to-and-fro of neighbours in the Lane. Young women and girls always wrapped their arms around themselves as they skittered from door to door. Most people hunkered down in heavy coats or scowled from under flat dripping caps. Only Dave strode easy and upright as if content in the knowledge that the rain was wet as God intended and the pleasure of a dry towel waited just beyond the door. Now and then there was a pause in the spatter of steps and the whine of complaining bikes and in that lull I felt every muscle relax and, out of focus, flowed with the rain down the grey-black slates to drop the down pipe to the gurgling Lane.

Picky (hopscotch) and skipping were girls games we were literally roped into by bossy young wans we daren't refuse. We grudgingly turned the rope as Marie Sullivan hopped in the middle but balked at joining her chant:

> Who's dat comin' down de street?
> Tom McCarthy, isn't he sweet?
> He's been married twice before
> But now he's knockin' at Kenneally's door.
> Bernie, will you marry me?
> Yes, my love, at half past three.
> Half past three is much too late,
> So marry me in the mornin' at half past eight.

Bernie blushed happily and Tom jerked the rope to catch Marie's ankle. Even worse was to be shanghaied into playing house. You were either the baby or the father. If you were the baby you got to lie flat out like an eejit while the young wans oohed and aahed at you. 'Isn't he very big all de same?' If you were the father, you drank imaginary tea out of tiny plastic cups, read an imaginary *Echo* and got to say things like: 'Ask your mother.'

Glassy alleys, or marbles, was a real game. You 'alleyed up' against one wall of the Lane while your opponent crouched with his backside against the other wall. His job was to hit your marble with a throw. If he missed, you got to throw at his wherever it came to rest. The rules were simple and timeless but the 'gaitch' or style was everything. I favoured the slow pendulum swing between splayed legs; others held it on the thumbnail above a closed fist and fired with ferocious power. The most important thing was to have a face on you as if you were trying to go to the toilet and couldn't. Neilus and I got tired of winning from and losing to each other, so, we hatched a sting. I was smaller and slighter than him but a better actor so I made the approach to the mark.

'D'ye want a game of glassy alleys?'

'All right. Heads or harps?'

'No, you can alley-up if you like.'

I was a pushover. I lined up my first few shots where he'd have to be spur to miss them and then Neilus would happen along. 'Can I fall in?'

'I don't mind,' I'd say magnanimously and yer man couldn't be a louser in the face of such generosity. The hook was in. Now I laid them up for Neilus and he wiped the two of us off the Lane. When the sucker was cleaned out or suddenly remembered a message for his Mam, we went back to my house and stashed our hoard in a sugar bag under the bed. We were into our fourth bag when Neilus made his first confession, got a conscience and ended a great partnership.

Runaway knock was a beginners game for aspiring cafflers. The theory was simple enough. We ran from one end of the Lane to the other, knocking on all the doors along the way. The real challenge lay in doing it twice, because the second time you were expected and could be helped on your way with a clatter or the flick of a tea towel. Influenced by Denis the Menace in the comics, I devised a new strategy. We tied a string from Mack's knocker to Brennan's on the other side and knocked on both. The tug o' war was glorious. Thunder up the alley was another notch up the daring scale. It had to be played midweek so that the pious promises of the previous Saturday's confession would have worn off and there was still ample time to work on a firm purpose of amendment for the following Saturday. We stuffed the chute (down pipe) with papers and applied the match. A roaring whoosh went up the down pipe erupting into sparks and flying fiery papers at the roof. It was worth the three Hail Marys as we hid behind Pop's wall and listened to the language.

This was Jimmy Mul's favourite game. Jimmy lived next door to us for a time and it was fire that brought us together. Shortly after the Muls moved in, their chimney caught fire, without urging from the *Echo*. The bells of the fire brigade brought us to the bedroom windows to watch the excitement. The Lane was a confusion of helmets and hoses. The women huddled in an assortment of dressing-gowns and curlers, blessing themselves with fright while the men ran around importantly in their braces, getting in the firemen's way.

'Boys, mind Jimmy now for a while and be good,' Dave said ushering a boy into our bedroom. Jimmy had a physique that Pop would have described as 'two bits of thread and a knot'. He was a pyjamas with feet, topped off with a white luminous face and a mop of hair that frustrated combs. His most memorable feature was a pair of dark dancing eyes. The minute we saw him we went mad. When Dave returned to collect him, the bedroom was a blizzard of feathers from an epic pillow fight and we were welded to the gawky boy who was game for anything.

All the boys around the place had a fascination with fire and getting our hands on a box of matches was the Holy Grail. Jimmy was very gullible so we primed him to the task.

'Go into Bridgie's shop and get a box on your mother's bill.'

Jimmy was gullible but not stupid. 'Me Mam will have a canary.'

'Den she'll have two bloody birds,' Tom Mack said sourly. 'Course, if you're affrightened?' Jimmy's reluctance crumbled. The Quarry was rich in combustibles; papers and scraps of lino were everywhere. We set up our fire and smoked papers in its companionable glow artfully building a pyramid of bubbling lino to hold the night and the imminent call to bed at bay.

Rainy days rarely drove us indoors. We huddled under a tarpaulin tent in the Quarry, deaf to the calls from home to 'come in outta dat,' absolving ourselves from disobedience with the thought that they didn't really want us 'draggin' dirt and filth' over me clean threshold'. When a decent-sized stream coursed the centre of the Lane, we raced sleek lollipop sloops and squat matchboxes, shouting encouragement as they swirled or stuck or surfed the tributaries from the gasping down pipes. The high point of my dam building /bursting career happened in the front Quarry off St

Mary's Road. It was the day I drenched the shawlies.

The North Chapel was the hub at the centre of five spoke roads. From their perch at the corner of St Mary's Road, the group of black-shawled women could watch the world go by. Whenever I passed on the way home with a message from Shandon Street, I left a bob of heads and a lapping of whispers in my wake.

'Who's dat now?'

'He's poor Maura Hartnett's boy; sure you'd know him outta dem. Isn't he de head off Christy Hartnett?'

'He is, girl.'

There were two brown puddles on a flat patch uphill of the shawlies and Neilus and I were armed with two hurleys. Our first plan was to splatter any children who passed on the pavement but they divined our intention from afar and crossed to the other side at Dineen's, well out of our range. We decided to cut a channel from the upper to the lower puddle and coaxed the water with the hurleys. I don't know what possessed me; there was something about the black shawls, sharp eyes and fidgety heads that reminded me of crows. Now crows, unlike our own spadgies, lived in the convent trees and could be shelled with impunity. They were not part of the tribe. Carefully we carved a track to a point above the steps where we built a dam of sods. Then we swept the lake with the hurleys, our stomachs tight and tingling with suppressed excitement as the water level rose behind the dam. One swift flick of a hurley and the torrent began to move. Everything seemed to happen in slow motion: the heads stopped bobbing and a surprised voice said, 'Madge, Madge, I'm soakin'.' Then the screeching nearly made us wet ourselves. 'Oh Jesus, I'm drownded, ye lightin' caffler.' The shawled sisterhood flapped in confusion, standing on each other to escape the flood. We raced for the sanctuary of the Lane, delirious with laughter, trying to run and breathe at the same time, our heads tucked down against a volley of threats and curses. 'Ye saucy scut, I'll go up to your Nan.' But, I knew they wouldn't. Nan could be a formidable figure in the face of complaint and had little time for that particular coven of connyshures.

7

DE PICTURES AND OTHER DREAMS

The first picture I ever saw was *The King and I*. It was on in the Savoy and Kay minded me in to the front seats where I sat dazzled and deafened for two horrible hours. When she got me to the bus-stop, she asked in a grown-up voice, 'Did ya enjoy the picture?' This was for the benefit of the queue. I threw up over her patent leather shoes. There were nine picture houses in Cork. The Assembly Rooms was the haunt of what the grown-ups called 'a rough element.' We slummed it one Saturday to check it out and, sure enough, the film was subtitled by shouts from the gallery. 'He's behind ye, ye flippin' gowl,' was the advice to the hero and, 'Get 'em off ya!' was the admonition to the heroine. The constant swaying seascapes of a pirate film were too much for one patron's bladder and with an expression of beatific relief he let fly from the balcony. Never again. The Lido in Blackpool, a local wag said, was Lourdes: you went in crippled, you came out walkin.' That left seven to choose from which meant seven different preferences and heated arguments every Saturday. It also meant one picture for each glorious day of the Christmas holidays when our pockets were flush. On Saturday mornings, we rendered unto God by going to confession and rendered unto Caesar by doing Nelly's messages for a bob. Then the debate started.

'Yerra dat one's a cod boy; dere's no shootin'!' That was out. 'Me sister said de wan in de Palace is massive.' Definitely out. 'In de Lee, yer wan get's shot at de start.' Definitely our kind of picture. Our idea of the perfect picture was where 'de wan' got killed in the first five minutes and 'de boy' avenged her with murder and mayhem for the rest of it. We pooled our money and headed for town. Before us lay the challenge of the queue. It wasn't easy for fourteen boys to jump a line that snaked all the way to Tyler's but Jimmy McAuliffe was a natural. He was slight and freckled with a drawly voice. He also smoked which made him seem older and gave second thoughts to would-be attackers. Jimmy joined the back of the queue listing from the fourteen shillings in his pocket and wheedled his way upward as the rest of us invaded the foyer pretending interest in the shop. The shilling seats were always up front where you'd be guz-eyed after five minutes. In the roar that greeted the dimming lights, our entire row descended to the floor only to reappear shortly afterwards in the good seats at the back. John Barrett nearly got us all thrown out one Saturday. If it was raining, his mother always insisted he wore a second pants, and as we settled nonchalantly into the back row, John dutifully stood up to take them off. There was an eruption of cheers and whistles and flashing torches as we pretended not to know him. 'Sit down, ye gom! I hope you get pneumonia.'

Undaunted, we shouted all the words of the ads, giving a special yowl for the nylons ad that promised, 'The magic of Mystic is yours for the asking.' Just after the ads, the spotlights picked out the two mortified girls serving ice-cream and ice lols, vying with each other for the scarlet blush award. More whistles from the fans. Then a roar went up as Fred Bridgman ascended from the pit astride a massive organ to lead us through a medley of tunes. We were itching for action and only mildly satisfied by a selection of trailers. At last, the picture. Oh the groans when 'de boy's' gun clicked on an empty chamber! Oh the screams when a feather poked over a boulder! Oh the mad hubbub of talk when the kissing started! And the roars of relief when the cavalry charged over the hill to the rescue. All the way home, we tried to walk like the hero, our coats half-open for a quick draw, our eyes in slits, making innocent people nervous at the bus-stops. As soon as we could, we replayed the picture in the Quarry. Everyone had at least one gun and hurleys doubled as rifles. The small ones were allowed a part if

61

they agreed to die early on and soon the Quarry was littered with small dead bodies in dramatic poses, the Lane treacherous with creeping Indians, and the villain taking twenty bullets to die. 'I'm only wounded, boy.' Jaded from our efforts, we lit a 'bona' and reviewed the trailers for the coming week, trying to sustain the magic by placing a can on the fire and getting an unselfconscious Indian to slash into it for authenticity.

I played for Cork in the 1956 All-Ireland Hurling Final and scored two goals. The second one was disallowed because it took a deflection off a jamjar. I argued the point but the referee, Mr Ryan, was adamant. 'Anyway,' he pointed out, 'it travelled over the sleeve of the goal post.' This fantasy was made possible by Mr Ryan, a bus driver from the Terrace. Up to then our games were haphazard affairs with everyone chasing the ball all over the Quarry. Everyone except me, I was as far from the possibility of injury as I could get, coursing and lifting an imaginary sliotar into my hand as my own radio commentary struggled to keep up. 'He's on the forty, he swings, he strikes and the ball is in the net.' Mr Ryan tamed us into recognisable teams and prefaced our All-Ireland by having us clear the Quarry of stones. We threw them in a pile against the concrete wall and that cairn survived to his memory until the Quarry was levelled and buried in smooth tar. Someone put sticks along the sidelines with scraps of paper for flags and we marched behind a band of small ones playing imaginary instruments. The team which lost the toss had to be Tipperary and the next question for the Cork team was who would be Ringy. Jimmy McAuliffe won that honour with the irrefutable argument: 'I'm de only one wit a cap.' Michael was Uncle Joe and I alternated between Joe Twomey and Johnnie Clifford. Mr Ryan doubled as the archbishop of Cashel and threw in the ball. It was here on a patch of mud that Michael and Patsy Harte served their time in short pants to the red jersey before they wore it with pride for their county. Even Neilus and myself were to have our brief moment of glory when we played as fullback and goalkeeper for the Cork under-fifteen team. But nothing ever matched that day of pure excitement as we scourged a final goal between two coats under the watchful eye of a bus driver.

As children, the world of fantasy, the world of the unconscious was where we spent our true energies. It was not different from the ordinary world, just deeper, and we moved in and out of it without noticing the boundaries. It was only as we grew older and self-conscious that we lost that grace and divided our world into the real and the imagined. Only Seamus stayed loyal to the vision, and I think in some part of our 'big boy' selves, we envied this permanent child. Because we grew up together, his difference was unquestioned, something we adapted to long before labels like Down's Syndrome could mark him apart from us. He hit me with an Indian club one day outside Geoghegan's. I was chalking a picky on the path and must have glared when he shifted into my light to inspect the work. Without malice or anger he picked up the stick and hit me. Nan's lap was a safe sanctuary for all ills and a repository for complaints.

'Seamus is the way God made him, boy. He couldn't help doing that no more than a baby. You're a big boy now; you'll have to learn to allow for him.'

Allowing for Seamus meant including him in all the matches. Sometimes we took on a team from Wolfe Tone Street or Redemption Road and it always amazed our opponents when we called a halt to the play so Seamus could get a puck of the ball. It wasn't all chivalry, Seamus usually owned the ball and he was quite capable of taking it home if he wasn't involved.

I remember two very special days in his life and ours. We were at our dinner one Saturday when the front door opened and Seamus wandered in. There was nothing remarkable in that; he was very fond of our Michael and would often take his chances at the table with the rest of us. But, this day was special because Seamus had made his confirmation. He had the biggest rosette and medal I ever saw. Pop said you would not get it in the war. I remember that he was very upright and steady and sat down with great majesty and I remember my Nan by the gas stove, fumbling in her purse with one hand for hansel and wiping her apron to her eyes with the other.

The other day that stays with me is the day he rode the bike. For weeks we saw Mr Ryan walk up and down the terrace holding with his hand to the saddle. 'Aisy now, Seamie boy. Don't be lookin' at the front wheel keep your two eyes out ahead of you on the road, good man.' And then, he was side -pedalling and swinging his leg over the bar and one glorious day he rode to Blarney with his Dad. His homecoming was a triumph with neighbours gathered in the Quarry and at the windows to see him glide confidently up the Terrace to the door, his cheeks ablaze from the wind and cheers.

8

ME AND TWO OTHER DOGS

A young fella from our place started a school essay one day with the immortal line, 'One day me and two other dogs went out huntin'.'

Dogs were part of the extended family and we had a succession of Spots, all named for Spot Hartnett, a legendary ratter who lived to be fourteen. Beaver was an exception in name and nature. Auntie Noreen had Pop plagued for a beaver fur coat. 'If that's what you want girl, that's what you'll get,' he said with a twinkle from behind his pipe and he was as good as his word. He came home one evening with a suspicious bulge under his coat. 'There's your Beaver now,' he said, and spilled a pup onto the lino. We rolled ecstatically on the floor and tickled his little bare belly until a little fountain of pure delight rose into the air. 'Ah lovin' God. Where's the *Echo*, quick. Put that dog out in the yard.' Now a dog called Spot belonged in the yard but Beaver was born for better things. We smuggled him up into the beds or in under the glass case in the front room. One day he fell asleep in the Caboose under the stairs and his scratching set Dave's nerves jangling. 'Rats, d'ye hear 'em. Dere's bloody rats in de house.' We made a complete fool of the dog, protecting him from anything that would make him streetwise. Small wonder then he wandered under the wheels of a car one day in Blackpool and had to be drowned in the stream behind the Glen Club. We washed Blackpool with our tears and were only consoled when another sawn off mongrel arrived in the door to us.

The three dogs in our Lane were called Tiny Leary, Patch Purcell and Spot Hartnett. Of the three only Spot would have known what to do with a rat. Tiny was well-named. He was a small ratty sample of a dog who rarely ventured beyond the handkerchief of concrete outside Leary's door. Tom Mack and I sat outside his range one day sizing him up.

'D'ye know he have one glassy eye?'

'Go way ou' da.'

'On me soul. A cat scrawled out de udder wan – me Mam told me.'

There was no contesting that authority; I was hardly going to ask Mrs Mack to put out her tongue so I could check the truth of it.

'Which wan?'

'Ha?'

'Which wan is de glassy wan?'

There was a long pause.

'He'd take the bloody hand off ya,' Tom said with finality and Tiny's glass eye, like religion, became a mystery.

Patch on the other hand had two good eyes, which always seemed to be closed. He had a fat sausage body barely supported by four short legs each of which seemed to have a mind of its own. For most of the day he lay dead outside Purcell's door only shifting himself to follow the sunlight. But Patch was part crocodile: he could lie like a log for days and then pin a new postman to the wall in a blur of black and white. Spot was a mongrel terrier with all the rough tongue and twitches of the breed. Pop had him half-trained when a rat caught him by the lip and damaged his confidence but he was a mastiff in comparison to the other two.

On Saturday mornings in high summer, we whistled the other huntsmen out of bed and gathered every ould God-help-us dog available to hunt the Brake. The Brake was a stretch of hilly land below Nash's boreen, littered with boulders dropped long ago by some tired glacier. The whole place was hip-deep in buttery furze, perfect cover we believed for rat and rabbits. We stopped at Riordan's to cut sticks from the lilac tree then faced into the hill, keeping our motley pack in order with hup hup as if we were driving cattle. Along the route there were many stops for ritual fights and tempting ESB poles and gardens offering relief. Finally we were whacking the furze and whipping the dogs into a lather of excitement. We never ever saw a single rabbit but there was enough shouting and barking and false scents to bring us shambling home, our dogs too tired to be fractious, their swinging tongues dusting the road before them.

Summer was full of hunting and swimming and endless light evenings for games of Release organised by the big ones. Nobody ever got sick in the summer. The small houses opened all windows, the front door and back to catch any breath of air available. We gradually went from tomato red to dirty brown. 'Wash your knees.'

'Yerra dat's me tan, Nan.'

It was the season for old neighbours sitting out before their doors, when Pop banned the electric light until the house was thick with shadows, savouring the last red flicker over Ryan's chimney, hoarding it against the long winter. We had reason to huddle close against the winter, to keep our fire roaring in defiance up the chimney. But death did not come this time in frost-bound days. It came when new grass peeped above the March mud in the Quarry and the long fast days of Lent sharpened our appetites for Easter eggs. When the bare trees of the convent were regaining their modesty and children ventured out again on legs as white as grass stalks covered by a stone, Nan died.

Some time earlier in the year she had a stroke. We were gathered one day on the landing so that she could see us from the bed. One side of her face was tight but she smiled on the other side and lifted her hand. The nuns came from the Assumption Convent to look after her and we were told to pray very hard. Maura's memorial card was full of prayers over four small silvery pages with extra ones crowded into the margins. Every prayer promised an indulgence to shorten Maura's stay in purgatory. Sometimes I had the mad notion that she was wandering around purgatory handing them out to the people we prayed for in the trimmings of the rosary, those 'who had no one to pray for them'. 'Here you are girl. That young fella has his knees worn away prayin' for me. Go on girl, sure I have the givin' away of them.' So we prayed and struggled quietly out of our beds every morning to the half-seven mass. I remember kneeling in the half empty church looking up at the golden doors of the tabernacle, asking silently would it be all right if we could keep our Nan.

'Maybe ye'd like to go out to Deasy's for a few days,' they said. It had echoes of before but we said nothing, just went to the Common's Road where they made much of us and Jackie Daly, one of our hurling heroes, came every day after work to build timber blocks with us on the floor.

'Any change Josie?'

'No Jackie, still the same.'

Joe took us walking with his own small boy to Fitz's boreen and we took turns on his tricycle. It was on the small bridge that he told us. Michael burst into tears and I wanted to but couldn't. The dark at the top of the stairs had broken free again and filled our little house. Our refuge from night-terrors and sharp memories was gone.

9

CHRISTMAS

They did their best to make Christmas for us that year. We were assured that Santy would still come and Noreen and Eily stood on chairs in their black skirts and cardigans to hang the decorations. This year, it was Pop who held the match with Bernie, our youngest, to light the red candle that would sit in the window in case the Holy Family came to call. I wasn't a bit surprised when they didn't come. Sure how could they face us?

As soon as September faded in, we covered our new and hand-me-down schoolbooks with brown paper and resurrected our sacks from underneath the stairs. Christmas was coming. October winds swept the Convent leaves into crisp kicking piles. We forswore sweets for the Holy Souls during the month of November now that we had two to release from Purgatory and finally December grudgingly arrived. At this stage we were jaded with waiting and the adults were addled from 'How many more days now?' As we ticked off the days, the rituals clicked into place. Letters for Santy were drafted and redrafted and then updraughted from the fireplace to sail in soft cinders all the way to the North Pole. It seemed to me that everything they could find in the house went into the pudding. We were allowed to squidge our fingers in the chocolate-coloured, raisin-freckled mess, before it was boiled and hung in a pillow slip from the nail by the gas stove. Michael and I took it in turns to sniff loudly like the boxers we saw in the City Hall and punch the pudding. Sniff, jab, a left, a right to the body, sniff. 'Would ye blow ye're noses and leave that puddin' alone.' Joe Louis retires to the neutral corner.

The crib was Dave's pride and joy. It was a brown hardboard

structure kept on the top of the tallboy upstairs. Coming nearer to Christmas he organised trips 'outlong' to gather moss so that we could clad the walls and roof and carpet the floor. The figures were swaddled in pieces of the *Echo* and were disinterred like dusty mummies from the biscuit tin. Only the Holy Family had set places, an elastic band keeping the baby Jesus from wandering off. I thought he lay there with his hands outstretched in indignation. The angels and other hangers on had a wandering brief and sometimes perched dangerously in the branches of the Christmas tree. St Joseph went missing one year and was discovered leaning casually against the rear wall admiring his reflection in a silvery tinsel ball. 'Out for a fag,' Michael said wickedly and got a clip for his sacrilege. There was a woman with a water jar on her head and she was moved a lot, probably to ease her burden. Another fella lay with his head on a pillow sleeping through the entire season every year. Dave bought the tree in the Coal Quay and made a big fuss of hanging the lights so that a red one shone through a hole in the roof of the crib. Some nights as we lay around the tree, there were mysterious toings and froings in the hall and a suspicious crackling of wrapping paper but we pretended not to notice.

It was always a shock to discover the baldy turkey laid out on the kitchen table, its head hanging down on the floor and a few drips of blood on the lino. On Christmas Eve, we crowded out on the step to hear the carol singers at the foot of the lane, joining in the carols we knew and shouting at the other children.

'He's comin' to our house first.'

'Get away, boy; we had our chimney cleaned.'

The final ritual was when the youngest and oldest held hands to light the candle in a saucer of water. We set out a glass of porter for Santy and a slice of cake for Rudolph, urged up the stairs by Dave: 'Go on now, let ye. he'll never come if ye're awake.'

'Michael, are you still awake?'

'Yeah.'

'I tink I heard Santy.'

'Naw boy, dat's a rat under the bed.'

I knew that was a lie. Under the bed were crates of Tanora and Little Norah and stout; there wasn't room for a rat. Still I tried to sleep in the middle of the bed hunched into the hollow of Michael's back.

It was the only morning of the year when we didn't need to be called. We were up with the light, fighting our way through the tight necks of new pullovers and racing down the stairs. The house rule was that we had to go to mass before we opened our presents and we pressed our noses longingly to the coloured glass of the front room door, the dregs of the stout and the crumbs of cake teasing us from the table. Mass was a torture. 'If 'tis the canon, we're knackered,' Michael muttered from between latticed fingers. 'He never stops raimeishin'.' But it wasn't the canon, we barely repressed a cheer as the bustling form of Fr Harte coursed the altar boy out of the sacristy. Fr Harte had better sense than to preach on Christmas Day. There was a God after all.

Another of Dave's rules was that we had to stay a decent interval after the priest left the altar; then we were off like hounds from the leash, tearing up the road to rip the coloured paper to bits in a frenzy of discovery. Naturally while our hands tore at our own boxes our eyes were sizing up what the others had. Uncle Paddy always sent magic presents from America. One glorious year, there was a four engined TWA constellation plane for me and a helicopter for Michael. One terrible year, he got a tricycle and I got a yoke on wheels with a horse's head. I demanded a steward's inquiry but the result stood.

'He's older than you boy. Maybe next year Santy will bring you one.'

I wheeled my horsey to the top of the Lane and took up a position outside Barrett's door. When Michael cycled out the front door, I gave the horse his head. The fall of ground was with us and we hit the tricycle at a fair lick. The horse's head fell off and looked reproachfully at me from the concrete but the trike was wrecked. I knew they'd never lay a hand on me on Christmas Day.

Most Christmasses, the only snow we got was on the Christmas cards, brittle sparkly stuff that came off on our fingers. But, one year it did snow! The weather seemed to be holding its breath and there was a funny yellow glow under the clouds. Just as the streetlights lit up on Christmas Eve, the snow began to fall. Huge cotton wool flakes filled the triangle of light under the ESB pole and when we woke in the morning, the whole world had changed. In the Yard, the dustbin wore a soft white helmet crisscrossed with the filigree footprints of sparrows. Even the knobs of coal in the shed had luminous bonnets, but, the clothesline was the wonder. A long slender line of snow balanced impossibly on the length of the line from end to end. Every surface was covered in white silence; even the irregular slates bumped up into rectangles, the borders around the chimneys shiny and black from the fires below.

The Quarry was a blizzard of boys and girls flaking half-made snowballs with purple fingers, noses running happily from the cold. The snowman wore Pop's soft hat and a bit of curtain material for a scarf and we checked him out the back window every night as he kept his watch. The women threw ashes in the Lane to provide a purchase but the bottom of Grawn was impassable to buses and cars, and we made a slide all the way to the cobbles at the cathedral gate. In the first flush of enthusiasm, we went down on our bottoms, spinning wildly, our arms stretched out in exultation. Our bottoms soon froze, however; so all manner of conveyances were stolen, borrowed and invented. In the space of a single hour I saw kamikaze pilots zooming by on tomato boxes, a wheel-less pram and a young wan from Wolfe Tone Street sailing sedately in a coal scuttle. I had to settle for the turkey dish from our oven and long after dark when Dave had given up whistling from the Yard we hobbled home on numbed feet, our ears stinging from the sudden warmth of the house.

The week after that Christmas was spent playing ice hockey with hurleys and a polish tin or waiting for shawled women to pass under the laden branches of the convent trees so we could shower them with a well-lobbed snowball. We took time out to visit the cribs in the city churches, comparing them unfavourably with the one in the cathedral. 'They have a dinky donkey in St Mary's,' someone remarked ecumenically. 'Yeah but our baby Jesus would make bits of dere's,' was the confident reply. We brought the thaw on our wellingtons in around the house and soon, too soon, the roofs were black again.

Christmas was also callers and card-games. Relations bowled in at all hours and reeled out after a sherry or whiskey from Dave's heavy hand. He had a 'pioneer's pour'.

'Aisy on, Dave; you'll have me on me ear.'

'Sure 'tis only the one day in the year.'

The hundred-and-ten was a serious business, usually played in number four where the leaves of the table were pulled out to accommodate the crowd. All the uncles, Dave, Pop, Seamus O'Brien and Dr Mack from Farna, bid and trumped well into the night. We did a tour from lap to lap, trying not to laugh as Paddy palmed the dummy hand or slipped the ace of hearts in the crack of the table for the next round. Bedtime was a movable feast because of 'the time that was in it' and one day blurred into another until the rituals of dismantling Christmas were begun. The decorations were concertina'd carefully into tins. The crib figures were laid to rest in paper habits, the lights unplugged, unstrung and coiled away. The tree, brittle now and shedding on the lino, was lifted out of the butter box and landed into the Quarry. Only the books lasted, read and reread before the fire. *Coral Island*, *Little Women*, *Kidnapped* and all the sensible presents from dutiful aunts and uncles lulled us into unaccustomed quiet wherever we could curl. The annuals were traded from one house to another criss-crossing the smoky lane to Mack's and Murphy's 'til the covers cracked and the spines gave way. I often heard adults say, 'Sure 'tis only for the children!' Not in our house, where Dave, in a new pullover, squatted on the front room floor, laying a track under arches of playing cards for a train that puffed real smoke. I remember Pop, puffing away on a new pipe, as argumentative as any child about the rules of Ludo. Years later, Dave told us of one Christmas when work was scarce and funds were low.

'On Christmas Eve, all I had left in me pocket was a shillin' for the gas and no tree bought yet. I was walking down Washington Street, wrapped up in meself, when I met Auntie Kitty. "Happy Christmas Dave," she said and pushed a ten-bob note into me pocket. Sure we were made up.'

Christmas brought out the best in them and if there was a worry about money, it was to their credit that we never knew of it. All we did know was that the fire burned brightly, the table was well laden, the visitor was welcomed night and day and we were surrounded by the secure circle of a loving tribe.

10

Neighbours

'Tis more important to have good neighbours than family because you'll always have your neighbours.'

This was one of Dave's great proverbs and in time I came to appreciate the truth of it. Our little ghetto was a model of interdependence. They often said that during the war, when tea was scarce, it wasn't unusual for our family to make a pot of tea and another to have the leaves for their pot. Before Nan's death, I was largely unaware of this safety-net of lives and ties but in the shadow days that followed, when our security lay in shreds, neighbours were our defence against aloneness, a concrete visible reminder of belonging.

Again, it was the women who set the tone of our lives. Any door on the Lane could be opened by a child's push and 'bates' of bread and jam were automatically offered and casually accepted.

Purcell's was one of my favourite ports of call. Mrs Purcell was a widow of long-standing. She was a small woman with grey black hair tied behind her head. She always seemed to walk in slow motion and never passed any remark on the small boy hovering in the hall until I took my courage to tour the laps of her grown-up children. I felt safe and accepted and ordinary in a house where I was referred to by name or as the 'child' and never as 'poor Maura's boy', a label that marked me out as different. Even when I adventured up her steep stairs and tumbled from the top, it seemed the most natural thing in the world that I would land in Jimmy's strong arms. Mrs Purcell's affections were doled out smothered in jam or in a cup of milk from the gallon in the kitchen. Jimmy worked the nightshift in Dunlops and it was my job to hush the boys if we played outside the door. It was small recompense for the hours I spent swinging my legs under their table. Sheila and Peggy, the daughters, were fiercely protective of me, keeping sharp eyes and sharper tongues to ward off potential bullies or 'tormentors' as we called them. But my heart longed for the Christmas and summer holidays when Neilus and Chrissie, their two emigrants in England, would come home. In the absence of nephews and nieces of their own, they ruined me entirely.

Leary's was almost an extension of our own house and Eily an adopted aunt. None of us begrudged Bernie a special place in Eily's heart, knowing instinctively that even though she lavished love on Bernie, our share of her heart was undiminished. Bernie blossomed in Eily's affections and snubbed poor Jimmy Walsh for ages when he had the cheek to marry her.

In all the other houses there were children our own age and, apart from the sweat and blood camaraderie of hurling, there was a brisk trade in swapped comics that took us over and back the Lane. Mack's and Murphy's were bottomless wells of *Beanos*, *Dandys* and *Beezers*, with the occasional nugget of a sixty-four pager. I remember that most of the comics were full of war stories. All the German soldiers had square heads and only about three words of German which we included in our play. *Achtung*, *schnell* and *kamerad* were added to our usual scripts. The Japanese soldiers had bandy legs, buck teeth and what we called City Hall glasses, round and flimsy. They had only one word between them, *banzai*, and it amazed me that they could have done so much damage working out of a vocabulary of a single word.

Through the girls, the circle widened to include the Keatings around the corner and the Ahernes in the Convent Lodge. There were only two childless houses that I can recall. A retired teacher lived on one side of us with his widowed sister. Mr Rourke was a gaunt dignified man, who made rare appearances in public. What's seldom seen in any neighbourhood generates the greatest number of stories. It seems he had our Uncle Michael in his class at one stage and when he was confounded by a sum, one evening, he knocked on Mr Rourke's door for clarification. 'The office is closed,' was the response and the door closed definitively. I remember him as a man who would sometimes appear at the door to the front room when we were hunkered over our homework at the table. 'Twould halt your heart to look up from an Irish book and see this apparition framed in the doorway, a top-coat draped like a cloak over his shoulders. 'The ghost who walks,' Michael whispered one evening, and earned a look from Dave.

'Good evening, Dave.'

'Good evening and welcome Mr Rourke; will you sit up to the fire?'

'No thank you Dave' (he never did).' I have a little message for these miscreants.' Then he'd open his coat dramatically and all the rubber balls that had been 'banished' into his yard from the Quarry, would bounce merrily around our front room. After he died, his sister gave us a set of encyclopedia from his collection of books. For years after, it mopped up the boredom of many a wet day and added an exotic spice to our school essays.

Even though she was no relation, we called his sister Auntie. It was the accepted thing that we would pause in our game, and 'hold up the ball' to let Auntie pass in safety. Someone would always take her string bag of messages as she struggled up St Mary's Road under her black shawl. We weren't as eager to enter her house, because we had invested it with ghosts and phantoms to match the noises that came through our bedroom wall at night. Auntie would get lonesome some nights and take consolation in a Baby Power. At some stage during the night, she'd part company with the bed and call out to Dave for help. In the first stages of sleep, we'd hear her thin voice, muffled by the wall.

'Dave! Dave!'

'Dad!'

'Wha'?'

'I think Auntie's callin' ya.'

Without complaint, he'd hoist his trousers over his pyjamas

and stumble off to the rescue. She was nearly the death of him. He told us how accustomed he got to lifting her off the floor in the gloomy house and tucking her into the bed like a child.

'Sure there was no weight in her and I was half asleep meself. Then I'd sit down on a chair and wait for her to nod off. Well one night I'm sittin' there on me own and ye know how dark 'twas. "David," she says, as clear as a bell, "you may go home to your own house now, boy, because my father has just come in to keep me company." The hairs on the back of me neck stood up to attention.'

Worse was to follow. As he felt his way carefully down the rickety stairs in pitch darkness, he distinctly heard a tapping sound follow his every step.

'When I got to the end of the stairs, I was in a bog of sweat. I went in me own door like a greyhound.'

And, though we had heard it over and over, we supplied his cue.

'And what was it, Dad?'

'Yerra, 'twas me braces hangin' down behind me.'

Twice a day, Bridgie's house was awash with children, and none of them her own. Bridgie had converted her house on St Mary's Road into a small shop and the house speciality was toffee. This was boiled up on the stove in the kitchen and poured out on a slab to cool into a brittle glacier. She hammered it into small crazy-paving pieces and packed them in a twist of paper for a penny. She was tall and gangly and an expert on crowd control. 'If you don't stop your pushin' I'll tell the teacher.' This put immediate manners on the pusher because everyone knew that Bridgie had a great leg of the nuns. In the summer, the school market dried up totally and Bridgie kept the shop open for company. I became a regular caller during the long summer evenings. I'd rap on the wall beside the curtained door to her inner sanctum.

'Are you there Bridgie?'

'Where else would I be! Come in and let me look at you.'

'I was wonderin' if you wanted any messages?'

'No, sit down there for a minute.'

Sometimes, she was sitting up in the bed with her crochet needle flying surrounded by a whirlpool of coloured threads and patches. Behind her on the wall over the mantelpiece she had a framed picture crowded with cameos of the leaders of the Rising. The only one I could recognise straight away was Padraig Pearse because he had his head turned sideways. 'That was because he had a squinty eye,' someone said irreverently at home. 'Wasn't he very vain all the same?' Instinctively, I kept that particular insight to myself. Occasionally, Bridgie liked to 'tour' the picture, giving a running commentary on her heroes.

'Dere's Connolly at the top, mud fat with a tash. Never darkened the door of church or chapel,' she sniffed. 'And dat mawkish lookin' fella was Plunkett, writin' poetry God help us and the GPO burnin' around him.' Another sniff. In Bridgie's world order, missing mass and writing poetry were reserved sins. She would meander down the picture as I sat, half shocked and totally fascinated by the contrast between Bridgie's version and the blood and glory stories we were fed at school.

Another evening, it would be 'de Tans'

'De sweepin's of English jails boy, roamin' de streets of Cork in their tenders, puttin' the fear of God into innocent people. But, dey got deir lot from our boys down here,' she'd say with satisfaction, stabbing the needle into the innocent ball of wool. I held my breath, wishing her on to the gory bits. Pop had fought the Tans and sometimes, could be wheedled into stories. But they were all about nicknames, and burying rifles up the Brake. Eventually I'd lose patience with him and blurt out the important question: 'Did you shoot anyone, Pop?'

''Tis very late,' he'd say. 'Ye're father will be wonderin'.' Having fought against them he had to go and make his living among them in the Dagenham foundry. During his exile, he developed a great respect for what he called 'the real English people' as he huddled into basements with them from Hitler's bombs. Bridgie had no such brakes.

'Dere was terrible bad tings done too, boy. A gang of de boys shot an informer over the road dere one night, and, God forgive them, wasn't he out of his mind with drink.'

She stopped, and looked beyond me and the sweet-smelling shop to hard and hurtful times.

Bridgie was the only one who spoke easily about Maura, my mother. She could switch with stomach-wrenching suddenness from an ambush to something Maura said to her on the road or a dress she had worn on a summer's evening. I sat there trying to be invisible, gathering these throwaway threads and weaving them into the sepia coloured memory I carried in my heart.

'Wait 'til your father comes home,' was a common threat in the Lane. I never appreciated that men who were gone to work before we opened our eyes and came home, tired in the evenings, got the short end of the stick by being cast in the role of the heavy hand of justice. I remember them as *Echo*-readers, kindly men who tossed my hair and said things like: 'You're gettin' very lanky, God bless ya!' or 'What book are you in now?' The Mack's dad was a foreman carpenter and clerk of works on the new church at the top of Grawn. Neilus' dad worked in Goulding's fertiliser factory out in the Glen. He let us see the vats of acid one day and lit a match by touching it to the surface of the innocent-looking liquid. His shirt had lots of tiny holes burned into it by the splatters from the vats.

Only two men didn't go to regular jobs. Thomas lived alone and rarely spoke to anyone but that 'was his way,' and no one passed any remark on him. Mrs Purcell made sure the gasman had access to the meter and his sister came once a week to tidy the house for him. Jack, the other one, had a hump on his back, a permanent cap and a passion for opera. Dave swore that Jack could have been on the stage of the Opera House 'if 'twasn't for his affliction.' Passing Keatings' door was an education as Gigli and Tauber swelled out of the house from his scratchy records. When Jack took a notion to cut sticks for his mother in the backyard, the neighbourhood men would take the *Echo* to the outside toilets to enjoy the arias in doubtful Italian that poured pure and strong from his twisted body.

The two men who were the supports of our world lived just two doors apart. Pop, my grandfather, smelled of pipe tobacco and trained me as his acolyte. I would take the moist plug in my left hand and the shiny silver knife in my right. 'Mind your fingers, for the love of God.' The whittled grains had to be rubbed into curls in my palm before they were mixed with the 'dottle' from the previous smoke. This dusty concoction was tamped firmly into the bowl and at last the match was struck. 'Always strike away from yourself, boy, in case the sulphur flies.' It was vital to keep the match away from the bowl until the sulphur burned away and then it had to be held over the bowl so that the flame was drawn into the tobacco. When this painstaking ritual was finally completed, he'd puff furiously for a few seconds – and the pipe would go out. 'Arrah, bad cess to it,' he'd say good humouredly, 'but the fella who invented the pipe wanted to sell matches.'

He was also my tutor in the mysteries of one-hundred-and-ten, dealing the hands on a chair set between the two of us before the fire. 'Five, Jack, Joker, Ace of Hearts, Ace of Trumps, highest in red, lowest in black,' I recited to his satisfaction at the end of our first lesson. I learned to hold my cards well up to my chest, to 'poke' against the dealer with a handy trump and never ever to renege. The cards were an excuse for talk about promising terriers and famous hounds, and a closeness grew between us until the night he broke the rules. 'C'mere,' I said, 'you reneged on my Ace of Hearts.' The apprentice had dared to question the master. He looked at me over the tops of his glasses. 'I did not.' But, I was like a Jack Russell in a ditch, answering to no master in my pursuit of prey. It ended badly. 'Well,' I said righteously, 'if that's the way you're going to play, I won't play at all.' I stormed out the door to my own house. Dave could read me like a book. 'What happened?' I related my tale, a little less assured now that my teaspaí' had worn off. 'Go up now. ye caffler, and apologise to Pop.' It was the longest walk of my life. By the time I got to his door, my eyes were dangerously full. He was sitting where I had left him, the pipe going full blast, the cards untouched. 'Tis your deal' he said, before I could open my mouth, saving me the shame and scald of tears. We played on far into the evening as if nothing had happened between us. He had great nature in him and I loved him fiercely for it.

Dave ordered our evenings around the homework. He had a great belief that 'de books,' would be our passport to good jobs and a better life. He hovered over us as we wrestled with sums which he had a gift for and Irish which he couldn't fathom at all. Kay was our reference point when deciding whether there was or wasn't a séimhiú. The wonder was that she ever got her own work done between us.

With the books away in the sacks at last, we would have a concert. The small hall off the kitchen had a curtain to catch the draught from the back door and we took turns before it, announcing the acts into the handle of the brush.

'And now, ladies and gentlemen, Bernie Kenneally.'

Loud applause from the audience as Bernie entangles herself in the curtain and then escapes to stand scarlet beside the gasstove. 'A bit of order now,' Dave commanded the unruly crowd in the gods. 'Now, Ber girl.' In her small tuneless voice she would start into 'Every lickle girl would like to be ...' Michael and I would be bent double in an agony of giggles.

'I'll soften the two of ye. Go on girl, don't mind them.' Michael and I sang a duet we entitled 'Off with the boys on an engine' and Kay sang 'De swallow now'. Maybe the same scene was being reenacted in the other houses up and down the Lane but nowhere with such energy and abandon, as if we had to try harder to keep the shadows at bay and fill the empty places. Reluctantly we set the table for the night supper and vied for Dave's lap as he sang in a sweet tenor voice:

Oh my baby, my curly headed baby,
Your Daddy's workin' in de cotton fields;
He's workin' dere for you.

This was the promise that would lull us up the stairs, knowing that he would be there if we called out during the night, waking from a dream, or just to check that we weren't alone.

'Dad.'

'What, boy?'

'Nothing.'

'All right, off to sleep now, 'tis very late.'

11

THE SEASIDE

We all went down to Youghal;
We let the baby fall.
Me mother came out
and gave me a clout
and turned me into
a bottle of stout.

It wasn't Shakespeare but that popular ditty perfectly expressed the madness, the sheer self-abandonment that infected us at the mention of Youghal. As city children we rarely ran for more than twenty yards in a straight line. There was always some obstruction, human or man-made that turned us jinking left and right like swallows. We seldom settled into the exultation of free flight. Youghal was a massive open space with an alarming expanse of sky. The mysterious sea stretched out and up to meet the sky without the blinkers of city walls.

The adults packed as if we were going to America, lumbering themselves with pannier bags of sandwiches and changes of clothing. These were carefully folded for children who would live in a togs for the day. We walked en masse to the railway station, savouring the soot and smoke smell, clinging close against the squeal of coupling carriages. At last in a sudden snort of steam we were off. The train grumbled and complained down the line to Dunkettle, picked up speed as we flashed by Midleton and tore through the sedate rich fields of East Cork, a scarf of smoke waving over its shoulder. We roared from the windows at bemused cattle and screamed under bridges, ignoring the order to 'come in outta dat; ye'll get smuts in yer eyes', vying with each other to be the first to spot the pale blue rim of the sea.

Outside the Youghal station, we clambered up the sharp-grassed sand dunes and stopped at the top overawed by the immensity before us. After much deliberation, the adults eventually agreed on a spot with 'a bit of shelter', where they spread the blanket and anchored the bags. Pop's concession to the seaside was to roll up the legs of his trousers and drape a hanky over his head. Nelly dressed in black, sat erect and unmoving, her pale face tilted up to the sun. Dave fretted at the notion of sitting on a patch of sand and wandered off on bare snow-white feet in search of shells and stones.

We hopped from foot to foot, dragging off our clothes, whingeing when a lace wouldn't loosen, mewling like pups in a cage until we were free. The first moments were heady and unforgettable. Running full tilt on the firm wet sand, we held our arms outstretched, mimicking the wheeling gulls, before we hit the water. I pranced in to the depth of my knees and thought better of it, contenting myself to race sideways in shin-deep water, holding an imaginary reins in one hand and slapping my backside with the other. It was a day outside time when we wandered back to the blanket at will for cup or crust, our eyes roving over our shoulders all the while, impatient for adventure.

Halfway up the beach one day, I found half a dozen mackerel floating in the water, a loop of twine through their gills. I couldn't believe my good fortune. These were the prized fish that sometimes sizzled on our pan in a sea of molten butter and God had gifted me with six of them. My return to the blanket was a slow and studied triumph. Men with red faces and women with red chests over cotton frocks called out from the blankets.

'Young fella, where did'ya get dem fish?'

'Back dere.'

I nodded nonchalantly behind me. In my wake children were shanghaied into going back the strand to buy the tea. My own crowd were less enthusiastic.

'God knows where they came from. Wouldn't you throw them back like a good boy?'

I wouldn't and didn't. No amount of cajoling or threats could stir me from my resolve to bring the fish home and re-enact my glory in the Lane. I hid them in a hollow behind the sand dunes and whiled away the day building sandcastles and burying Bernie. Finally, we tiptoed up the cooling sands, lips blue and teeth chattering to a huddle of towels and the tired trek to the train.

In latter years, Dave recalled what happened then.

'Dem bloody fish were a mixed blessing. Dey were as high as kites so we had a carriage to ourselves and we had to take turns putting our heads out the window for air.'

Uncle Christy had summed up an individual one time by remarking that parts of him had died years before. God alone knew when these fish had died but their stench filled the carriage. Dave and Pop were throwing dangerous eyes at them but I threatened to make a disgrace of them and they kept their distance. We cut a swathe through the crowds in the Cork Station, the fish held out before me like Moses' staff over the Red Sea. Nelly prevailed where all the others failed. Outside the Coliseum Cinema in MacCurtain Street, she asked me very quietly if I would 'throw them away, alanna, 'cos they'll bring a fit of sickness into the house.' My stubbornness, which had stiffened against the threats of the men, melted away under her soft gaze, and the fish fell at the side of the road. I thought their eyes looked up reproachfully at me from the rubbish.

Crosshaven was a different experience altogether. It is a small village tucked into the elbow of the estuary, just around the corner from the sea. Spike Island is the centre hub of the vast circle of water that separates brash Crosshaven from the stolid cathedral town of Cobh. The twin arms of the harbour extend to Roche's Point on the Cobh side and Church Bay on the other. They are straddled by two large navy forts. The one on the Crosshaven side is called Camden, and it hulks over the harbour under a camouflage of scrub grass and gorse. The stretch of rocks and small bays snaking to the sea from the foot of Camden was the Corkman's Costa del Sol.

I went there just once on a northside expedition, organised by Auntie Nell and Auntie Noreen. The troop who pitched camp in a tiny bungalow on a bend in the boreen above Graball Bay also included Auntie Eily, Kay, Bernie, Michael, Auntie Noreen, her husband Seán, their baby Brenda and myself. The bungalow was so small that when Eily asked a fella she had met on the beach up for tea, he said he'd leave his bike in the shed. Mortified, she had to explain that the shed was our bungalow. There were two beds in the inside room. Noreen and Seán had one and the rest crowded into the other. When they were all safely installed, Seán pulled the high pram in behind them. Michael and I slept in air beds on the kitchen floor. The last ritual every night was blowing up the beds and climbing in to sleep with the aftertaste of rubber on our tongues. The beds must have had a slow leak for halfway through the night the cold of the floor brought me awake and Michael was in the same predicament. I sat up in the dark and clocked myself on the open door of the dresser. 'Jesus Mary and Joseph,' Auntie Nelly exclaimed from the inside room, 'we have burglars in the bungalow.'

'Auntie Nelly,' I called out plaintively, 'our beds are after going down.'

In blessed relief, Auntie Nelly started to laugh. That drove me mad altogether, so I added, 'And I'm after clocking meself on the dresser.' That set the rest of them off. Brenda, who was normally a placid child, woke up and started to give tongue. That set them shrieking and gasping. 'Where's Auntie Nelly gone?' Kay asked in the middle of the racket. 'I'm here girl, under Eily.' The little wooden bungalow seemed to rock and sway with the force of their laughter. Despite my self-pity, it was a moment I would never forget. Their laughter teased me into good form again, and, without further grumbling, I blew up my bed, every puff fanning fresh gales of laughter from the women. I pulled it away from the murderous dresser and settled down again, ready to add my own three half-pence to the fun.

'Burglars? Sure there's no room to break in here.'

At that stage, Nelly took a fit of coughing and that put a halt to our gallop. At last, I went to sleep, satisfied with the thought that Michael, as usual, would remember nothing in the morning and I could add legs to the story without fear of contradiction.

Almost every other year, I went to Crosshaven with my south-side Auntie Nora, who was a demon for it. Nora was a small, bird-like woman with dancing eyes and a great tongue for slagging. Whenever Dave trooped us over her threshold for a visit, she'd cry out in mock horror, 'Hide de bird; dey're here from the northside.' Despite the fact that her two girls went to St Al's school, which we thought snobby, and her two boys favoured Sully's Quay, our mortal hurling enemies, we were the best of friends.

They lived in a house that hung precariously to the foot of the barrack wall, overlooking the south channel of the river. Kyser's Hill was a cliff of steps leading to their front door, and the air was always spicy with the combined smells of the Mills and Beamish's brewery. Their father, John Scannell, was a small stocky man of massive dignity. He was a builder who laid floors, dashed walls and mended roofs and so, the northsider's claimed, Nora prayed for storms. John had two worker/acolytes called Willie and Jimmy who always cycled the requisite bike length behind their boss or manoeuvred the hand-truck laden with ladders called 'the iron maiden.' His own house was a collection of architectural after-thoughts, dropping from a high front door down two steep steps to a meandering hall that wound out and up to a back kitchen hanging out over a quarry. It was a warm welcoming house polished to a glow by Nora's mop and bucket. As soon as summer warmed the Barrack wall, the swallows flew in from Capistrano and Nora flew out to Crosshaven.

She always invited me for a fortnight and then forgot I was there for about five weeks. We had different bungalows over the years on the hill above Graball Bay but the most memorable was a lean-to affair, grafted on to the side of a family home. The pro-prietors were called Heaps and they had a sign hanging out on the fuchsia hedge advertising 'Boiling Water.' This was a great challenge to our creative skills and we'd drive them mad, skipping in and out of the yard singing, 'Boiling water, pots of tea, made from Mrs Heaps' wee wee.'

The Crosshaven shoreline was a relief after the dizzying spaces of Youghal. Fingers of rock stuck out from the cliffs, carving the beach into hundreds of small cozy places, perfectly comfortable for families accustomed to the confines of two-up two-down houses. Nervous of the water, and influenced by Dave's yen for discovery, the stretch from Camden to Church Bay became my area of adventure. Nora never minded what time we fell out of the beds. Breakfast was a casual cup of tea and a bite of whatever was going. Then I was off on a lone voyage. Rock pools were a rich seam that took hour to mine. I would smash a barnacle on a rock and peel out the flat leathery creature, rinsing away the yellow stuff in salt water. A length of twine, weighted by a stone with the barnacle bait tied on at the end and I was crab fishing. The trick was to lower the bait close to the foot of the rock and watch it wave tantalisingly to and fro 'til the crab scuttled out and grabbed it. Then slowly, very slowly, I would haul the prize up on to the rock. I was much too cautious to chance my fingers against his pincers and usually hoofed him back into the water. The pools had their share of small crabs with flaps on their bellies that we called purses. Blood-shot anemones waved their hairy heads, sifting the water for food. I often obliged them whenever sprats did a kamikaze on the beach, pursued by mackerel. Any flicker of a rockfish meant hours of bailing with a tin can just to hold the wriggler by the tail for a few seconds. The shark was a shock.

I was sitting under Camden, on a warm and reasonably ridge-free slab of rock, resting from my labours at the rock pool. The slow green swell had lulled me into a daydream when a sleek grey shape slid from the corner of my eye into full focus. The perfect creature turned lazily in an impossible space and was gone again. I remember a feeling of exhilaration spread out from my stomach, as if the sea had singled me out, a child of the shallows, to experience something special from the deep. I never told a single soul. Partly because I didn't want to risk a slagging but mostly because I though the magic might be diluted in the telling.

To Nora's eternal credit, she never stood in my light or limited my scope with expectations of playing with the others or staying within sight of the blanket on the strand. I remember when Dave visited she said, 'I never see that child from one end of the day to the other.' She said it in a tone of acceptance rather than of accusation and I felt grateful to her. There was a healing in the long lone hours scaling warm rocks, and comfort in the regular inhale/exhale of the tide that loosened old knots and made me, for a time, carefree.

The estuary was always busy with boats. Small trawlers could be seen in the early morning swell, appearing and disappearing in the waves, pushing for the fishing grounds beyond Daunt's Rock. Petrol tankers seemed to have only a front and aft, their low-slung bellies invisible from the shore. I got used to the passage of high and low boats, only occasionally pausing from play to watch a navy corvette, grey and purposeful, slicing out the bay. One ship was different to all the others. I remember watching its passage in silence, allowing it the respectful pause from play we gave the Angelus. The *Inisfallen* was well-known to all Cork people. Over the years, it had carried someone from every northside family to exile in England. Some returned and some didn't, and this potential for bereavement froze the walkers on the cliffs as the gulls keened behind the massed decks of the black and white ship.

Wet days were a killer, whiled away with card games on the lino between the bunks. The hours were marked off by the mournful bellow of the foghorn from Roche's Point. Fog settled like a suffocating facecloth over the bungalow erasing the ditch at the foot of the garden. The light outside was headachy bright as the sun fought loyally to burn our mood away. By the second day cabin fever was rife and petty fights broke out over what was trumps and we were banished to the bunks to brood through books we'd read already. Hutchie's father broke the spell. 'Awful day, missus,' was his passport to the teapot.

'Desperate, boy! I'm driven demented.'

'Sure I know, me own crowd are like a parcel of cats. Listen, boys: I have news for ye. Accordin' to the paper, there's a liner due in tomorrow mornin'. About half five she's due.'

Despite the weight of the fog, our gloom lifted. A liner, Janey Mack.

The following morning we tiptoed out the door, catching it before it could lash back on its spring and wake the house. Graball Bay was mysterious with fog and the tolling of invisible buoys. There was a grassy hollow half way over the cliff and we hunched there, miserable with damp. Then as if in answer to our unspoken prayers the fog rolled up and a city of lights appeared before us, floating on throbbing engines up the channel to Cobh. Our hearts beat in sympathetic rhythm as this apparition from another world eased slowly out of sight, only the high breakers on the strand beneath convincing us that it hadn't been a dream.

In Crosshaven, the day belonged to the sea and the night belonged to the merries. At the start of every holiday, I measured out my money for the merries. There might be the odd lop (penny) for a few sweets or an extravagant threepence for an ice-cream, but the merries merited a full shilling for every night of the week. When the tea was over, we quelled our impatience kicking a ball outside the bungalow until Nora wheeled out the go-car. At the first bend of the road, beyond Driscoll's farm, we cut across country, along the flank of the cross-topped hill and quickened our pace with the fall of ground to the lights below. The merries spun and sparkled to loud music behind a whitewashed wall. Trailers and generators formed a rough square, and, as daylight ebbed to stars, this was our patch of magic.

We were spoiled for choice. The swinging boats had the double advantage of being cheap and not too adventurous. There was also a fair chance that the man would get forgetful about regular customers and we'd have two or three gos for our money, before he'd raise the plank and judder us back to earth. We became expert at timing the pull on the downswing for maximum lift and raising our bottoms to avoid the friction from the plank. The bumpers were mostly a spectator sport. We thrilled to the whine of the engines as they charged about under their pilot light spark and held our breath as the attendants rode the rubber rims to turn the wheel for helpless girls. But we watched our chance and sometimes approached a lone grown-up.

'Can I go round with you, sir?'

This gambit worked wonders on fellas with new long pants and pimples who didn't have to pay for the passenger anyway. For the next frantic five minutes I would clutch the rim, pretending to steer Mick Scannell's bumper into the retaining border, all the while changing gear and revving in my throat.

The large wheel that loomed high above the merries made me dizzy looking at it so I gave it a wide berth. A sawn-off, butty little man in a posh waistcoat took bets on metal coloured horses that ran round a turntable on his stall. Tuppence on the right horse could boost our stock to a full shilling. If Mamie was with us, we were made. She spent her whole night on the wheel of fortune and never came away without cups and saucers or, if we could get to her on time, a football. It was usually a light plastic one that put up with a few kicks on the strand before it headed for England on an off-shore breeze.

No night in the merries was complete without chips. The chip shop was strategically placed right opposite the entrance and had seduced our noses long before our bellies urged us out. It was always boiling with people. The ageless woman behind the counter, shovelled, bagged and shook salt and vinegar all in one smooth movement, shelling change and shouting orders all the time. Out of good manners, we offered a chip to the adults and happily they rarely accepted. This was the feast for the road home, to be eaten with mouths opened wide for relief from the scald of salty chips. It was always with a sense of disappointment that we groped our way to the crunchy bits of flotsam swimming in vinegar at the bottom of the bag. Night supper was a cup of milky tea and talking softly so as not to wake Catherine and Gerard. Mamie and Nora, freed from the laundry and the house on Kyser's Hill, swapped stories over and back about that foreign country, the southside, answering the questions in my head about the other half of my tribe. At last the beds and the final satisfaction of putting my feet on Mick Scannell's sunburn before the memories of treasure pools and rhythmic waves lulled me off to sleep.

12

ALTAR BOYS

In our lane the only kind of boy to be was a Mon boy. The North Mon was where big boys went after their first holy communion to play hurling, be taught by 'de monks' and get good jobs. That was the dream of parents who had never gone there themselves but who would put up with any hardship to make sure their children did. Like all traditions it had its private and public heroes. Our uncles had all soldiered there and hadn't Jack Lynch been a Mon boy himself. But first, there was the hurdle of first communion.

Sr Eucharia chanted us through our prayers and tapped a spoon on our tongues in the nun's chapel to prepare us for the day. The more delicate among us had qualms about being down the queue for the spoon. Nobody wanted to be behind Whacker, convinced he had the mange at least and the spoon would give us 'a fit of the gawks'. Communion was preceded by confession and it was a shock to discover that most of what we had done for the past seven years was a sin. There was also a serious practical problem. How could we do a reasonable stock take of seven years black-guarding in just a few minutes? I settled on a formula that stood me in good stead for years. 'I told lies; I didn't do what I was told; I threw stones; I back-answered me father.' Three Hail Marys was a fair penance for that list of misdemeanours. Some of the des-peradoes in my class had more serious matters to confess.

'I stole a Woodbine from me Daddy's box.'

'I kept the change from the messages.'

'I put pepper in me Nanny's snuff.'

The prospect quietened them for weeks before the event. On

the dreaded day we were shepherded up Gerald Griffin Street by Sr Eucharia into the candle-flecked gloom of the North Chapel. I had my fingers crossed that I'd get either Fr Harte or Fr O'Sullivan. They were pushovers when it came to penance and my prayers were answered. Other 'seeds fell among thorns.' In some of the other boxes, there were a few red faces, the odd tear and one or two puddles of perfect contrition.

The communion suit was got from a tailor in Castle Street. Pop and Dave nodded approvingly while a small fidgety man made me nervous sticking and slashing with pins and chalk. It was a good suit but not a miraculous one like Michael's. My brother's communion coincided with bad times at the factory. Dave was working some days and 'idle' more. Nan had worried about the expense of the suit and took the worry to her prayers at the side of her bed. 'During the night I opened me eyes and there was Maura. "Mother," she said, "you'll find the money for the suit in the leaves of the front-room table."' Over a cup of tea the following morning Nan shared the apparition with Auntie Noreen and the two of them ventured to the front room. 'When I tugged at the table, didn't a roll of notes drop at me feet on the floor.' My communion was not as dramatic but just as rewarding financially. After the tour of the tribe I had a satisfying crackle in every pocket of the new suit.

In a fit of religious zeal, I decided I wanted to be an altar boy. 'Well, your brother is a very good altar boy,' said Fr Cashman. 'He's always on time for the early mass. I hope you'll be just as good.' I didn't point out that Michael's punctuality had more than a little to do with Dave's threat to 'flake the backside off him' if he didn't get out of the bed.

Nelly and Noreen brought me up to the Good Shepherd Convent in Sunday's Well to be fitted for an altar boy's outfit. I wasn't too mad about that idea because the Good Shepherd nuns ran an orphanage and we were regularly threatened with it when we were bold. The altar boy's 'togs' was made up of a long purple soutane with too many buttons, and a snow-white surplice to put over it. This was topped off with a scarlet cape that went around the shoulders and was fastened with a hook and eye under the chin. We wore knee-length scarlet socks that could double as football socks and a pair of black 'rubber dollies'. The interesting thing about mass at that time was that nobody understood a single word of it. Apart from the sermon and the announcements it was in Latin. The congregation usually rattled their beads or read their prayer books and left everything else to the priest and altar boys, who had their backs turned to the congregation to 'keep their business to themselves'.' Fr Cashman was a slim, slow-moving man with high eyebrows and a beautiful singing voice. He was another one who should 'have been in the Opera House,' according to Dave. He was firm but kindly and explained the words carefully as he went along. I was fascinated by the long musical sounds and began to pick it up fairly fast, aided by tutorials from Michael at home.

'What are the two of ye doin' with the good cloth off the table?'

'We're practising Benediction.'

'I'll bless ye're backsides with the brush, if ye don't go out and play.'

The Latin did nothing for Towser. ''Tis all double Dutch to me, boy' he confided one Monday evening before Fr Cashman came for the lesson. 'It's easy!' I said innocently. 'When the priest turns around and says, "Dominus Vobiscum" we have to say, "Et cum spiritu tuo".' Towser went into convulsions. 'Lads, d'ye hear dis?' He turned to his eager audience and spread his arms. 'Dominic, did de biscuits come?' Then he joined them reverently for the reply. 'Yes, but father, I got none.' Pandemonium broke loose in the presbytery room 'til one of the priest's housekeepers put her head in the door and snarled us into silence.

Fr Cashman trained us to genuflect without falling over and to strike the consecration bell a glancing bow with the padded side of the stick. For our inaugural flights, he apprenticed us to the big fellas. 'Whatever they do, let ye do too,' was his final word. With this motto emblazoned on our hearts, we dogged the footsteps of the regulars. Michael glanced down the bench one evening during Benediction at David McGrath who was picking his nose. 'Hey, sham, cut that out.'

'But you were doing it,' came the indignant reply. Another evening, one of the old stagers was short taken during a long sermon to the women's confraternity. With all the self-conscious grace of an ambitious monsignor, he genuflected before the high altar and made his escape to the waste ground at the side of the chapel. He was standing there with his soutane hoisted, tracing his initials on the wall, when a sudden premonition made him wheel round. Two small altar boys were standing behind him, their hands joined perfectly before them.

Most of us managed some semblance of grace and composure on the altar but Theo had an extra elbow and no coordination. Every time he came out to light the candles, he clattered the sanctuary lamp with the taper. His most effective method of quenching candles was to knock them. Towser kept up a commentary from the benches: 'Four down and comin' into de straight. Can he make it a full house?' Theo poured the cruets up the priest's sleeve, banged the communicants under the chin with the paten and got a bong from the bell that was painful. 'D'ye know' Michael observed wisely, 'I'd say he's drainin' the wine cruet.' It wasn't unheard of and some fellas took a terrible chance blowing out the candles.

The new bishop was Dr Lucey and he said the eight o'clock mass in our chapel every Sunday. He was a slight man with a pale face and black eyes thatched thickly with enormous eyebrows. We waited inside the sacristy door to slobber all over his ring when he arrived to vest. Adults seemed to go stiff and awkward in his presence but we were easy with him, sensing that underneath the ascetic exterior he had a warm heart. Sometimes he'd prod us into telling stories from school and shock the priests with a burst of laughter. On one such occasion, an old neighbour completely forgot herself. She touched him gently on the arm and said, 'C'mere me lord. You should laugh more often, it takes years off ya.'

Some of the priests we admired for their sanctity and some for their humanity, and a few we revered because they managed to combine both. Fr Harte was my favourite. He had a red face, topped by a head of hair the colour of a rusty Brillo pad. He had the temper to match his colouring and could deliver a clip to a rubber-necking altar-boy that would 'soften his cough for him'. But we saw his kindness and patience with the old people and the effort he put into the mass, and felt comfortable in the company of a truly holy man.

The women of the parish flocked to Fr Jerry's confession box. Auntie Nelly swore by him.

'If you told dat man you were after murderin' your husband, he'd say, sure you didn't mean it darlin'.'

Nearly all of our priests were bony farmers sons from West Cork and coming to our parish must have been a terrible shock to their systems. For one thing, there was the language problem. On any Saturday night in the box they could hear that someone had been 'connyshurin'', 'doin' a foxer' or 'slockin' and with the secrecy of the confessional, who could they ask for translations? The majority, very wisely, opted for the most charitable interpretation and were acclaimed for their understanding. Small wonder then, that one little woman who had appeared stricken before going into the box, bounced out with a light step and a broad smile. In a loud whisper, she confided the source of her happiness to her pal: 'He's in from the country, girl, Sure he haven't a gowrie's, tank God.'

Over the years priests came and went but there was one special man who stayed and had a profound affect on generations of altar boys. Paddy Dwyer had all the best virtues of the priesthood and none of the power. He was known throughout the northside as Paddy the clerk. Paddy was the man who arrived at first light from his home in O'Connell Street. He unlocked the church, hung up his coat and hat and put on his vestments for the day. With his grizzled grey-black hair and big build, he was an impressive figure in his spotless black soutane. Paddy's breviary was the *Cork Examiner* and the first altar boy through the door every morning was dispatched to Statia Cahill's to buy it. I always tried to be the messenger because there was a tanner in it. He would lay it out on the big bench in the sacristy and as I dressed in the altar-boys passageway I'd hear his prayers: 'Well, my God, hah. This fella wasn't at the same match at all.' In preparation for the priest, he laid out the flat dalmatic and pooled the alb, curling the cincture in two perfect loops so that the tassels hung straight. Lastly, he placed the stole in a perfect inverted vee and draped it with the amice. He went through that ritual many times every day and I never recall him touching and folding with anything but gentle reverence. Certificates of baptisms and marriages, mass cards for a coffin, palms for pictures and ashes for foreheads, as well as unruly altar boys, were all part of his function. Sometimes, in the evening, he would kneel up on the bench that ran under the window and with his elbows on the sill watch the passage of people in Roman Street. He was a man who noticed and pondered. 'D'ye know, boy,' he said to me once, 'I saw a marvellous thing today. We had two coffins down at the back of the church and one of them was covered in mass cards. The other poor craythur was from one of the lanes and hadn't chick nor child. Well, I declare to God but after the ten-o'clock mass, wasn't there a procession to the door of people looking to have mass cards signed for the bare coffin. Isn't there great nature in people all the same!'

In the summer we made a fortune from the weddings. After the mass we'd invent reasons to hang around the sacristy until the best man got the message. The other perks of the job were, ringing the Angelus bell for sixpence and going to a Presentation Brother's funeral at the top of Blarney Street. The Brothers always gave a party for the altar boys after the burial and I firmly believe we decimated the Order with our prayers for their happy release.

The mission was always standing room only. Fellas who owed their religious allegiance to the Harrier Bar and Flaherty's pub all year, pooled self-consciously around the chapel doors and spilled into the seats at the last stroke of the bell. This was the only time in the year that we had to leave the altar for the sermon, under strict instructions from Paddy to be back in time for Benediction. With the thundering roar of 'We Stand for God' in out ears, we scampered down to the opposition. Shandon Steeple looked disdainfully down on Dominick Street and between the steeple and its graveyard, there was a perfect place for soccer. Someone always had to keep an eye on the Shandon's clock in case we missed our duty, but Shandon had four clocks that often disagreed. It was known to the locals as the 'four-faced liar'. At the last minute we'd burst into the sacristy and drag on our togs in the passageway that smelled of socks and incense. Then we'd bustle out the door to the altar before the missioner who was cloaked in gold for Benediction. We got some funny looks from the priests but none of them ever queried our sweaty faces. Maybe they took our flushed appearance as a compliment to their preaching or as a kind of solidarity with the fellas sweating in the seats below.

Characters and crying children were things we took for granted. Visiting priests would startle to hear a loud voice from the back of the church roaring 'Holy Mary, Mudder o' God ...' We never turned a hair; sure 'twas only Dinny Daly. To ring the mass bell, we had to manoeuvre around Dan at the foot of the stairs. A deaf mute, he would mime his frantic mass, the cap stuck like a biretta on his bald head. Dogs were regular massgoers, only ejected by a wary altar boy when they got too ambitious and wandered inside the rails. Jenny's dog was always in the chapel. He sat devoutly at her feet through three masses and was often pointed out as an example to fidgety children. One night, he took a turn for the worst and laced into Jim Keating at devotions. Poor Jenny was covered with confusion. 'You'll have to excuse him, Jim,' she said apologetically. ''Tis his first time doing the Stations.'

13

OUTLONG

My father and Pop, my grandfather, were castaways on a concrete island surrounded by the green sea of 'Outlong'. Outlong was the Cork pidgin-English word for the countryside. After my mother died, it seemed to hold a terrible fascination for the men; they saw it as the antidote to all ills. Like all city dwellers, their knowledge of the land was limited to growing dusty geraniums in the window but they invested that huge green space beyond the concrete pale with magical powers.

Every Sunday morning, after mass and breakfast, they would twitch up and down the lane until my Nan took pity on them.

'Will ye take them two out from under me feet and let me get the dinner.'

They needed little encouragement. 'Them two' were my brother, Michael, and myself, reluctant acolytes to the two adult druids. Girls didn't go 'Outlong'. In some weird aboriginal way, Outlong was reserved for men and boys, a Sunday ritual akin to walkabout. Michael would have preferred to puck a ball in the quarry and I longed for nothing more than to nest on the mat before the fire with a book or comic but, when the call came to coats, caps and boots, we knew better than to argue. Of course, we whinged a bit for form's sake and it elicited their favourite mantras.

'You can't bate the fresh air' and ''twill make men of ye'.

We knew, from hard experience, that 'Outlong' was a place for men in flat caps with hawk, hairy, runny noses, removable teeth and jutting chins, water-skiing behind asphyxiating hounds. Outlong was for stick men with stick-greyhounds, Lowry on a loose leash. Outlong was for twitchy men with ear-blind cockers; ferrety men with chesty Jack Russells ratting up and down the ditches; soft-hatted men with mangy mongrels shambling sullenly at their heels; old men with snuff-green overcoats. It was a sting-nettle, rain- sodden, sharp-stoned place outside the security of streets and we wanted no part of it. It was no place for girls, the men concluded sagely.

'Lucky bitches,' Michael whispered.

'What did you say?'

'I said I'll get me ould britches Pop.'

We kicked the hollow metal ESB pole outside Cremins at the end of the Lane, tolling our reluctance, sending out a message on the tom-toms to our pals the Macks and Murphys.

'We are sacrificial victims dragged to the martyrdom of wide green spaces, wind-weeping noses and thighs afire with ire. We who are about to die salute you.'

Bong, bong, bong, bong.

'Are ye ringing the Angelus or what? Come on now, stretch ye'r legs.'

We leant into the slope of Fair Hill, accelerating past the North Mon gate, snatching a glimpse at the building, brick-red from the week's exertions. The Fair Hill Harriers Club slipped by, a cloud of wet dog smell, the bell of an old hound sounding from the yard behind, too old for nosing hare or flesh, snuffling warmly in their beds of straw.

'Lucky bitches.'

Auntie Nelly's house beckoned from the left over the high wall, the last beacon of civilisation: Cap St Vincent, the High Flame of Alexandria, the Pillars of feckin' Hercules, all rolled into one. Our eyes clutched the gate, the hedge, the bright clean windows. We conjured smells of erupting scones, lava'd with whipped cream. Our stomachs grumbled in protest, but the march continued.

Finally we crested the Hill and edged along the cliff over

Spangle Hill, the last frontier of settlers from the city, Cork's Negev.

'Bloody boxes,' Pop muttered.

Beyond Fairfield, Mikey Sullivan's pub afforded a glimpse of men's feet marooned in puddles of patient dogs. There was the faint possibility of Tanora or, please God, a timely shower that would drive our two pioneers to reluctant sanctuary. But God goes outlong with the other old men on Sunday, freighted from a morning full of prayers.

We were outlong. The funny smell? Fresh air. Nash's boreen wound along a ledge overlooking Corkery's stream where, in summer, we stood in leprous white feet trawling the weeds for toirneens to be jamjar'd home. A farmyard loomed rotting to our right, velvet with cow plops.

'You can't bate the air.'

'Right you are Pop.'

We held our breath to bursting point. The men are striding now, hungry for road, trying to outpace their pain, sluicing their raised faces in the flow of damp air.

'Will ye stop.'

'Haw?'

'Ye're going too fast. Ye have the legs run off me.'

Michael sidled to the men, standing shoulder to hip with the Sanhedrin. Judas!

His face was a mix of dread and delight.

'Now there'll be sparks. Now there'll be music. Now this caffler will have his backside reddened and the two legs torn out of his body. Now they'll dance on his grave.'

My father marked time, pacing on the spot, struggling against this choking lead. Pop was softer in his way.

'We're going up to see the view boy.'

I started to cry a miserable silent crying that had little to do with cold hands and feet. He crouched down before me, his round face tautened by the wind that teared his eyes.

'Don't be crying now, like a good boy. Here, blow your nose.

Don't sniff, blow. Good man. Dave, let yourself and Michael scove away ahead. We'll meet ye at the Croppy Boy.'

My father slipped the lead and was gone. Michael drag-ged in his wake, his head turning back. Pop lifted me up by the elbows and planted me on the ditch.

'God, you're a ton weight. Stand up there now 'til I show you something. D'ye see that furze bush below the small tree. That's where we buried the guns during the Troubles.'

'Guns?'

'Yeah. I had a Lee Enfield rifle and when the spotter plane came over, I took a few shots at him.'

'You shot down a plane?'

'I missed by a mile boy, but I got a right rantantan from the others. They were afraid I'd bring the barracks down on top of them.'

He turned me to look at him.

'That's a secret. Promise you won't tell anyone. Word of honour.'

'Cross me heart and hope to die Pop.'

'No, don't say that boy, don't say that.'

He lifted me clear of the ditch, high and close into his pipe-smoke smell, his bristled face sandpapering my face with goats' kisses. I felt the wind breathing over the small fields, heard a lark chipping at the high stone silence of the sky, and my heart steadied.

'Will we go on so?'

'We will Pop.'

They were waiting for us at the Croppy's cairn, and we lobbed stones on the pile in memory of a long-lost boy.

'Michael, you know the song, dontcha. Give us a few verses.'

Michael's boy soprano notes lifted the verse across the valley:

I cursed three times since last Easter day
At mass time once I went to play
I passed the churchyard one day in play
And forgot to pray for my moth …

'He's forgotten the words,' I thought, until I saw his stricken face.

'Come on now or the dinner will be burned,' Pop said quietly.

It was all downhill home and our spirits rose with the fall of ground. We picked up the pace around the aromatic pines of the Mon field, coursing past Sheas, our cousins. There was a man relieving himself in a gate.

'Great view Pop' Michael said slyly.

'Walk on ye cur,' Pop said, but his eyes were laughing. As we rounded the last bend, our canter broke into a gallop. We angled into the lane pressing our numb fingers to the hot spot on Cremin's gable wall, hopping from foot to foot at the agony and ecstasy of restored circulation.

'Is the dinner ready?'

''Tis ready this ages. I'm killed trying to keep it warm in the oven. Where in God's name did ye go?'

'Just outlong.'

14

LIGHT AND SHADOW

The North Mon primary school was bright and busy and 'de monks' weren't the ogres the older ones had promised. Brother McCormick was a 'new' monk fresh and lively, enthusiastically coaxing us through our Irish and driven to despair by my handwriting. 'Maybe you'll be a doctor, boy,' he said hopefully. But despite my leaning scrawl, I loved the challenge of new words and the complexity of fractions. We came across the word 'brazier' one day in our reading book.

'Boys, who can pronounce that word for me?'

'Brudder, brudder.'

For once, my hand caught his eye.

'Yes, Christy.'

'Brudder, brassiere, brudder.'

He had to threaten them with the leather to still their roars.

I remember that excuses for not having our exercise done were an art form. Some offenders opted for the epic approach, launching into an account of how 'Me Auntie den called down wit her crowd and sure you couldn't do a tap wit dem in de house,' safe in the knowledge that the teacher would get browned off with the narrative and roar on to the next fella. Others favoured the understated and creative line: 'De baby et me eck.'

The lay-teachers were all called 'de masters' and the Brothers were 'de monks'. 'De monks' came in all shapes, ages and humours but Lofty was unique. He was the giant who stalked the big boy's yard during Play, his long-limbed prowl as dogged and unswerving as an ice-breaker through a solid pack of boys. I fell foul of Lofty and it was Dave's fault. Among Dave's sermonettes were two particular gems.

'Never answer to a whistle. Dat's very demeaning; only dogs do dat. And never answer to "hey" remember you have a name.'

One particular day, I was freewheeling around the yard, when a sharp whistle struck my ear. I faltered, remembered Dave's caution, and continued. 'Hey you,' came ringing into the other ear but I pretended not to notice. Suddenly, I found myself nose to navel with Lofty. 'Are you deaf?,' he asked. 'No, Brother,' I answered, 'and I'm not Hey either.' I never even saw the clatter coming. Reeling away to become invisible in the mob, I made a mental note to be more selective in my acceptance of Dave's proverbs.

Sports were big on the Mon curriculum. A fever seemed to sweep the school when the senior team got into the final of the Harty Cup and the weeks before were fraught with posters and colours and bringing in the money for the small cardboard train ticket. At the crack of dawn on final day we were out of the beds without urging and racing for the railway, our pockets sagging with sandwiches. Before the train roared into daylight beyond the tunnel, we were hoarse. By the time we reached Mallow, we had eaten and drunk our entire store. From there to Limerick we took turns being sick out the windows or standing in the shaky place between two carriages for air. We strode off that train in Limerick, bristling in blue and white and ready for action.

I can remember only the times when we won and the happy havoc as the train rocked homeward to Cork. There was always a impromptu procession from the station up the middle of MacCurtain Street, until the crowd was siphoned off into sidestreets. At last we coasted in the front door, ready to replay the day before the fire.

Religion ran a close second in terms of interest and involvement. Every class was started with a prayer. 'Grace before meals' as one Brother was heard to remark as he watched a timid new teacher stand up before 4B. The prayer was a kind of spiritual sedative; an effort at quelling our restlessness into a semblance of receptivity. Religion class was always before lunch and we listened to the wonderfully horrible deaths of the Christian martyrs to a background of rumbling bellies.

The scamper home at the end of the day was full of shouts and flying caps and tossing the ponytails of sniffy young wans from the convent school. I favoured the horse approach, whipping my imaginary steed past Mullane's shop, giving him his head on Wolfe Tone Street, before we took the corner for home on two hooves in a scatter of gymslips. By the time I hit the Lane I was beginning to flag. The empty house held no attraction. The sack of books was dumped in the caboosh under the stairs and I was off to the Quarry.

The Quarry was an oasis of calm after the energy of the school day. Sometimes I liked to climb the high wall behind the 'new houses', just to sit and be still. Gradually my eyes would go out of focus and I would float off into a daydream. The sensations I can remember are of the wind tickling the hairs on the backs of my bare legs or the shimmering of green from over the convent wall. Sometimes, I was lulled to the point where I welcomed the impact when I jumped back to earth and trailed my hand for reassurance along the stubby faces of the houses, as I walked down the Lane.

I was also getting lanky and strong and though I knew I'd never match Michael's gift with a hurley, I could hold my own among my own and that was enough. It was in the Mon that the little spark I had for writing was first noted and fanned with praise. Compositions were my joy, and the more difficult the topic the more I relished the challenge. Our teacher in fourth class was quick to oblige.

'Now, boys, for tomorrow, I want four pages on "An Old Football Boot Tells its Story".'

I hardly heard his warnings about 'wide margins' and 'big writing', my brain was racing with possible approaches. When he brought our corrected copies into the classroom the next morning, I noticed mine was at the top of the heap.

'Christy, stand up. Tell me now boy, what does "melancholy" mean?'

'It means to be sad, sir,' I stuttered.

'Sit down, boy. Now, lads,' he said to the class, 'I want ye to listen to this,' and he began to read my composition. It had taken me ages to write it and I had to defy Dave's command to 'hit the stairs' to get it finished. But I had polished it into a tale of the football boot which had scored the winning goal in the county final, only to be discarded for a new pair by an ungrateful owner.

'And listen to the last line, boys: "I was very melancholy".'

I sat in the scratched desk with throbbing cheeks and the kind of feeling in my chest I often got before crying. 'Never in all my years as a teacher …' he was saying, and I had to distract myself in case I'd disgrace myself. It was a moment of the purest joy. There was something I could do and do well and the future seemed less frightening than before. I remember that feeling vividly to this day because it lasted so briefly.

Neilus, my best pal, had a look on his face that was half fearful, half concerned. It betokened bad news.

'Christy, I think Auntie Nelly is after gettin' hurted. You'd better go down home.'

I was rooted to the schoolyard. All around me, boys were boiling after ball and playing chasing in the sunlight, their shouts rebounding from the concrete shed. I put my head down on the low wall and started to cry. Neilus called the Brother and I was sent home. Our little house was in agony. The women rocked back and forth on chairs as neighbours fussed around them. I saw Eily Leary filling a kettle from the tap, her tears dripping into the sink. Over the next few awful hours, the story emerged. She had finished tidying up in our house after the dinner and was heading home up Fair Hill, in her black shawl. The small children from the parish schools were surging all around her on the path. At the top of the hill, a parked tractor began to move. ''Twas an act of God it didn't hit a child,' the neighbours said. But it hit Auntie Nelly.

'What kind of God would do a thing like that?' Kay asked angrily, voicing the question we were afraid to ask. No one could answer her. It was the first time I ever saw my father crying. He held himself all the way from work and crumpled just inside the door. We heard his terrible sobs from the front room as the women tried to console him. But there could be no consolation. The little woman with the bright face and clouded eyes had followed Maura and Nan, and left us. And that evening, forgetting I was a 'big boy', I crept into Pop's lap, burrowing into his broad chest for comfort. I knew then that my childhood was over.

Nothing ever goes back to normal and nothing stands still, School became a place of refuge from the heartbreak at home, a place of rituals where the day was chopped into orderly and survivable sections. When the school bell rang, we formed reluctant twos and shuffled into our classroom. The Brothers usually moved with purpose to their classes, zealous in the war against incomprehension they waged daily. The lay teachers dragged the last of a fag or hung about in conspiratorial pairs as if delaying the dreaded moment. One or two shambled down the corridor as if pushing a mighty boulder before them, with all the fatalism of Sisyphus. They knew from hard experience that whatever heights we scaled today we would be standing at the foot of the same hill tomorrow.

We were now in fifth class; a motley crew with scuffed shoes, socks at half mast, short pants and an array of moth-eaten pullovers. Our new classroom was lit with wall-high windows that baked and dazzled us in the late summer light, taunting us with memories of Crosshaven and Youghal. The room smelled of old floor polish, ink, chalk, pencil shavings, wilted flowers and fresh boys. This was the anvil on which we would be forged for confirmation and we awaited the blacksmith, the hammer of the Lord.

Mr O'Sullivan exploded in the door of our classroom every morning burning with religious zeal. He was a man with a mission. His 'sacred calling' was to prepare us northside heathens for confirmation. Our indifference to the coming of the Holy Spirit drove him demented. In his more apoplectic moments he would rail, 'Yea, the Holy Spirit will come upon you and burn you to coke if you are deemed unworthy'. The Redemptorists came to the northside once a year for the 'Mission' to scatter fire and brimstone.

They could pack the confession boxes, empty the pubs and reduce grown men to tears, but they weren't a patch on Sully: 'Verily, the bishop would smite us on our unwashed cheeks and should there be blot or stain, taint or blemish on our immortal souls, we would bear his handprint like the mark of Cain forever and for all eternity as well.' In his darkest hour of travail, and they were a daily occurrence, he would fling his arms in the air and lament his failure in the civil service examinations. When we lapsed into the local vernacular and said 'he do' and 'he have' he would throw the window wide and cast our dinkies, fudgies and other such distracting perversions to the grateful mob who knew his form and waited under our class window. We never batted a collective eyelid; this was par for the course. Sully could 'maudlin' for Ireland, slobbering on in endless anguish about the fate of our immortal souls and the definition of Trans-sub-stant-iation, and we would nod comfortingly. He was from the southside, 'nough said. He might, in extremis, rush to the cupboard and grope feverishly for the stick and though we called out helpfully, ''Tis on the second shelf, sir', he somehow failed to find it. He would cast around the room, eyes darting into the unlikeliest hidey-holes, all the time berating us for escaping righteous chastisement.

He could out-opera *Boheme*: Sully's 'tiny hand' was fallin' off with the cold; hand him a pencil and he'd stab himself; a confiscated sweet paper was Desdemona's hanky.

'He's off his game,' Towser remarked, and we nodded wisely, anticipating the van and the men in white coats, the jacket that zipped up at the back and Sully foaming a fond farewell as they escorted him to the big house up the Lee Road. There, at last, he would find solace with the fella from Shandon Street who thought he was God. We loved him.

We savoured Sully for one mad, glorious year, learning to parrot the lines that soothed his demons.

'Why do we call God our father?'

'We call God our Father because He gave us life and provides for us with fatherly care.'

'Yes,' he'd mutter gratefully, 'Oh yes.'

In the month of May, those who took the catechism to heart and dwelt upon such things scoured the Brake and under the Eight Arch Bridge for bluebells to intoxicate the statue of the Virgin on the class altar.

'Oh Mary we crown thee with blossoms today,' Sully sang joyfully, his eyes uplifted.

The sons of Adam among us deflowered every garden between home and school so that lilies, chrysanthemums, pansies, and every manner of cultivated plant sang hosannas to Mary the mother of Jesus with their country cousins. And behold, the principal was summoned by Sully to gaze upon it and found it 'good'.

God help you if his raging sentimentalism focused on your unruly head.

'Christy Kenneally, boys. Chris-ty Kenn-eally. His mother is … dead.'

'What happened her?' Towser asked, suddenly full of interest.

'Cut off in her youth,' Sully proceeded tearfully. 'Those whom the Lord loves he takes unto himself. No one home, no one to answer the door, no nighttime kiss …'

'I have me Nan in the southside sir,' I said defensively.

'I have my Nan,' Sully said, never breaking stride. 'My Nan, my Nan, the old woman of the road. Oh to have a little house to own the hearth and stool and all … a little house, a house of my own out of the wind and the rain's way.'

'Is yer nan a knacker?' Towser inquired.

'Will you shut your gob, dún do bhéal you blasted heathen,' Sully roared, his misty mood evaporating. We heaved a collective sigh of relief. Sully was back.

But, sometimes, he despaired. The black dog would shadow him in the door and he would gaze mournfully upon us and sigh. 'Why, why,' he breathed and his breath was of mint.

'Look at ye, look at ye.'

We looked and shrugged.

'Ye'll be lucky to end up as messenger boys,' he quavered.

'Jesus, that's great,' Towser murmured, 'messenger boys have bikes.'

'He who takes the name of the Lord in vain shall be cast into infernal fire,' Sully shouted but his heart wasn't in it.

Sully lapsed deeper and deeper, up to his leather-padded elbows in the Slough of Despond as the dreaded day hove nearer. The bishop was coming.

The bishop came. He knocked and entered shyly. He was a spare man with a shock of white hair and loads of red buttons down the front of his black frock. The principal closed the door behind him and fled. Sully was already on his knees, hobbling across the room to slobber the ring.

'Are they good boys?' the bishop asked.

'The best my Lord. The cream of the crop, your lordship, never in all my years preparing boys for the sacraments ...'

The bishop gave us a wary eye.

'What is Chrism?'

'Oil of olives mixed with balm and blessed by the bishop on Holy Thursday,' we thundered.

'Very good,' he said cautiously, fixing his little red tea-cosy on his head with one hand and trying to raise Sully from his knees with the other. Sully was having none of it. Eyes locked on the plaster Virgin, he held his arms aloft like Moses willing us to victory.

'Is the Father God?' the bishop asked, his eyes falling on Towser.

'Yeah,' answered Towser enthusiastically.

'Yes, the Father is God,' Patsy Burke interpreted.

'Is the Son God?' the bishop persevered.

'Bloody full sure He is,' Towser said, all fired up to proclaim his faith.

'And the Holy Spirit?' the bishop asked faintly.

"Course He is,' Towser exulted.

'I look forward to seeing you all on confirmation day,' the bishop said quickly and backed out the classroom door to rapturous applause.

'Did we pass sir?'

'Never in all my years teaching,' Sully whimpered.

'Three cheers for Sully. Hip Hip …'

15

MASTERS AND MISCREANTS

They told us that school was the best time of our lives. It was typical of hard-working people whose rose-coloured view of education was reflected in the Irish poem, 'aoibhinn beatha an scolaire a bhios ag deanamh leinn' (ah, the blissful life of the scholar who passes the time reading). Retrospect is always twenty-twenty vision and nostalgia has a way of blunting the hard edges.

Baby school was a place I dreaded going to and then never wanted to leave. We would learn the three Rs, Reading, Ritin' and Rithmetic, and our mothers would have the benefit of the fourth R, Rest. We were Sister Eucharia's boys, to be hugged and hassled in equal measure but we knew our destiny lay beyond the cosy classroom and riotous yard of the North Pres. All too soon, we would leave that happy sinless state and be wafted by a thermal of expectation to the all-male world of Brothers and masters in the North Mon.

We were enthralled by the young tousle-haired Brother who skipped enthusiastically into our lives. He had a life-force that was infectious and swept us along through the excitement of story-books, the tongue-protruding exactness of traced maps and the mysteries of long-division. The introduction of the 'leather' was a discordant note. If we acted the 'caffler' at home we got a clip and rarely felt hard done by. The punishment in school was for 'not knowing' or for homework sloppily done. Not everyone had a memory for lines of poetry and some shared the kitchen table and their homework with unruly small ones so that their exercise copies, badged with jam stains, were often testimonies to effort rather than neatness.

I remember he'd say, 'this hurts me more than it hurts you'. Even as a small boy, I had difficulty squaring stinging palms with his genuine efforts at being a good teacher. Fellas developed 'slapping strategies'. Some 'rode the punch' by dropping their hands at the moment of contact to lessen the force of the blow. Others contorted themselves into the most amazing shapes, offering as little bare skin as was humanly possible. The result was always the same; we hurried back to our seats our flaming hands tucked in our armpits for comfort and bowed our flaming faces to the desk fighting back the tears. The powerless always develop survival techniques to subvert the oppressor. We took refuge in the cruelest nicknames and spread mythological stories about a boy's father who had turned up at the door one day and clocked the Brother. But, we never said a word at home. We knew only too well what the answer would have been. 'You must have deserved it', and 'here's another clip for annoying the Brother'.

Secondary school, we believed, would be different. We would be big boys, dedicated scholars, and the Brothers and Masters would be our companions and motivators in the great learning adventure. Human nature being what it is, some teachers rose to that challenge and some didn't.

We met Brother O'Brien in first year. His initials immediately destined him to be known as Bob. He was a lean, ascetic man with a shock of white hair and we thought he must be ancient. He underlined our belief by enthusing about Fionn MacCumhaill, Cuchulainn and the Red Branch Knights as if they were past pupils of the Mon like Jack Lynch. His eccentricities only endeared him to us. I remember he would greet the class with 'bail ó Dhia ar an obair' (God's blessing on the work), and we would chorus, 'An bhail cheanna ortsa' (The same blessing on yourself). Some of the more militant said 'volcano'. One day he introduced a small clicking instrument. 'Look boys,' he said gravely, 'fifty years ago, a teacher clicked this at the start of class and an immediate and attentive silence reigned in the room.' We were amazed. Our unruly mob could have shrugged off a klaxon and fire hose.

Bob was a lover of all things Gaelic. If he had been president instead of Dev, the whole country would have been jigging at the crossroads and away up the boreens as well. His special love was the 'language'. 'Nil aon tír gan teanga,' he reflected, more as an aspiration than an admonition and there was a sadness in his voice. Luckily for us, his teaching methods were very different from those who reduced a beautiful language to the irregular verbs and who substituted casual violence for motivation. Warily, we took his measure during the first term, waiting for the affable mask to slip under the pressure of our undoubted indifference and un-ruly nature. Eventually we concluded that there was only one Bob; what you saw was what you got, there was no homicidal Doppel-ganger waiting for an excuse to 'come the heavy'. Hearted by this we held a meeting to discuss something close to our hearts but alien to the culture of our school. The North Mon promoted Gaelic games, exclusively. Every Wednesday afternoon, we made the pilgrimage to the Mon field to don our armour in the metal shed and wield our hurleys on the pitches. Every other day, in our 'real lives', we played soccer on the streets. We looked longingly at the potential of the Big Yard in school. The Yard was a traffic-free zone that plucked invitingly at our twitching, soccer-playing feet. We needed a spokesman to enter the lion's den, a 'sacrificial offering' and Terry Buckley was the unanimous choice. Terry had captained the school hurling team in primary and his family was 'falling down' with County and All-Ireland medals. The icing on the cake was his name in Irish, Toirdhealach Ó Buachalla, the mighty warrior Buckley. If you pronounced it properly, you could hurt yourself, but it rang of ancient Ireland of the Gael and would surely resonate with Bob.

'Brother, the lads were wondering like if we eh could like you know eh play like eh you know soccer in the yard.'

We exhaled collectively. It was out, the great taboo, the relic of the colonist and barrack yard, the game that 'dare not speak its name'. As Terry finished, the delegation edged away quietly. If there was lightning, no-one wanted to stand beside a conductor.

Bob chewed on the request for a moment, nodding his head as he digested the enormity of it.

'You may,' he said, smiling to take the harm out of the correction.

'Wha ... Brother? You mean we ca ... may play soccer?'

'Yes, if you play in Irish.'

Ah, the canny little man. How quickly we picked up the Irish words for wide, throw and penalty, as well as a host of Irish phrases that weren't technically necessary but were incredibly descriptive and offensive. Bob had the gift of blending the ideal with the real and somewhere inside we knew he saw us as more than our rough manners and optional grammar.

There were some teachers who never saw outside the blinkers of their own prejudices. These were the ones who could reduce a boy by comparison with another or mark him as non-academic because of his address. A priest told me once that when he was in secondary school the principal decided he wasn't fit material for the leaving cert. 'I had a notion I wanted to be a priest,' he said, 'and that was a total non-starter without the leaving.' He brought his burden to his mother. Fathers might bellow and bluster but it was the mothers who went to battle, particularly where education was concerned. She put on her hat and mass-coat and confronted the principal. 'What is his father?' the principal asked.

'He's a carpenter, Brother.'

'Then let him be a carpenter like his father,' the pocket Solomon declared wisely.

'And Brother,' she countered, 'what was your father?'

Not every boy had a champion in a small hat. No boy had armour against sarcasm; that is an illness peculiar to adulthood, and every boy lived with the humiliation and powerlessness engendered by corporal punishment.

I think sometimes of boys whose spirits were broken by excessive beatings. Usually, they were 'gabby' fellas, reared in the verbal give and take of 'slagging', in a community that rightly regarded the tongue as the most powerful muscle in the body.

Most lads would enjoy this verbal facility all their lives and develop the 'cop on' to know when to stop or never to start at all. Jerry was a master slagger who had skipped the 'cop on' classes.

The new teacher was a tall young man with a self-conscious stoop. He was also blessed with a buttered country accent and pursed his lips as he spoke as if savouring his flawless Irish. Knowing Jerry's weakness and fearing lateral damage, Patsy nudged him warningly with his elbow. What was a rein to others was a spur to Jerry.

'Are you a country boy, Sir?'

In anticipation, we hunched small in our desks putting our joined hands together between our knees. The monotonous drone clicked off and a silence frosted the room.

'Tar amach anseo a bhuachaill.'

This translated into 'lay your head on the chopping block'.

We watched the leather strap slide from his sleeve to his palm. It wasn't the shiny black one whose slap was worse than its sting. This one was brown and rigid and he raised it high over his head.

One ... two ... three ... four.

Jerry stumbled back to his desk, blowing on his fiery hands. The voice resumed as even and measured as before, as if nothing had happened. We all knew the drill. Almost everything was a slapping offence. If you were late, brazen, or caught copying your homework, you were slapped. Instinctively, we knew it was better than the verbal slapping, that ridiculed accent or appearance and 'wondered at the kind of homes we came from'. Most slapped out of frustration or rage and the fact that they could 'lose the rag' and lash out was something we already had experience of at home. We would never speak of it there. Where would we find words to express our horror at a grown man hurting a small boy to establish or buttress his authority? In our community, like the Sicilians, we had a code of Omerta, a code of silence. If someone did break the code, the response was immediate: 'it'll make a man of you'.

We would grow to be men anyway. I have met men who were once these boys and when the talk turned to the slapping teacher, they would tell their tale and laugh. But the laugh was that of 'gaire Seán doite' (the laugh of burnt Seán), who is unsure whether he should laugh or cry.

There were others whose authority came from their enthusiasm for their subject and their perception of their pupils. These were men who were secure enough in their own skins and skills not to find threat in a boisterous boy: men who had the intuition to see beyond the sullen or angry boy to a boy who carried baggage to school every morning beyond his years and strengths. These men shone a light on whatever was best in us and, under their tutelage, whatever was best in us blossomed.

As a man, I met a man who had achieved a great deal. He had travelled to many parts of the world and realised his dreams. As we found common ground in our conversation, I discovered he was 'a neighbour's child' and had attended the same school as myself. He told me of the misery of his childhood, a misery compounded at school by teachers who fixated on his faults and were blind to his pain. I wondered how he could have survived that kind of childhood and risen above it to become a rounded human being and successful professional. 'Ah, but there was one Brother …' he began.

'There was one Brother who did something very simple and effective for me when I was in the height of trouble. He just took a minute every now and then to take an interest, to listen, and to keep me in touch with my dreams. I never meet him but I was the better for it.'

It was a story I carried and quoted over the years and then, the world turned. I was filming in Zambia in Africa some years later. The order of nuns I was working for got me digs up the road with the Christian Brothers and as I walked in the door, I saw him sitting reading a magazine. It took just an instant to strip the years from his face and his name tumbled to my tongue. He remembered me, my brother Michael, and our Uncle Joe.

'What brings you here boy?'

Just at that moment I felt as if some Providence had brought me to that particular spot on the surface of the world at that particular moment.

'I have a story for you Brother,' I said.

I related the story of the boy who had found a calm place in the hurricane of his life; a boy who had found a friend and the man that boy had become. At the end of my story he was weeping quietly and many miles and years from school and boyhood, I sat and patted the arm of a true teacher.

16

KATIE BARRETT

Even the river takes sides in Cork. The Lee sneaks away from the monastic boredom of Finbarr's Gougane Barra, tumbles head over heels through Ceim an Fhia, wades with bog-browned knees through Ballingeary to be checked by the stern wall of the Iniscarra dam. Having had 'manners put on it', it sidles down to Cork, splitting indecisively below the weir at the Lee fields baths. The quieter sibling opts for University College Cork, the goldy angel of the Protestant St Finbarr's Cathedral and the mock Greek columns of the City Hall. On the way it holds its nose passing Lunhams Bacon Factory and the Employment Exchange. That channel, the northsiders sniffed, flows 'with an accent'.

The North channel holds to some measure of decorum as it threads through the eye of the 'Shaky Bridge' and passes under the sniffy high houses of Sundays Well, then it lets rip round the Mercy Hospital, whoops beneath the North Gate Bridge, ignores the arias from the Opera House and the stalagmite of Shandon, each of its four clocks telling perfect time in Cairo, Marrakesh, Tokyo and Rio de Janeiro. Demure once more, it joins its more sedate sister below the docks.

A famous professor of mathematics in UCC once warned his students that there were three kinds of students who undertook the study of maths: those who could do maths and those who couldn't. Therefore it's safe to say that like Caesar's Gaul, Cork is divided into three parts, the northside and the southside. There is a bit in the middle between the arms of the encircling river called the Middle Parish. Much like Belgium during the war it lies uneasily between the great powers on either side, crouching low for anonymity.

Born and reared on the alpine slopes that stepped in terraces and winding lanes from the hunched shoulders of St Mary's to the summit of Gurranabraher, we were imbued with the spirit of competition that had evolved between the two sides. By the time we arrived on the scene, there was a kind of civilised détente between the opposing factions, but whenever the Glen met the Barrs in bloody combat, we reverted to our primal instincts. These were titanic confrontations where the word 'quarter' always followed the words 'hang' and 'draw'. As one local wit remarked wryly: 'they should both be sponsored by the Blood Transfusion Board'.

Geographically, if not morally, we knew we held the high ground. We had the Cathedral, the North Chapel on our side and for the annual Eucharistic Procession, our troops massed in the streets that radiated from the cathedral and marched in serried ranks before the Monstrance into the DMZ of Daunt's Square. The bishop was flanked by sword-wielding officers from our barracks and marched to the stirring strains of our Buttera Band. As soon as the Monstrance had been waved impartially over the bowed heads of both tribes, we closed ranks and marched the Messiah back home.

Love knows no boundaries and so my father crossed the river to woo my mother. In school, the Brother explained how the invading Normans had 'married in' to the native Irish clans and become 'more Irish than the Irish themselves'. Patsy Burke looked relieved at that and I forgave my father for being born on the wrong side of the river. It was exotic and exciting having three aunts and a gaggle of first cousins 'over there' and, as we grew, we became firm friends despite the great divide.

My southside grandmother posed something of a dilemma for us. We called our northside grandmother 'Nan' and the southsiders called theirs 'Mother'. What should we call her? My own mother didn't help.

'Remember, your Nan is in the northside and I'm your mother.'

My father was a dutiful son who took us to visit regularly. We managed to avoid calling her anything for a long time, taking the earliest opportunity to dance out the door and play with Eileen, Catherine and Teresa, our cousins, coming in at my father's whistle for a peck and a lop. Cornered, on one occasion, I called her Missus Kenneally and she nearly left me for dead.

We knew in a vague sort of way, from judicious eavesdropping, that she worked as a cook in the Penny Dinner. This was a charitable institution, a refuge where knights of the road could be fed for that princely sum. We also gathered that she had been 'sent into service' as a young girl to a wealthy Cork family but had returned unexpectedly to her mother late one night. She said a man had come into her room and said, 'Katie, this is not a good house. Go on home to your mother.' 'And who was the man?' they asked. 'It was that man in the picture,' she said, pointing to the picture of her father who had died when she was an infant.

I remember we would push in the door and find ourselves in a small hall, screened from the rest of the house by a curtain. When we appeared, she always gave a mock cry of alarm. 'Kitty,' she'd call, 'come down quick the northsiders are here.' She had a high wheezy voice and would gather her breath like a pump organ before speaking. Her speech was the slow plain chant of the southside so different to the excited coloratura of the northside. Lines, like the spokes of a bicycle radiated from her eyes and we had to be careful not to squeeze her hands because her knuckles bloomed with arthritis.

As we got older, my cousin, Michael Scannell, and I would often stroll up under the arch to see my southside grandmother. Being a native, Michael had a vocabulary of people and places that were lost on me. Occasionally he would explain who they were talking about as a person might interpret for a foreigner. He had a great grá for my father, his Uncle Dave, and often braved the northside to ask his advice. One evening he asked our grandmother why her only son had never continued in school after the age of fourteen. I thought she bristled a bit at what might have seemed a criticism of herself. Quietly, she spelled out a scenario that was common to many families in Cork at that time. A boy could go from fourteen to forty, from freedom to factory, on the death of his father.

'I never stood in his light,' she said simply.

And we walked home chastened.

In her younger years she had a great reputation for organising outings, but we had to wait until we were older to get a more rounded picture of Katie Barrett, as she was always known to her neighbours. In one of his more relaxed moments, my father told this story.

Kitty, my father's younger sister, was very friendly with a girl in the Terrace. This girl disappeared suddenly from the group of friends and the gap was filled with whispering and rumour. Auntie Kitty came home one evening weeping salty tears. She had the worst possible news, the kind that would be murmured behind a hand and acknowledged with a sign of the Cross. Her friend was in Sarsfield's Court, the sanatorium outside the city. She was just one of the hundreds consigned to premature death by T.B. Katie listened to her story sympathetically and straightened in her chair.

'Send down to D. Forde for a car,' she said.

D. Forde ran a taxi service from the top of Kyser's Hill in the shadow of the Barracks. The word went out to Kitty's friends and the taxi brought mother, daughter and friends to the girl's bedside. For a few sweet hours, they lit up the ward with tales of dances and fellas, bringing a smile to the dying girl's face. All too soon, it was time to go. They trooped disconsolately to the steps outside, the girls weeping freely now for the friend they would never see again. Katie turned and looked up at the forbidding building and from the steps she began to sing.

I remember, even in her later years, she had a powerful voice for such a small woman. But, more than pitch and tone, she had passion and her song rose up and tapped at the windows. And, as if by magic, the empty windows filled with the faded faces of young and old, drawn by the small woman's song. When she finished, the faces smiled and mimed applause from behind the glass.

As my father finished the story, his eyes misted and he looked away from us, nodding his head in approval at the courage and character of his mother, our grandmother, Katie Barrett.

17

HYMNS AND ARIAS

Charles Lynch, the famous Cork pianist, once announced to his audience: 'I will now play Debussy's "Clair de Lune".' A voice called back from 'the gods': 'Good man Charles, give us Clare's Dragoons.'

Lest you get the impression that Cork people considered Debussy a form of public transport and, musically speaking, didn't know their arias from their elbows, let me assure you to the contrary. A Cork conversation was opera without the orchestra, sliding up and down the scales with an alacrity that would have given Maria Callas the bends. Every Saturday night, the Cork Opera House would be packed to the rafters to hear the touring opera companies and the performances would be dissected in homes and factories for days after with the same forensic intensity as the hurling match in the Park on Sunday. Debates raged regularly on who was the greatest tenor.

'Dere's no one to touch Gigli, boy, can't he break a glass with his top note.'

'Yerra not at all, he's not a patch on Bjorling, isn't he the tenor's tenor.'

'What about McCormack,' some patriot would interject.

'Sings through his nose,' they countered dismissively.

The sing-song was the pidgin-English for what happened at home. Every wedding, wake and coming together of the tribe would inevitably end up in our front room in a welter of sandwiches and Tanora. The few who took something stronger were served massive measures by innocent pioneers and would ricochet home down the narrow lane, slurring sentiments of undying friendship.

The sing-song was a highly ritualised affair, preceded by the election of the M.C. He would require the wisdom of Solomon and the tact of a diplomat to ensure all branches of the family were represented in the choice of performers. The wrong call might not lead to the division of babies but it could split their parents into years of sniffing silence. He would have to be the Oracle of Delphi, squatting on a tripod stool that separated North from South, to divine the sensitivities of both sides. Otherwise, a voice might insinuate itself from the throng.

'Yerra that fella thinks we have no songs in the southside.'

The rituals were equally rigid for the singers. Everyone called was required to protest that they 'hadn't a note', despite the fact that they had been practising for half an hour in the outside toilet, to the amusement or discomfort of the queue.

'Hey, Nelly Melba, hurry up ou'dat, I'm burstin'.'

Modesty was the required virtue. Eight hundred years of domination by one of our offshore islands did not breed a people comfortable with their giftedness. If modesty had been an Olympic event, the Irish would have a certain gold every four years but would be too modest to go up for the medal.

Everyone knew the script. The request for a song was always followed by mock surprise, quickly followed by a half-hearted attempt at delegation.

'Me! Yerra no boy. Kathleen Kenneally is sitting there all night and not a squeak out of her.' Misery loves company. Excuses ranged from the self-serving: ' I'm hoarse from singing in the choir', to the illogical, 'I can't sing, I have a sore leg'.

The relief of those who escaped the call was converted into persuasion of the victim.

'Mary will you give us a song girl?'

'God, I'm a crow.'

'Go on now girl, sure you have a lovely voice.'

'Sure what would I sing anyway?'

Someone 'in the know' would mention a particular song and she'd be off.

Songs were territorial, there was a whole raft of them that 'belonged' to someone and they were taboo. Singing someone else's song was a mortal sin. This was a matter of dread to me when I was forced up in front of the company. I would warble my way into some song with a small breathy voice and a throat that closed before the end of the line. Somehow I'd manage to ignore the stares and headshakes of my aunts, misinterpreting the message and pausing to check that my pants were all right. Then I'd go sailing on to wreck myself on the glare of the offended party. No amount of beseeching glances could rally support for the chorus and I'd trail away to resume my seat with a burning face and a bursting bladder. There'd be a half-hearted clap; the Zen concept of one hand clapping was never a mystery to me. In absolution, the injured party might remark, 'Sure he haven't a bad little voice all the same.'

Michael and I decided to develop a party piece that would sail well clear of other people's preferences. We decided a duet was the best way of sharing the burden. The song we settled on was 'Whispering Hope' because we knew the harmony. Unfortunately we misread the first line, 'Soft as the voice of an angel' and, on our debut, sang 'Off with the boys on an engine'.

The adults, as they say, 'drank their tears'. Kay, our big sister, always sang as if she was at the Feis, with a poker-straight back and her hands clasped demurely before her. Bernie, our baby, lisped 'Skippy the Bush Kangaroo' and bolted back to bury her head in the nearest lap to wild applause. Pop, our grandfather, sang an old eviction song:

Spare the old mud cabin sir,
The home I love so dear
For it has sheltered me and mine
For over fifty year.
My poor old wife is dying sir
And I'm not worth a nail.

Spare the old mud cabin sir
And I will go to jail.

We always had the sniffles when he sang that, even though we
knew the absent son 'a jolly jack tar' would turn up in the last
verse and thwart the landlord. Sometimes he sang:

In cellar cool I sit at ease
Upon a wine cask seated

And we would take turns putting our ears to his belly and
scream when the deep bass notes tingled our cheeks.

My father's song was 'Sorrento' and it always brought immediate 'order' on the throng, partly because he had a sweet tenor
voice, but mostly because the sentiments expressed in the song
reflected his loss of my mother. When he concluded with:

Then say not goodbye
Come back again beloved
Back to Sorrento
Or I must die.

There wasn't a dry eye in the house.

Uncle Paddy boomed them all back into good form with
'Granada', and they practically blessed themselves with shock
when Auntie Eily sang a particularly jazzy version of 'I've got you
under my skin'.

Sometimes, a person could become identified with their song,
so much so that they were referred to by the title within the circle
of family neighbours and friends.

'D'you remember "The Minstrel Boy" from Wolfe Tone Street?'

'I do well.'

'He's after getting married to "Far Away".'

'Imagine. Isn't she "Beautiful City's" daughter?'

'She is, she is, there you have her.'

If singing someone else's song was a mortal sin, laughing during a song ranked fairly high on the venial scale. I could usually
avoid making a show of myself if Michael, my brother, was

somewhere else. One fateful evening, we were planted cheek to cheek at the bottom of the stairs and the house filled up so I had no escape. I was too old to take political asylum in someone's lap, where I could be earthed against 'skitting'. Michael was an incurable 'ballhopper' and, sure enough, once the singing got started he kept up a lively commentary without ever moving his lips. A girl was called to sing who was generously built.

'She have big bones, God bless her.'

She launched into 'Three Little Maids from School'.

'She's all three of them,' Michael whispered and I dug my nails into my palm. She was followed by a man who wasn't noted for hard work. As Pop put it, 'An ounce of his sweat could cure you of anything.'

'I hear you calling me,' he sang, hanging on the top notes so long his false teeth began to wobble dangerously.

'Get up and go to work, ye waster,' Michael murmured, and our backsides drummed the lino with the dint of swallowed laughter. When Auntie Mamie was called, I knew I was doomed. Auntie Mamie was a lovely singer but she always widened her eyes and she had a tremor in her voice that sounded like a lorry about to stall at the top of the Green. She sailed into a long note and began to chug. 'She'll never make it,' Michael said, 'get out and push.'

Tanora foamed down my nose and I rolled out on to the floor.

'Go out to the back kitchen, ye caffler,' they hissed, 'or I'll mangle ye.'

'Good girl Mamie, I wouldn't doubt ya.'

Other houses had other traditions. The Deasys in the Commons Road were a revelation to us. The boys would slag their sisters unmercifully right through their songs even getting up to mime behind them. Everybody took it in good part. The only one granted diplomatic immunity from the heckling rule was Mother Deasy. She sang 'After Aughrim's Great Disaster' in a sweet plaintive voice; a lament for yet another chance at freedom lost, and we saw the adults moved by the sadness in her voice and the heartbreak of her song.

'Come on Joe,' they called. 'We need a bit of a gee up after that. Give us "Sean Éirinn na nGael go deo".'

Uncle Joe, with arms crossed, eyes downcast, and his feet splayed for purchase on the floor led them to the rousing chorus:

> For hurrah the night is ended
> We can see the dawn's red glow
> And we shout it high
> It's a free man's cry
> Sean Éirinn na nGael go deo.

They were still singing when we grumbled off to bed. Sometimes my father would sit on the side of the bed and end our day with 'Little Boy Blue':

> The little toy dog is covered with dust
> But sturdy and staunch he stands
> The little toy soldier is red with rust
> And his musket moulds in his hands
> Time was when the little toy dog was new
> And the soldier was passing fair
> And that was the time when our Little Boy Blue
> Kissed them and put them there.

Typically, Little Boy Blue died in his sleep and the toys remained steadfast, waiting until he would awake again:

> But as he was dreaming an Angel's song
> Awakened our Little Boy Blue
> Oh the years are many the years are long
> But our little toy friends are true.

We knew it was the way of our world that someone could lie down and not wake up. We knew also that the man singing at the edge of the bed would continue to sing long after we slept. Always true.

It was a time when a woman might sing at the sink in the kitchen, radiant in the light from the little window and lost in her song. A man might sing to his summer backyard as he dazzled the walls with whitewash and blessed the shore with Jeyes Fluid. Someone passing by in the Lane might call 'rise it' as a compliment and a token of thanks. My people could take all the joys and sorrows of everyday life and transform them through someone else's words and music. For us children, a gathering of 'our own' was an antidote to our loss and the predictability of who would sing what was a kind of security. I have heard the 'Chorus of the Hebrew Slaves' sung in Rome's Caracalla and been moved to tears by Welsh choirs singing 'All in the April Evening'. But it is the old voices that echo in my heart and bring it comfort even now.

18

THE CLUB

Hurling was the only game in Cork. Gaelic football was the county game played occasionally by the city teams to keep them fit for the hurling. Soccer was a street game and rugby the preserve of those with adenoidal accents and money. Sometimes, in the church, we had moments of religious fervour like at the end of the Parish mission when a Redemptorist whipped the congregation to a frenzy and held the edge of the pulpit with whitened fingers, like Captain Ahab before the onslaught of the Great White Whale as the combined male voices of the northside thundered through 'We stand for God'. Every hurling match was do or die.

Every Monday night, I did a lap of the laps in Pop's house. The men in our lives went to the Confraternity in the North Chapel on Monday night and gathered uncles, cousins, friends and an assortment of Glen Rovers aficionados for an autopsy of Sunday's game. The sermon might get the odd dutiful mention but the main item on the agenda was hurling. As soon as a boy could stand he was measured for a hurley. If the grip nestled against the bone in your hip, you were ready for the fray. Most of us played with 'cut down' adult hurleys, ringed with leather at the top of the amputated shaft and banded with metal strips. We honed our skills in the Lane, the Quarry and up the Mon field. And our collective dream was to play for Glen Rovers and for Cork. From the table talk, we learned the pantheon of great Glen hurlers. They were always retired or dead; the wisdom was that the current crop couldn't hold a candle to the hurlers of 'long 'go'. Our anti-heroes were Brohan and Cashman from Blackrock, Shaughnessy from the

Barrs and Paddy Barry from Sars. The titanic games were played 'up the Dyke' and 'down the Park' and, when we were old enough, we were dragged to both arenas to support the Glen.

'Up the Dyke' meant crossing the North Gate Bridge, loitering to marvel at the blanket of mullet floating in the light-green water. Swans were an added distraction at the Mercy Hospital and the small stream that bordered the tree-lined road to Fitzgerald's Park always promised the fleeting excitement of a swimming rat. We passed the sedate cricket grounds with all the disdain of a Roman mob passing a game of marbles on the way to the Colosseum. If we took the Sunday's Well route and crossed the 'Shaky Bridge', someone might 'stroke haul' a salmon from the river and casually rejoin the crowd. A flapping trouser leg would hardly be noticed in the general excitement. When the teams erupted on to the field, the pent-up expectation was released with a roar that seemed to suck the oxygen from the air and left me light-headed.

The players were familiar; we had a gallery of their mug shots in the photo album at home. Standing between the posts, Davy Creedon looked slender, a mere wand against the bulk of John Lyons the fullback. Vince Twomey looked as if he was made up of the spare parts of other players. A gangly, ungainly figure, he was poetry in motion when he oiled his way out of defence and struck the sliotar as if in slow motion, sending a high arching clearance to relieve our lines. Seanie Kenefick was the Jack Russell of the team, nipping and snapping at the heels of attackers and striking short-stick passes to the forwards. Our favourite was Jackie Daly. He was a hurler who would solo for the pure joy of it, the ball glued to the boss, taunting the opposition and supporters alike. 'Hit it, hit it,' they screamed and when he seemed to have run down a cul-de-sac of vengeful blue, he would flick the sliotar almost casually over the bar. Our focus was always on the front line where Uncle Joe ruled 'the forty'. Joe had a reputation as a tough hurler. He preferred to go shoulder to shoulder with an opponent and pull. Men who knew the game were of the opinion that his physicality blinded people to his skill, nevertheless, the hard-man image prevailed and became a source of wry amusement and even satisfaction to him in later life.

While visiting a hospital in Cork one day he encountered a man of his own vintage who introduced himself as a one time opponent in the Barrs blue.

'We were to play ye up the Dyke on Sunday night Josie,' he related. 'I was picked to mark yourself. I was getting married the following Tuesday and tried to "cry off" but they wouldn't hear of it. Sweet suffering God Josie, I went up the aisle sideways.' Legend has it that they were waiting in the dressing-room one evening to take the field against feisty opponents. The Glen captain was standing at the door and noted the small physique of their opponents. 'Lads,' he drawled, 'look at the size of 'em. We'll have to lower the blade.'

Christy Ring played with a fixed wide-eyed stare, his body constantly adjusting to the run of play, waiting to make the darting run that would slide the sliotar to his hand and curve like a shark on goal. I spent the weekdays trying to emulate their feats in the Quarry behind the house, trying to read the hop of the ball on the rough ground and smashing it against the Convent wall. Gradually, the painful realisation dawned that the best I could be was 'handy', and that my brother Michael was exceptional. To be a sub on a Glen team was no disgrace. Once when someone from another club taunted my sub status, I asked if it was better to be a sub with Brazil or play with Liechenstein. If by some miracle I was called to duty from the bench, I had to put on the jersey of the displaced player and can still remember playing in the heady scent of another man's sweat.

Training sessions were held in the Glen field in Goulding's Glen. Gouldings, the fertiliser people, had always been patrons of the club, drawing most of their workforce from Blackpool and its hinterland. We always began with a round of the field, to limber up. The old hands would try and 'box in' the eager youngsters to slow the pace. There were endless sessions of hitting the sliotar on the ground; 'scourge it' the mentors roared from the sideline. After the usual banter in the dressing-room, we went to The Pantry in Blackpool for milk and cakes, hardly a balanced diet for a race of supermen. My moment in the sun came in a match we played in Cobh.

By some quirk of fate, the mentors decided I should start the game, and I resolved to give it my all, chasing lost causes and risking my head where you wouldn't put your hurley. It was a summer evening and the hard surface was slick from an earlier shower. Trying to copy Ring, I gathered the sliotar and spun for goal only to find myself flat on my back, my left knee sticking out at an interesting angle. 'Get up,' the mentors screamed, but the traitorous knee had slipped its casing of cartilage and locked solid. 'I can't,' I called plaintively. 'Come off,' they yelled. This manoeuvre involved using muscles in my buttocks I never knew existed to inch off the field of play. I sat on the bench, trying to ignore the leg that pointed towards Crosshaven across the Estuary, ignored by subs and mentors alike who were consumed with the passion play unfolding on the pitch. At the final whistle, they all trooped victoriously to the dressing-room and, belatedly, discovered my absence.

The doctor in Cobh was a harried man whose waiting room resounded with competing coughs and fractious babies.

'Where are you from?' he demanded, looking over his glasses at my jersey.

'Glen Rovers in Cork.'

'Go to a Cork doctor,' he barked.

I contemplated reciting the Hippocratic oath but thought better of it and hobbled to the bus. We had all the obligatory stops on the way home at various taverns and a long stop so that my teammates could make a long relieving contribution to the environment. By the time we arrived at the North Infirmary, it was inevitable that the two who had 'drunk not wisely but too well' should volunteer to carry their wounded comrade. We wove to the door of Accident and Emergency, my champions using the stuck-out leg to open the double doors. We ricocheted down the hall and they hopped me on the examining table. 'There you are now boy,' they said with satisfaction, and reeled back to the bus, their duty done.

The next morning, I was given a general anaesthetic and the knee was clicked back into place. As soon as I was conscious, I grabbed my trousers and limped for home.

Some years later, I was playing for the Maynooth College hurling team in the Sigerson Inter-varsity Championship. We were in pursuit of our first title and needed a 'friendly' match to sharpen our skills. As a student of English literature, I should have recognised an oxymoron but impulsively I suggested we play the Glen. It was a measure of those men that they agreed to a request from a sub and arrived in the College on the appointed day. They decided before the match that I should play for the Glen and appointed me captain for the occasion. On reflection, I suppose they had qualms about maiming 'one of their own'. I can't remember much about the game but I treasure the team photograph and remember the intense pride I felt and still feel at seeing myself smiling 'like a half-head' among the men who were my heroes.

19

SNAPS

We hanged our ancestors in the northside.

Every house in our Lane groaned with the weight of pictures on the walls. Of course we had the Virgin with sorrowful eyes that followed you around the room and no home was complete without the Sacred Heart picture. My sister went to the Coal Quay market once, in search of a Sacred Heart to replace the one that had crashed mysteriously to the floor, probably under the weight of intercession. Perched on a chair outside the shop she spied a likely candidate.

'Ma'am, d'ye know the Sacred Heart outside on the chair?' she enquired.

'I do girl,' the shopkeeper replied. ' Isn't he handsome?'

Where pictures were concerned, familiarity didn't lead to contempt but to invisibility. We never noticed them at all until the spring cleaning. The troops were marshalled to scour the house from top to bottom, armed with rags, sprays and polish. The vast white expanses of the windowsills were swept of dead flies and the air was heady with Windolene. The youngest were dispatched like miniature miners to harvest the dust balls under the glass case and beds, giving rise to a conversation between a small boy and his mother on Ash Wednesday.

'Mam, is it true we all came from dust?'

''Tis boy.'

'And we'll all go back to dust?'

'We will boy, why?'

'There's someone comin' or goin' under my bed.'

When the house was immaculate and we were manky, the

pictures were liberated from the walls, their cords whiskered with dust so that they could be hawed and polished.

The oldest pictures were of men and women gazing mournfully out of a yellow fog. Next, in order of descent, came the formal studio or wedding portraits of parents, aunts and uncles. I have travelled among peoples in various parts of the world who wouldn't let me photograph them because they believed the camera stole their spirits. Once, filming among the Masai warriors in Tanzania, the video tape recorder slipped from the technician's shoulder and crashed to the ground. One Masai warrior turned to another and said sagely, 'It had too many people in it.'

Was it this primal fear that froze the figures in the old photographs into such formality? The men always looked uncomfortable in high collars and choking ties. The women were buttoned up to the point of asphyxiation, their knees pressed together and slanted slightly off-centre, their hands resting demurely in their laps. Only their eyes revealed any emotion and these were usually resigned or anxious.

When it came to our turn, we were marched up to Auntie Nelly's the night before for a 'proper bath' and warned to keep ourselves clean or face dire consequences. On the fateful morning, we were slathered with a face-cloth, buttoned into our 'good clothes' and advised to 'smile when the man tells ye, or I'll dance on ye'r graves'.

I remember we were marched across the North Gate bridge to a high house with a dark echoing stairs. The upstairs room was umbrous with black drapes. It had straight-backed uncomfortable chairs on a raised dais and an umbrella leant on a stand with a light in it. The photographer was a stooped shambling man who looked as if he could have done with a lick of the face-cloth and a rake of the comb himself. He prodded the four of us into formation while my father glared us into reluctant compliance. 'Smile,' the man commanded from under a black cloth and we were flash-frozen for posterity. Michael and I are dressed in our new suits on parole from the wardrobe and smelling of mothballs. Kay, our big sister, is bisected by a chair and has a beautiful ribbon in her hair. Bernie, our baby, sits in front, glowering like a suspicious little Buddha.

Snaps were a different art form altogether.

Snaps were taken with my father's box Brownie camera, usually when the subjects were unsuspecting. Maybe it was a consciousness of the Famine that dictated that ninety per cent of these involved food being transported to gaping jaws. But, snaps were much more accessible and revealing to a child than the posed photographs.

My favourite was a mixture of the two genres. It was taken by a roving photographer in Fitzgerald's Park. The park was the ideal demilitarised zone for my parents' courtship; a green oasis between the rival factions of my mother's northside and my father's southside. They are resting in the shade of a tree, my mother sitting upright, my father lounging. To my child's eye, she looked wonderfully normal unlike the formal coldness of her remembrance card picture. Even more intriguing to me was my father's relaxed pose. As I recall him in later life, he was usually tightly coiled with repressed energy prone to sudden shifts and hand movements, some of them in the direction of my rear end. He rarely spoke of my mother and as children often do, we took our cue from him, more for his sake than for our own. One evening we were sorting through a box with him when this beautiful photograph rose to the surface.

'You know,' he said, 'your mother turned to me at that second and said "this is going to cost you money".'

We discovered our 'real' family history bracketed in the pages of the family album and, like the Bible, it needed interpretation.

'Who's that Dad?'

'He played for the Glen years ago. Someone told him he had a lovely head of hair. That's why he always has his head down in the photographs. He was weak for himself.'

'Who's the woman eating the ice-cream?'

'That's so and so, she have a lovely mouth for it. God help her if she was chocolate she'd ate herself.'

The album was swollen to bursting point and seemed to sigh with relief when my father opened it; something he did rarely and with reverence. The pages were made of the cheapest paper so that splinters of wood were visible like fossils embedded in a brown stone. Snaps of 'long 'go' clung to the pages with the help of a dollop of solution, an industrial glue my father had 'liberated' from the shoe factory. This was the history of times past; a time when uncles were gangly and knobbly in short pants and aunts were young and carefree in summer dresses. There was an air of suppressed mischief in their expressions that scandalised and comforted us in equal measure. There were also shadows in the happy scenes.

'She died young, Lord rest her. 'Twas consumption.'

'He went to England and never hide or hair heard of him after.'

'And who's that Dad?' we asked, pointing at a young woman laughing in a group of fellas and girls.

'That's your mother. Time now to start the homework.'

'And who's the fella beside her?'

'Arrah sure they all went around together in those days. Come on now with the reading and no skipping mind, I'm listening to you.'

He left us this treasury of memories: the faces of those who surrounded and supported our fractured world. It was comfort to page through the family album and realise that we belonged. There are other 'snaps' that were never captured on photographic paper. These were the moments imprinted on the mind and held for slow-parsing by the heart. As time goes by, the world turns and we who were young have young of our own, who ask,

'Who's that Dad?'

'That's your Granddad, boy.'

20

THE DOC

Most of the priests in our parish walked and talked like John Wayne. They were big-boned countrymen from West Cork, with footballers' chests and slow drawls. When it came to humour, they were a bit like the cowboy shot at the pictures every Saturday who gazes with amazement at the hole in his chest before realisation dawns and he topples over. The quick wit of the northside always took a few seconds to strike home, then they would smile broadly and tilt back their heads to laugh. I remember they had no 'quick'. 'Quick' in the northside involved stringing all your words together in a rapid-fire burst. 'Quick' meant darting in and out of a conversation like a Jack Russell terrier in a dogfight. It had only a fifth gear; it allowed for no commas or full stops and regarded breathing as best left for later. These solid men were appointed to our concrete Gulag, served their sentence and were parolled to country parishes. Those who were reckoned to have 'fought the good fight' went to the bliss of parishes like Bantry; the others ended up in Schull. Doc Harte was different.

He had a roundy kind of figure, like a chocolate sweet left out in the sun. A West Cork man, he came to us from the seaside village of Kinsale, via Blackpool and only left the city in his latter years for Watergrasshill, a place where lorries changed gear at the summit before coasting down to Rathcormac.

A priest has no armour against the scrutiny of an altar boy at the 7.30 a.m. mass. We knelt on the bench inside the Sacristy window and sussed the celebrant's body language as he crossed the road from the Presbytery. Some arrived wrapped in the Rule of

Silence they had learned in Maynooth. Others carried their own particular humour like a burden that threatened to overbalance them so that they bent their backs and knees and placed their feet with great deliberation. Doc Harte always seemed to wave at some fella on a bike or swap a few words with a woman in a shawl as he negotiated the road. It was too early in the day for chat so Paddy the sacristan and 'the Doc' as he was called, would communicate in short sentences.

'Good game Paddy.'

'All over them Father.'

When he turned to the vesting bench he became a different person. He seemed to withdraw into himself as he slipped the long white alb over his head and tied the cincture at his waist. Paddy stood attentively behind him pulling at creases in the vestments but no amount of tweaking could streamline Doc Harte. Finally, he would lift the chalice in his right hand, lay his left across the top and bow for the door to the Sanctuary. That internal focus had the effect of calming our unruly group so that all of our early-morning itches, twitches and compulsive eye-rubbing would abate and we moved deliberately through the ritual even though he could aquaplane through the Eucharistic prayer to the delight of a congregation who were anxious not to be late for work. After mass he was full of fun, teasing us unmercifully and teasing stories from us of Masters and school-room pranks. I noticed that if someone came to talk to him, he would bring them to the end of the big table in the Sacristy and create a little cocoon of privacy. Although he spoke in an abrupt manner, he was very soft at Baptisms, particularly when the baby began to wail. 'He has a fine pair of bellows on him,' he'd say and the couple would relax.

Whenever we had a mass card for signing, my father always insisted I bring it to the Doc. 'He has no meas on the money,' he'd say. 'Someone who needs it will have it soon enough.' Gradually, I was granted easy access to his sitting-room. He was a chain smoker who declaimed, 'Never start on these bloody things boy. They have me poisoned.' There was always smoke, and books and talk.

We would range over many topics from the humour of P.G. Wodehouse, to the ethics of hanging Lord Haw Haw, always returning to his beloved Latin and how it was the root of the everyday English we spoke. When our stomachs started to rumble, we descended to the kitchen in the basement for tea. I had been brought up to say 'no thank you' and he would always roar 'he will, he will, sure that fella has a hollow leg for food'. Mouths full but still talking we took chunks out of the evening until he declared, 'Go on home you ruffian or your father will be out searching for you.' I can remember the few times he spoke of his mother, and he did so wistfully and softly. It gave me permission to relive the loss of my own mother and I cherished these moments.

In my day, being an altar-boy was a lucrative occupation. Baptisms, funerals and weddings were a 'nice little earner'. When I turned fourteen, I remember having my first long pants which were scalding the legs off me. I was chivvying some small altar boys into tidying their altar clothes when the Doc took me aside. He suggested gently that when an altar boy grew taller than the priest, it was time to retire. I was stunned. It was true that my soutane was at half-mast and my surplice riding like a pelmet around my shoulders but I was reluctant to go, fearing I'd lose contact with this special man. I needn't have worried. I became his apprentice, shepherding altar-boys on outings to Youghal and acting as sacristan at various scout camps. We still discussed the books and he began to ask my opinion about the crossword clues. I cut my teeth on the Simplex version and began to chew on anagrams.

At fifteen, I declared I wanted to be a missionary. Fired up with tales of clerical derring-do from the African Missions magazine, I longed to become Father Indiana Jones, swinging like Tarzan across piranha-infested rivers in the service of the Gospel. There wouldn't be a Jane of course but that didn't bother me then. I took my fantasy to the Doc and he listened carefully before suggesting I might think of joining the diocese. 'A spell in the local seminary might give you a chance to make up your mind,' he said.

On a September morning, in 1966, when my generation was

kicking over the traces of the glum 1950s, I was boarding a train in Kent station for Maynooth. Six of us huddled for comfort on the platform, self-conscious in our black overcoats and Frank Sinatra hats. We were the unlikeliest Rat Pack imaginable. For the next seven years, he kept up a stream of correspondence, always full of banter and trivia and always signed S/H. Parcels of books arrived in the post, a ragbag of Waugh, Maugham and Wodehouse, never anything vaguely spiritual or theological. 'God is in the human condition,' he wrote. At my ordination, he joined the queue of priests who placed their hands on my head in blessing. I reached up and held his hands on my head until he whispered, 'You'll be all right boy.' For the next six years I saw him fairly regularly and yet, we were always man and boy, master and apprentice. As my doubts grew about my continuation in the priesthood, I began to withdraw from him, perhaps to shield him from the pain and when I left the priesthood, I had another life to construct away from Cork and we lost contact.

It took a death to reconcile us. One of his old friends and a companion on numerous scouting adventures died. The Doc was pacing the aisle of the cathedral before the requiem mass, muttering his Rosary as he always did. I stood and watched him until he turned at the top. 'God took one and gave one back,' he said quietly and hugged me.

I can remember mad moments like the time he came to Dublin for a 'check-up' in the Bons. Waiting on the platform, I got chatting to a couple. 'Who are you waiting for?' they asked. 'Wait and see,' I said. When the door opened he alighted to the platform shouting, 'I have come to pare the parrot's claws.' Before I could explain that this was a quote from a P.G. Wodehouse story, they asked, 'Who in the name of all that's pure and holy is that?' 'That's the Cure of Ars,' I said simply. He was the genuine article in a long black coat, an umbrella held like the staff of Moses before him and a beret perched at a rakish angle on his head. In due course my first-born arrived and I summoned the Doc to the christening. He barrelled into the house, called Linda 'missus' and waved a hand at the baby. His duty done, he pulled me aside. 'Do you want me to pour the water on that fella?' he whispered. 'No,' I answered, 'I want you to sit in the front seat with the family.' 'Thanks boy,' he said, squeezing my arm. He was a man of enormous sensitivity and affection who went to great lengths to mask those emotions. I wrote to him regularly, always writing from the baby Stephen and always including long tirades about the ineptitude of his parents. He replied in kind, sympathising with Stephen on his unhappy fate and always signing himself S/H. When he wrote that he was now a canon of the diocese, I replied wondering if that meant 'a big bore'. The reply fairly sizzled through the letterbox. And then, he retired. Typical of many priests, he withdrew totally from the scene to give the new man 'a clear run at it'. He moved out of the house into a much smaller one outside the village and his health deteriorated.

I was giving a lecture in Cork and Linda suggested I should take him out to lunch. 'Are you paying?' he bellowed.

'Yes.'

'Good. I'll have wine so.'

He was a bit unsteady getting out of the car and, without thinking, I linked my arm through his. We strolled together down the street singing 'The Man who broke the bank at Monte Carlo'.

Inside the restaurant, he spread the *Examiner* on the table and we started into the crossword. I got Rambo; he got Pyx. He said they summed up the intellectual abilities of both parties. When we got back to the house, he settled in his armchair, still wrapped in the long overcoat for warmth, his Biretta perched precariously on his head. As old friends do, we talked about inconsequential things and lapsed into comfortable silence. He began to reminisce then about places we had been and people we had encountered over the years. Then he spoke as he had never done before of his age, his health and his loneliness. I found myself reminding him of the many lives he had touched and of the long list of those who held him in genuine affection. He smiled and nodded, and then reverted to the old Doc.

'Go on home outta that ye ruffian, look at the hour of the night.' And then he said softly, 'You have a long road before you boy. If anything happened to you I'd never forgive myself.'

It was as close as he had ever come to saying he loved me and my heart was full as I left. Outside the door I paused to rap once on the window. It was a sort of code, a kind of final goodbye. I knew that would make him smile.

The phone rang early the next morning and I took the call in the kitchen. Maura Corr, his dear friend and mine for many years, told me he had been found dead inside the door. Numbly, I went upstairs and sat at the edge of the bed. 'The Doc is dead,' I said. Something in my tone sobered the small boy frolicking on the covers. He came and knelt beside me and stroked my hair. 'You'll be all right Daddy,' he said. I wept for him then.

THE PREMATURE PRIEST

When I stand naked before Him,
a carrion name
and cancerous with failure,
He will look gently upon me
and wryly smile a welcome.
For clowns are His special children
who laugh that they may not weep
and ease men's yoke a little
as they pass.

I was a premature priest.

In the year 1973, Cornelius, by the grace of God and favour of the Apostolic See, Bishop of Cork and Ross, sat down to rotate his clergy. He found his perfect plan was foiled for the want of a single curate. Pragmatic as ever, he decided to make one. Me!

It never occurred to him that the Maynooth authorities might have something to say about their deacon being ordained a few months shy of the seven regulatory years. We had our own pope in Cork. When the small man with the bushy eyebrows railed against the government of the day at the haemorrhage of people from the land, we said, 'Sure he's the boy for them!' It didn't faze us that he made his thundering denouncements at confirmation ceremonies to a congregation wilting in white dresses or strangling in new suits. Their biggest theological and social questions were: 'When do we get the clatter?' or 'How much money will we make?' Cornelius was following in a long line of episcopal 'disturbers' from Delaney through Coughlan. The former was reported to initiate clerical changes by saying, 'Give me me pen 'til I scatter them.'

The latter, hearing on his deathbed that the Protestant bishop had predeceased him, whispered with some satisfaction, 'Now he knows who's bishop of Cork.'

Naturally, I was the last to know. After all, a deacon was about one step above an altar boy in the hierarchy of the Church. He could bless bread and baptise babies but anyone who had reached 'the use of reason' could do that. In matters of notification, I fell into the limbo category between those he might favour with a phone call and those who would receive only the handwritten pale-blue envelope that could raise the blood pressure of many a comfortable curate.

The call came to Maynooth from the vocations' director of the diocese. In a formal voice he said his Lordship would ordain me on the fourteenth of April and because the official ordinations would happen in June, I would be 'done' in a convent chapel. This should have been the greatest anticlimax of my life. After all, in theory I had been preparing for ordination for the best part of seven years. But I was still shell-shocked. In reality, Maynooth had become a world and life of itself and now, standing in a cubicle under the stairs, I realised it was over. When the shock wore off I made a call to a priest of the diocese who had been my friend and mentor from secondary school. Then I called the vocations' director.

'Father, please tell his Lordship that I will be happy to be ordained on the fourteenth of April. However, I consider my ordination as official as any other and I would like to be ordained in my home parish, the cathedral.'

Within the hour, he was back on the line to say the bishop had said yes. I was always a nice rather than an assertive boy but I had been reared by an independent man. Years before, his Lordship sent a messenger to my father to say he had organised a scholarship so that a society would pay our portion of the college fees and the bishop would pay his. The messenger made two mistakes. He refused a cup of tea at the oilcloth-covered table and he misjudged the calibre of the man he was talking to.

'Tell the bishop I'm grateful for his offer but the society can pay his share of the fees and I'll pay mine.'

Then he courteously showed him to the door. He belonged to a generation that 'had their pride'. If it couldn't be paid for then it wouldn't be got. And if we needed help we would go to 'our own'. When I asked him about it, all he would say was, 'I wouldn't have a child of mine beholden to anyone. You'll always have your independence.' As a widower and a factory worker with three other children, he could have done with the help, but his home was his castle and his children his treasure. Cork and Ross could pay for their priest; he would pay for his son.

Before any great event, people take refuge in rituals. Soldiers check their equipment and write inadequate love letters they pray may never be delivered. Hurlers band a hurley, fold a knee bandage or pack and repack a gear bag, keeping the mind at bay with mechanical tasks. What do deacons do? I remember needlessly polishing my brand new shoes and checking the soles for price tags. As a former altar boy, I could recall more than one bridegroom who had snared our attention with a tag for seventeen and six when he knelt to take his vows. 'She's getting a right bargain there,' some wag would whisper. The black socks, a present from Purcell's, were rolled and snuggled into the shoes; the plastic collar, scrubbed with Parazone, coiled whiter than white on the bedside locker; the soutane, stippled down the front with bright buttons, hung deflated on the door, waiting for the man to fill it in the morning. This would be my last night sleeping in Pop's house, two doors up from my own. This room had become mine during the holidays from Maynooth so that I wouldn't wake to Michael rolling in from the Arcadia ballroom late at night or Dave rolling out to the Hanover shoe factory early in the morning.

Auntie Eily and her husband Pat Daly made a succession of night suppers – 'Sure we'll have one more cuppa before the stairs' – as if we were holding fast to something we sensed would change and be lost forever. Finally we checked and double-checked that all my gear was ready for the day. The old house groaned and leant against its neighbours for comfort as up and down the lane our ritual was mirrored in the small houses where 'good clothes' were laid out and curlers were rolled in before the doors were banged and locked. As I lay in Pop's bed, Shandon tolled the end of day. I tried to pray for the souls of the dead: for Maura my mother and Pop and Nan and Auntie Nelly Dorgan, but the memories welled from the walls and drowned my prayers.

I am back again with Michael by the fire as the old women wail for my dead mother; raised from sleep at the bottom of the stairs at Eily's twenty-first, sick from sweets and bursting with Tanora, to be ferried off to bed in Uncle Paddy's arms. I am hit-and-missing my way two-fingered through 'The Minstrel Boy' on the piano or sitting companionably, an empty briar stuck in my mouth, as Pop blows smoke rings like a Red Indian message from behind the *Echo*. Much later, turning the awkward corner of fourteen, I am soaking up the books for the Inter Cert at the table by the window, safe from the seduction of boys with hurleys calling at number six to lure me out to play. And always, I am swinging like the needle of a compass to the pole star sitting in the corner, secure in the knowledge that though my firmament had suffered more than its share of black holes, he would continue to shine, steady and true.

The aurora of memory shifts in the darkness and I am ten. We climb into pyjamas in the night light. Beyond the window, the grass of the quarry is brittle with frost; every humble puddle sports a silver moon. 'We'll say our prayers in bed,' he says, in deference to the lino's sting. I absolve myself with the thought that the holy souls have waited millions of years for the pardon of our prayers and another hundred days won't make a difference.

'Pop.'

'What, boy?'

'I'm frightened, Pop.'

'Of what, alanna?'

'The woman in the picture is watching me.'

'Arrah, sure that's only St Anne, Our Lady's mother. She won't do you a bit of harm.'

'But her eyes are looking at me.'

'Suffering God, 'tis only the way the picture is made. Close your eyes now and I'll give out the Rosary.'

I curl into the curve of his back, my feet questing for the warm pocket behind his knees. 'The first Sorrowful Mystery, the Agony in the Garden. Ah, St Anthony, your feet are frozen. Our Father …' Like two oarsmen, we rhythmically Hail and Holy Mary into the dark until the old man takes the strain for both of us and I am rocked to silence by the smooth sweep of supplication. One night, right at the threshold of sleep, I asked, 'Pop, sure you won't die?'

'No, boy,' he replied strongly. 'I won't die.'

And I believed him. I continued to clutch that promise through the fall from the barracks roof that shattered his leg into eight pieces, and through the heart attacks that pulled him down so that my head bobbed above his and mine was the arm he leant on. I believed it up to the day the dean called me from the noise of the Maynooth refectory to say, 'A grandfather of yours has died.'

And now, lying in the same bed the night before my ordination, I curl up and stretch my feet to where he would have been. Pop, I'm frightened, is my last thought.

On the day, there was one final ritual to be performed. Auntie Eily washed my hair in the sink. Her baby was overdue so she wouldn't be in the congregation. 'With all the excitement, we might get more than we bargained for. I'll sit here and start my prayers when I hear the bell. D'ye know, you have loads of grey hairs?' she said, starting a banter for both our sakes.

'Better grey than green.'

'True enough, boy! 'Tis a bad tree won't blossom.'

She worked the shampoo into my scalp with a rare tenderness and I knew that this was the last simple intimate service a woman of my tribe could do for me. I was glad of the excuse of suds in my eyes when I raised my head to the towel.

'Shave carefully now, boy, and don't disgrace us with pieces of the *Examiner* stuck to your face.'

Nearly a quarter of a century has passed since that day. My memories are like sparks from the fire that flare unexpectedly, but they are always the same. I remember Paddy the sacristan, checking and rechecking the oils and keeping a wary eye on the spotless finger-towel reserved for the bishop, in case some grubby altar boy would leave his *imprimatur* on it. My white alb and cincture looked suitably humble among the cloth of gold the main concelebrants would wear. Occasionally Paddy would kneel up beside me at the window bench, keeping me company as we watched people file towards the church doors. Gradually the sacristy began to fill. The canons of the diocese came with their fur-trimmed garb and formed a purple pool at one end. Assisting curates in plain black soutanes and spotless surplices handed out copies of the rituals and chivied the altar boys to line up with the cross and candles. There was a palpable air of expectation in the room; then the door swung open and the bishop walked in. Though a small man, he had an aura that extended before him and quenched the murmur of talk. As if he sensed the effect his entrance made, he smiled and engaged one of the canons in conversation. The talk resumed, but more muted than before.

'How're you feeling?' he asked as we approached the bench.

'I'm fine, my lord,' I lied.

'Good boy!'

As the bishop dressed, Paddy unsheathed the two ends of the crozier and screwed them together, handing it to him only after he had donned the mitre. Paddy then stood behind me as I threw the folds of the alb over my head, catching the hem and pulling it down. Then he held the cincture taut behind me so that I could swing it into a loop at my waist. For a moment he pressed his palm between my shoulder blades as if saying goodbye to the boy he had known. At last, on the first stroke of the clock, we moved in solemn procession to the church. The choir surged into a Latin motet from the balcony and there was something unbelievably comforting in hearing the Latin sung in unmistakable Cork accents.

In the solemn sway of the procession, against a background of blurred faces, my mind went again to Pop. He rarely spoke of the war against the Tans. When he was cajoled into a story, it was usually about something trivial.

'We were told never to use a comrade's name, in case the Tans would hear it and trace him. Well, we were involved in a bit of a … eh … tussle like and they were after us. Now there was a low-sized fella from the Terrace and his nickname was Toy. And as we were harin' down Gerald Griffin Street he started to go astray. Paddy Dullea shouted after him, "Toy, Toy!" When he caught up with us he was foamin' at Paddy for using his name and he shouted at the top of his voice, "Paddy Dullea, Paddy Dullea!"'

I was disappointed and amazed. Disappointed because he hadn't told us the real stuff like did he shoot a Tan and did he take half an hour to fall down and die like the fellas in the pictures. I was amazed that all he could remember from these heart-stopping moments were the funny bits. And yet, maybe that's how people cope in moments of high tension; they seize on something inconsequential to block out their fears.

I remember lying flat on the floor of the altar as a litany of saints and martyrs with unlikely names was intoned over me, and thinking, did I double-check the soles of my shoes for labels. I remember, when the monsignor declared that 'upon enquiry among the people of God' I was deemed worthy of ordination, wondering who did they ask. Hardly the owners of the windows I had smashed with a football, or the woman who declared affectionately that I was 'a saucy caffler' and should 'be sent to Greenmount industrial school'. And certainly not Bina, our neighbour, who wasn't shy about saying that my brother Michael should have been the priest. These memories were what people would call distractions at their prayers, and yet on that day I felt that they were at the heart of my prayers, drawing me into the presence of a God who had revealed Himself to me through the lives of those who now filled the seats behind me.

I remember glimpses of faces on the altar. The lived-in face of the priest from Grawn who said a gruff and saintly mass for my mother a couple of times a year, the man who had baptised me and then become my professor in Maynooth. One day in physiology class he shot a question at a sleeping student: 'What's the capacity of the bladder?'

Jerked by an elbow from his slumber, the student caught the prompt from behind. 'Twenty gallons, Doctor.'

'You should be in the fire brigade,' came the dry reply.

I remember the ecclesiastic who always managed to have a sour face in repose so that my grandfather had dubbed him Suck-a-Lemon. And time and time again, my eye was drawn to the round, reddened face of my mentor and friend, Fr Harte, who was known to the boys of the northside as 'Doc'. This was the man who had lent me Greene, Maugham, Waugh and Wodehouse, and who sent pages of stamps to Maynooth so that I could write to him. These are the threads I have left from the tapestry of light and music, wax and incense, question and response that was my ordination. And then, it was over.

In the sacristy there was a group photograph with the bishop. My father, grandmother and aunts representing both sides of the river gathered together. Instinctively I stood at my father's shoulder. 'No,' the bishop said firmly, 'the new priest must stand beside his bishop.' I glanced at my father's face as he struggled with his composure.

I sense now that my grandmother, who was a witness to this scene, felt deeply for the pain of her own child at that moment. For just then the bishop turned to her and asked, 'Are you proud to have a grandson a priest?'

In a rare show of public affection, she took my father's hand before replying, 'Indeed and I'm not, your Lordship, but I am proud to have reared a son who reared a priest.'

He laughed at that. What else could he do? He'd met his match in Katie Barrett.

THE HONEYMOON

The honeymoon started with goodbyes. I remember a sinking feeling as the friends from Maynooth piled into cars for the long journey back. For seven years I had lived on the draughty plains of Kildare, often driven by homesickness to a top window for a glimpse of the Dublin mountains across that featureless, flat landscape, to remind me of the hills of home. But I had made my own of it in time, forging friendships and developing interests, finding a security in a life regulated by bells. And now, like many a traveller who has come at last to his destination, I valued the journey more than the arrival. Cork was no longer a place for the holidays, where neighbours hailed me with that peculiar Cork greeting, 'You're home. When are you going back?' For a man who had left home for Farna, the minor seminary, at fifteen, this was not home and there would be no going back.

Officially, I was to be a curate in the cathedral until the bishop could juggle a niche for me somewhere in the diocese. A prophet in my own country, I was decorative rather than functional, too familiar to be taken seriously. Reminders of my limbo status were all around me: in the old woman who stroked my face in Shandon Street and said, 'Sure I knew your poor mother Maura', or Paddy the sacristan in the flurry before mass calling me 'Christy' and then correcting himself with my proper title. It was a time for grieving, for letting go of what I had known and learning from the new life what it was to be a priest.

Most curates and parish priests in the diocese lived alone, but the cathedral had a presbytery. It was a large draughty building with creaking wooden floors. The priests' rooms were at the top of the house and their individual kitchens and housekeepers were in the basement. I knew the geography of the place reasonably well. The front parlour was where we learned 'de Latin' from Fr Cashman as altar boys, and where Towser, my pal, wondered why the Lamb of God should be called 'Agnes Daly'. Regular pilgrimages with mass cards for signing or sprints at night for a priest for a dying neighbour had opened up the inner sanctum of this rabbit warren. It held no strangeness for me. It was my brother curates who were a bit distant towards the 'new fella'. The tidal wave of the Second Vatican Council was still surging through the church and, while some wanted to surf the freedom of the movement for change, others trod water or swam frantically against the current towards the firm ground of what had always been. That tension was evident among the clergy but it took a local woman to put words on the confusion and pain: 'Father, I preferred the mass when I didn't understand a word of it.'

The church was caught in a whirlpool between the passing of what was familiar and cherished and the assimilation of what was new. Small wonder then that my brother priests should be a little wary of the latest product of a seminary that had changed so radically since their own day. I needed expert guidance; so I went to see Jim Keating.

Jim was an old neighbour who had been reared around the corner from our lane. He was brought up in a house that swelled to bursting with operatic arias from a scratchy gramophone. He had been 'head and tail' of the boys' club and the underage GAA competitions, and respected by all for his good humour and sense of fairness. He had also been a master carpenter until arthritis had twisted his fingers into the kind of knots that defied his saw. Over the years the passage of his illness took him through sticks to crutches and finally to the bed. Occasionally he made a foray in a wheelchair but it was a painful pilgrimage endured only for special occasions such as my ordination. Like a china teapot in the glass-case at home, his visitors handled him with exquisite care; even the slightest pressure on his fingers could flood his eyes. Jim's door was permanently 'on the push', his wife Bridget warm and welcoming, the teapot never cold. I found him napkined with a spread *Examiner*, enthroned on a mound of spotless pillows.

'God bless all here!'

'Come in outta that, ye dirty dog. Not comparin' you to the blessed animal.'

'Dear God,' Bridget said in mock horror, 'if anyone heard the two of ye!'

'How are ye, Jim?'

He held up a caricature of a hand. 'D'ye see that small finger? That took a turn for the worse this mornin'.'

This was a familiar ritual of banter he used to put his visitors at their ease. Over the teacups I poured out my tensions and my shock at taking the men's confraternity the night before. In my youth the cathedral was always packed with men for the Rosary and sermon every Monday night, and I could recall the hairs standing on my head when they rose in full voice to sing 'We Stand for God'. The night before, I had looked down on a sea of empty spaces where islands of old men floated in the shadows.

'Did you ask them to move up the front?' he asked.

'Ah God no, Jim, sure they have their own places for years.'

'Good boy,' he said approvingly, bending his head to the cup he couldn't raise. 'Dere's good men above in that presbytery,' he said after a while. It was a northside question couched as a statement.

'They're a bit wary of me, Jim. I don't know what to do.'

'Well now, I remember lads like that in the club – fellas who'd be watching you, trying to get your measure like. Sure as soon as we'd get an oul match going, they'd all pull together and be grand.'

The Holy Spirit had spoken and I was filled with inspiration.

'Jim?'

'What, boy?'

'Can I have a loan of the bowl?'

The twenty-eight ounce iron ball was a joke-present I had

given him years before. He kept it in a drawer beside the gramophone, and sometimes, when he had visitors who did not know his form and were inclined to lament his condition, he'd say, 'I threw a score of bowls against Mick Barry last Saturday.' This always put a brake on the comforters.

'Did ya, Jimmy boy?' they'd ask to humour him.

'I did faith, and I had one of the Shea boys from the Mon field to show me road.' They were speechless at this.

'He was a bowl of odds up on me when we reached the Viaduct. "Doubles or quits on the loft," says I.'

'"You're on," says he.

I left her loose and she sailed over like a swallow. Barry's bowl took a bit outta the bridge. "You're a better man than me, Jim Keating," says he. Bridget, show them the bowl there in the drawer.'

Bridget, a willing accomplice, reverently opened the drawer and there was the iron ball in a nest of clean hankies. The visitors would make their excuses fairly handy after that, leaving him laughing in the bed, the tears streaming down his face from the effort.

''Tis dere in the drawer, boy.'

'I think 'tis punctured.'

'Bridget, would you have a bit of steel wool? We'll have to patch the bowl.'

'You're worse than him,' she laughed, drenching me with holy water at the door. My heart soared as my pocket sagged. I had a twenty-eight ounce key to clerical integration.

'Bowling?'

'Yes.'

'God 'tis years since I threw a score.'

Kevin's tone was doubtful but his eyes were dancing. Donovan, big, broad and hearty, was game for anything.

'Who else could we get?'

Misery loves company. The following Wednesday we had two teams on the back Blarney road, dressed in the assortment of mismatched casual clothes that only celibates can manage. Kevin was rusty but he was a natural and soon swung into his rhythm. I watched him dance a little skip sideways before he wound into a short run. Then, hopping into the air, he loosed the bowl to spark sweet and true along the camber of the road, driving us up the ditch with wild cries.

'Doubt'ya boy, all the way.'

Coordination was not a word in Donovan's vocabulary. He had the mind and the muscle, but under separate contracts, and his run-up warned us of impending disaster. When he released the bowl we were already competing for available cover. It shot straight up in the air and landed in a field of cabbage.

'The bloody shooting season is over,' Murph grumbled from a tangle of briars.

We were wading shin-deep in green stalks when a woman's voice asked, 'And what do ye cafflers think ye're doing?'

She was standing at the back door of her bungalow like John Wayne, ready to draw.

'We're looking for the bowl, ma'am,' Kevin said lamely.

'Get yer arses and yer bowl outta my cabbage,' she roared. Then a shock of recognition shook through her as if a particularly heavy someone had walked over her grave.

'Oh, God bless us, Father, I'm very sorry. Will ye come in for the cup of tea?'

'Ah no thanks, ma'am; sure we've found it now, so we'll go ahead with the score.'

We reeled back over the ditch, laughing like loons. Our first excursion may well have been a cause for confession for one poor soul but I had found friends.

After that the basement teas became less formal. I began to discover that the lads were reading the signs of the times and fretting for the future of the church.

'We have the whole week tied up in duties, for God's sake; masses to be said, children to be christened, anointing the sick and burying the dead. I'm not taking from them; they're part of it too. But we should be doing less and listening more. It's going to pass us by. Mark my words, we're minding the shop instead of selling the goods.'

Indeed, the duties could very easily become a narcotic against thought. A full diary could give the illusion of a worthwhile service and these men were aware that busyness was a subtle and fatal temptation for any priest. With the oil still fresh on my forehead, I was blind to that. I immersed myself in first fridays and communion rounds, confessions and masses. The theology I had learned from the neck up was now being parsed into practice by the needs of the people. I began to realise that the demands on the priest challenged him to move from the head to the heart. To be 'in the world and not of it' was a scriptural slogan that had been overused to the point of cliché in our training. The people who were now becoming my tutors would never ask me for a theological explanation of original sin but they would draw me into involvement in their lives and loves, and face to face with what it meant to be a man who was also a man of God.

This was the beginning of my journey out of law and into love, and I had gifted guides. The elderly couple in Blarney Street sat side by side in the kitchen for confession. When he saw my hesitation the old man smiled.

'Sure she knows all my sins anyway,' he said.

I began to grow accustomed to the fact that a twenty-year absence from the 'box' might need a few pints of stout to oil the cogs of repentance and that my job was to hold my breath and judgement as the heady odours of Murphy's brewery wafted through the grille; and that it was more important to comfort the child who had dropped the host on the floor than to fuss about how to raise the body of Christ from the dust. The bench outside my box was packed with penitents 'tryin' out de new fella'.

I remembered the story often told in the diocese of the parish priest who ruled alone and with a rod of iron. He was a tough confessor and would often exclaim loudly, 'You did what?' to the shame of the penitent and the entertainment of those wading through a long penance outside. Out of the blue, the bishop gifted him with a brand new curate, a round-faced, jolly boy who was as sweet-natured as his superior was sour. On Saturday night the tide of people ebbed from the parish priest's side of the church and overflowed the curate's benches.

After a time sitting inside the silent grille, the parish priest could contain himself no longer. He thrust his head out through the curtains and roared, 'Is there a slope in the floor or what?'

'Doc' Harte and I had a gentlemen's agreement never to discuss theology but privately I had him labelled as a conservative. Yet he was my faithful teacher and led me gently to the heart of the priesthood. Many's the time he said innocently, 'We'll go for a walk', and led me to to the kitchen of a widow who was obviously expecting us. There would be a fine cloth on the table and the good ware set ready. She would happily fuss over us for hours.

'Eat all that now, boy, and put a bit of weight on you; sure there's not a pick on you. Father, I often saw more fat on a grilled rasher.'

'Yerra, that fella has a hollow leg,' he'd say indulgently. And for those few hours we simply kept her company and gave her a reason to rise above her loneliness.

I remember the woman who helped me into my coat after one such visit.

'Wisha, God bless him,' she whispered at the door, 'but he takes me outta meself.'

He was an easy touch with an open pocket.

'God bless ye, Father, but I'm a bit short like.'

'That fella's making game of you,' I said irritably. 'Sure he'd drink out of a sore heel.'

'Wouldn't it be better to be taken for a fool than a miser,' he'd say gruffly.

He was shrewd enough to spot the danger signs of righteousness in his curate, so he sent me to take catechism classes in Eason's Hill school.

The school was tucked up a lane, the filling in an ecumenical sandwich between Shandon and the cathedral. In deference to both persuasions, the pupils took the time from the four clocks of the former and religious instruction from the clergy of the latter.

'They'll knock the corners off ya,' he said with relish.

I remembered with a sinking heart the day a few years before, when he had cornered me into going with him on the school outing.

'We're going down to Fr O'Leary's grave in Gougane Barra. It'll be great gas.'

They boiled onto the bus, laden down with bottles of Taylor Keith orange and bags of crisps. The first hiccup happened before the driver had time to let off the handbrake.

'Father, Tony can't go without his Mam.'

'Let her come,' he said cheerily.

'Father, I can't leave Mary at home.'

'The more the merrier,' he shouted, seemingly immune to the sounds and smells of raucous boys. I sat across the aisle from him, trying to maintain some clerical dignity, wondering uneasily if the character perched on the seat beside me had been to the toilet before we left.

We sailed down Roman Street with loud cheers and ribald comments from the windows. A line of mothers stood out at the doors waving with relief as we turned the North Infirmary and crossed the North Gate Bridge into the uncharted wastes of the southside. The noise abated a little when we hit the Straight Road and ran out of houses.

'Jay, look, lads, fields!'

It was too good to last.

'Stop de bus, Mary's pukin'!'

I walked up and down beside the bus as Mary and a few sympathisers made their contribution to the environment, wondering if the Doc would notice if I made run for it. However, we screamed into Gougane Barra to the strains of their favourite song, 'McCarthy's Party':

'Twas at McCarthy's party
Everyone was hearty;
Someone knocked Maguire round de room
With the handle of a broom;
McCarthy and his cousin
Paralysed a half a dozen
Down at McCarthy's party.

The monastic quiet of Gougane Barra was soon ringing to happy shouts as they played hide-and-seek in the monks' cells. The more energetic waded into the holy well in search of treasure, or chipped the pennies from the pilgrims' cross. The teachers, Doc Harte and myself, took political asylum in the hotel for lunch, and a line of squashed faces followed every forkful from the windows.

'Father,' said the owner, 'will you come out and talk to them. They're chasin' the sheep.'

With a few bellows and the odd clip to the ear of an overenthusiastic sheep-chaser, Doc Harte got them into order for the photograph. They massed proudly on the flat slab of Fr O'Leary's tomb and then we took the long sleepy road home. Of course there were the obligatory stops at convenient furze bushes, but finally I fell off the bus outside the presbytery, vowing, 'Never again!' And now, like Daniel, I was being garnished in collar and new soutane and dispatched as a tasty morsel to the lions' den.

As I stepped into the hallway I heard a young fella call out, 'Lads, will ye look at Sandeman.'

It was a portent of doom if I needed one. The class was a disaster.

'Lads, God is like our father.'

'If He's like my oul' fella you can keep him.'

'Father, Father, Jimmy stuck his tongue out at me when he had communion on it. Isn't that a mortal sin, Father?'

I began to wish I was a missionary so that I could distract them with stories of snakes in the sleeping bag and crocodiles in the bath, but that sort of adventure was rare enough in Kildare.

'Lads,' I shouted, in a moment of inspiration, 'we're going to have a play.'

'Hurray!'

'Can I be the oul' doll?'

'Now boys, did ye ever see a passion play?'

'Yeah, down behind Shandon on a Saturday night.'

'No, no, where do they have a passion play?'

One studious little fella raised a tentative hand. 'In Yobber-amegum, Father.'

'Good man. So who wants to be Jesus?'

'Father! Father!' A forest of hands. I searched for the hand that wasn't there, working on the principle that he who is not for you is against you.

'Josser, you're just the man for the job.'

Josser was twelve going on thirty. His shirt opened all the way down to his navel and his hair was watered back into a 'duck's ass', so tight it would make your eyes water. The props were simple enough.

'Where will we get the whips for the scourging?'

Two fellas disappeared out the classroom window and dispossessed two 'young wans' whipping tops in the lane.

'Now, what about the crown of thorns?'

This time the volunteer was gone a little longer and returned with a floral wreath.

'Where did you get that?'

'From the graveyard, Father.'

I had visions of clambering into the Protestant graveyard in my new soutane and explaining to the rector how I happened to have a wreath under my arm.

''Tis perfect.'

Josser's swagger began to slip a little at the whipping scene when the whippers became overenthusiastic. He started to growl ominously when the rabble pressed the wreath over his head.

'He's like de May procession.'

Finally he stood up on a chair with his hands outstretched for the crucifixion, flanked by two bickering small fellas on lower chairs.

'I'm de good teef, boy.'

'You are in me eye. I'm on de right side, see.'

'Oh yeah ...'

'Now, lads,' I said, remembering long-ago drama courses on improvisation, 'you're the crowd and you must mock and taunt him.'

They were totally caught up in the play at this stage.

'Come down offa dat cross, ye knacker.'

'He was so smart healin' everyone else. You're a proper daw now, aren't ya!'

It was more than Josser could bear. With a roar, he was off the cross and had two Pharisees in a headlock before I could drag him off.

'You were magnificent, Josser.'

'Piece o' cake,' he said, sauntering back to his seat.

I crawled into the Doc's room on my hands and knees. 'Hail, the conquering hero!' he laughed.

'The divil rot your purple socks!'

'Will ya have a cuppa tea?'

'I'd prefer a pint of blood.'

I had to give him a blow-by-blow account and he laughed so hard I hoped he'd choke.

''Tis a long way from John the Evangelist,' he said between gasps, 'but 'twill make a man of you.'

I couldn't wait to tell Jim Keating, but a sick call came through from the North Infirmary and I had the oils in my pocket.

'In here, Father.' The nurse took me straight to casualty where the cardiac arrest team leant back so that I could anoint the elderly woman on the table. Then they jolted her again with electricity, lifting her body convulsively off the bed.

'Her son is in the waiting-room, Father. Would you like to go out to him?'

In shock myself, I sat beside the young man until the doctor came through the swing doors and shook his head. 'I'm very sorry,' he said awkwardly, and moved away to the next case. The son began to cry and I sat beside him feeling inadequate, rubbing my hand between his shoulder blades until he stopped sobbing. It was what my father did for me whenever I had a nosebleed.

'I'll have to go and make the arrangements now,' he said, blowing his nose. 'And thanks very much, Father.'

I put my back against the wall outside on the street and tried to breathe. I had buried a mother, a grandmother and grandfather and a much-loved grandaunt, and had never come so close to seeing someone die. It took the heart out of me.

Jim read my face as soon as I walked in. 'Bridget, tea and loads of sugar.' I sat by the bed and began to tell him but the tears overtook me and I put my head down on the bed beside him. He stroked the back of my head with crooked fingers. 'You had a fright, boy; that's all right. Cry away now; sure what are you more than any man? 'Tis something you'll have to get used to.'

But I wanted to be more than any man. I wanted to be Christ Himself in all His passion, weeping blood through hands and feet, and not be crippled by the man I was. I wanted to be Damien of Molokai and Mother Theresa all rolled into one. I wanted to salve the agony of the world, to lose myself in prayer, to flare and burn and in some way appease this cruel God who stopped that woman's heart and stole away the mothers of small boys. How could I tell this saintly soul how much I raged at his disease and his acceptance of it? And how could I face the fear that one day, one awful day, I might 'get used to it'? I might climb into that protective shell where hurts can't come and priests don't cry and it's enough to do what must be done. And who would I be then?

23

LIMBO

One of the most famous of the northside characters was known as the Rancher. He went from door to door with a box car, selling bundles of sticks for the fire, but his gait behind the box car was that of a prince. The story goes that he was scavenging for bits one day in Cork's biggest lumberyard, when he was confronted by the owner.

The Rancher saw himself as the equal of any man and won a new disciple when he started the conversation with, 'Tell me, Mr Haughton, as one timber merchant to another ...'

He believed in barter and would slam a bundle of sticks on Statia Cahill's counter in exchange for a *Cork Examiner*.

Very few northsiders believed in buying anything directly, so when I said that I was interested in buying a car someone said they had a 'mark'. A 'mark', I discovered, was a fella who knew a fella who was doing a line with the sister of a fella who worked in a garage. In this Byzantine way, I came into possession of a black Morris Minor. It was the visible proof that Polyfilla could be driven. Maynooth had given me two degrees in almost seven years but neglected to teach me how to drive. The Doc took me for instructional spins and drove me into spacious fields so that I could 'have a go' at the wheel without decimating the parish. He was a devout coward. I got my brother-in-law to park the Morris at the presbytery and pretended it didn't exist, making all my calls on foot, until the sick call came from Clogheen.

Walking was out of the question, so, wearing the purple stole around my neck like the Red Baron's scarf, I climbed behind the wheel of the Morris. Through divine inspiration I got it started at the third try. What followed was a proof of God's existence and power. Shandon Street was busy at the best of times and shoppers tended to desert their cars rather than park them. This turned the steep hill into a slalom to test the skills of real drivers. Fourth was the only gear I was comfortable in and I roared away, weaving around trucks and prams and shawled women who shouted, 'Bad cess to ya!' in my wake. There was a hairpin turn into Blarney Street and the Morris took it on two wheels, making a noise of protesting rubber straight out of *Bullitt*.

I kept the pedal to the floor until I was in open country and watched for the boreen on the left as instructed by the flight crew before take-off. Again the Morris protested on the bend, but now I was barrelling down a narrow lane with grass growing in a line down the middle. The hysteria I had felt earlier was replaced by euphoria until I rounded the bend and there, before me, dead centre in the lane, was a big man in a helmet, dwarfing a small scooter. He was serenely putt-putting along, blissfully unaware that Fangio was racing for the chequered flag.

The Morris had one dud headlamp, and the steering wheel had the loosest of relationships with the wheels. More important still, the brakes were optional. As if in slow motion, I saw the look of serenity turn to surprise and then terror on the biker's face as we raced towards each other in a classic Mexican stand-off. Then he was doing the Wall of Death along the ditch, flying horizontally by the passenger window.

I ran back to where he was sitting on the verge, a bemused expression on his face as he watched his bike resting on its handlebars in the other ditch.

'Sorry about that. Are you all right?'

'N'yah,' he said.

'Ah, thank God. Am I right for Donovan's farmhouse?'

'N'yah,' he said again, nodding his head, a wavering finger pointing in the direction I was heading.

News travels fast. 'Doc,' I said when I got back to the presbytery, 'I think I'll take a few driving lessons.'

'Yerra, not at all, boy,' he said drily. 'You'll put the fear of God into more people with your driving than you ever will with your preaching.'

But the news everyone wanted to hear was where would the bishop appoint me.

Kevin gazed at the boiled egg with all the trepidation of Howard Carter at the threshold of Tutankhamun's tomb. He sighed as if the inevitable could be postponed no longer and tapped experimentally around the rim before cautiously lifting the cap.

'Soft,' he muttered darkly, 'again. I'd say Bantry,' he declared around the first mouthful.

'No way,' said Donovan, waving his arms for emphasis. Kevin shifted the milk jug out of range; a discussion with Donovan could be chronicled in the stains on the tablecloth.

'Schull,' he said, 'definitely Schull.'

They both laughed. In Maynooth the Cork students had their own croquet pitch. It was reasonably level except for one deep depression. To generations of Cork seminarians that hole was known as Schull. My laugh wasn't as hearty as theirs.

'Maybe he'll send you to Peru. Have you any Spanish, Christy?'

'*Un pocito.*'

I could see they were impressed by this, unaware of the fact that it had cost me half of my Spanish vocabulary. The diocese had adopted parishes in Peru some years before, and occasionally we saw photographs of the priests working there. The black-and-white pictures were usually posed before a blinding white wall, and because the lads wore white shirts, we saw two rows of black pants and two uneven rows of smiling faces. I remember sitting on the altar boys' bench as Fr Michael Murphy spun yarns to the men's confraternity about the mission in Peru. Towser and I were engrossed in working out how far we'd have to edge down the bench before Falvey fell off. But I gathered that the Peruvians lived in galvanised houses like the ones we built in the quarry behind our houses.

'Of course,' the preacher said, 'the priests have to come down from the mountains to the coastal regions at regular intervals.'

'Das in case dey get de bends,' Towser remarked knowledgeably. 'Me Mam sez me uncle gets dem if he gets down too quick from the high stool in Flaherty's pub.' The bench nodded sagely. Schull began to look more appetising.

The neighbours weren't immune from speculating either.

'You might be sent out the country.'

Rose, our next-door neighbour, said this with an expression of horror. To northsiders, civilisation paused at the North Gate Bridge and stopped dead at the city limits. 'The country' was lovely for a day out, but how could a body be expected to live there, 'miles from anyone'?

'You'll have to start watchin' The Riordans on the telly if you're sent out to the buffers,' Rose laughed. At the time, she was hugely pregnant and way overdue.

'Any move, Rose?'

'Yerra no, boy; sure he'll be talkin' back to me.'

I was sleeping next door in number six, still scaring myself at the sight of the black soutane looming on the wardrobe door in the morning. Some time during the night Rose nudged Jerry in the bed beside her.

'Jerry.'

'Wha'? Wha'?'

'The baby.'

'Wha'?'

'I think he's comin'.'

'Jesus!'

Jerry catapulted himself into the sleeping lane and ricocheted from door to door.

'Madgie, Norma, Eily, Mary, the baby's comin'.'

The men turned over as the women tumbled out. Swathed in dressing-gowns and prickly with curlers they gathered around Rose.

'I think the baby's comin'.'

'Oh, St Anthony,' Jerry prayed, 'what'll we do!'

'Never mind St Anthony, boy. Put on the kettle.'

'D'ye want tea?' the poor man asked in amazement.

'Ah lovin' God, Jerry, we need the hot water for the baby. D'ye know, there's an awful want in fellas.'

'Madge, what'll we do if the baby comes before the ambulance?'

'I think you pick them up by the ankles and slap their bottoms.'

'Go 'way!'

'On me soul, sure didn't you have your own?'

'Yerra, I was as high as a kite, girl. My fella said I was using language you wouldn't hear down the docks.'

They were stumped.

'D'ye know what,' said one, clutching her dressing-gown tighter for authority, 'we should send in next door for Christy Kenneally. They do a course in that class of thing.'

This was all the inducement the baby needed and he sensibly presented himself in the bed. Within minutes the fire-brigade ambulance was winking at the end of the lane and two large and jovial firemen were settling Rose on the stretcher.

'That's a grand cabinet, ma'am. Where did you buy it?'

'Jim Mack made that for me. Sure you'd swear it grew there!'

The house was suddenly silent and the women sat at the kitchen table, exhausted and slightly hysterical from the excitement. Jerry broached a bottle of brandy to 'steady me nerves' and they were persuaded to join him in christening the new arrival.

'I'll just wet me lips.'

'Mary, give us an oul' song.'

'Is it off your game ye are!'

'Ah go on, girl! Jerry, fill up her glass.'

Years before, in a plain black gymslip and scarlet sash, Mary stood on the stage at the Feis and swept the judge's table of silver with a voice of the same alloy. Now she straightened her back, tilted her bright face and sang:

Oh land of love and beauty
To thee our hearts we bring ...

The women around her were no strangers to loss and hardship and now the lilt of the old song soothed their tired faces to a sweet serenity. Their gaze turned inwards in contemplation of other songs and other voices, long stilled in this world but echoing always in their hearts. In the absence of my mother I had tuned myself to voices such as theirs; voices that chided me in off the road from danger or into kitchens smelling of ironing for the 'baat' of bread and jam and a heat to the fire with their own. These were the faces that changed now with the mood of the song as the lane they lived in changed when clouds roved over the crack of sky between their roofs. I remember at parties and weddings nestling in their closeness as they honoured the 'noble call' or, tucked in bed, smelling of smoke and smuts on Bonfire Night, drifting away to their chorus from around the dying embers in the quarry. Now, as if to soothe the pain of the past and welcome the sign of the future, they rose to the chorus:

> When you cry we hear you;
> When you weep we weep.
> In your hour of gladness
> How our pulses beat.
> Ireland, mother Ireland,
> Let what may befall.
> Ever shall I hold you;
> Ever shall I hold you,
> Dearest, sweetest, best of all.

I was the boy who had 'gone away to the priesthood' and that night I did not hear their singing through the wall that divided us.

The second delivery of the day was waiting for me in the presbytery. The handwriting on the blue envelope was inimitable.

'I hereby appoint you as chaplain to St Patrick's Hospital in the Wellington Road.'

I wasn't going to Schull after all or 'out the country', or even to Peru. I was about to embark for a different world entirely.

24

THE INCURABLE

Someone said
The air had smelled of urine.
Their hollow coughing kept her from her sleep
And there are those
Who still must cross themselves
To hurry past the gates
But I had known
Their spittle on my fingers from the rounds,
Their secrets whisper-woven in my stole,
Their sometime laughs,
And time and time goodbyes.
Small wonder then that I still weep
Estranged from Paradise.

St Patrick's had always been a place people mentioned in whispers. Generations of northsiders sprinkled their doorposts with holy water against the red-robed angel of tuberculosis, hoping, like the people of Israel, that the terror would pass them by. And when the dreadful coughing began and couldn't be contained, the shadows of their loved ones were finally 'shifted' to St Patrick's. Old memories die hard in our community and it was still common practice for people to go out of their way to avoid the iron gates or to bless themselves as they quickened their step on the Wellington Road. It was known as 'The Incurable'.

And it kept that name, long after TB had lost its lethal sting. Now it was the last resting place for those who carried incurable cancer. All of mine had died in Dublin or in the North Infirmary and I had only the vaguest idea where the hospice was. Growing up in the northside meant knowing the web of streets and lanes that stretched to within a half-mile radius of home. Blarney Street, Grawn, Spangle Hill and Blackpool were home to some of the diaspora of people who had married out from the core. These were places we adventured to and got familiar with as we grew older. We organised outings to the pictures on the island between the two arms of the river, and that was 'Town'. Occasionally we went in formal procession across the river to my Nan and aunties in the southside, always relaxing into familiarity as we recrossed the bridge into Shandon Street. I knew St Patrick's was somewhere on the hill above the railway station and below Montenotte. These were exotic places; to qualify for residency in Montenotte, the locals laughed, you had to have adenoids and money.

The reactions increased my apprehension. Jim solemnly folded the *Examiner*. 'You're very young for that,' he said quietly. My father reached across the oilcloth and squeezed my hand. He tried to say something and couldn't. Even the bishop seemed hesitant. Since my ordination he had been careful to use my formal title any time we met. Now he held my elbow at the door of the palace.

'You'll do your best, Christy?'

I followed the directions: 'Cross Patrick's Hill from Leitrim Street and you're on the Wellington Road. Christian Brothers College will be to your right and a high footpath to your left. Go up the hill 'til you strike a high wall. That's it.'

There was an iron gate set in the wall with an tidy apron of cobbles before it. The drive meandered left and then right through the garden to the front of the building. The hospital itself was a mixture of plain and fancy. It had a ruddy, honest face of Cork sandstone bordered with white limestone. This reminded me of the South Gate Bridge, which the locals claimed showed sandstone to the country side and limestone to the city side, for grandeur. I looked up from the bottom of the steps at three storeys, and down one to the basement. The windows were rimmed with yellow brick and, over to my right, a small balcony hung out from the top floor. A cluster of wheelchairs glinted in the sunlight, their occupants vivid in coloured shawls and blankets. A man in a wide straw hat waved tentatively. I waved back, just as cautiously. I felt like Gary Cooper in High Noon, totally outgunned and the sun in my eyes.

The first person I met inside the door was Pat, the receptionist, the only other male on the staff. TB had brought Pat to St Patrick's as a patient. Remarkably, he actually got better, to the consternation of the sister, who had him measured for the habit and ready for a divine departure. He told me the story himself, punctuated with long, ruminative drags at the ever-present cigarette.

'She says to me, "Pat, I think you're not going to die". God, I felt like apologising. "Not yet, sister," says I. "Maybe you'd get up," says she. "We need the bed." Lazarus was back from the tomb, boy, and nobody knew what to do with him. Well, to make a long story short, they needed someone to answer the phone and direct the visitors, so here I am.'

His kingdom was a small glass cubicle in the corner of the hallway. He had to fold his long legs almost into his armpits to squeeze inside, but every morning Pat travelled across the city on the Ballyphehane bus carrying a brown briefcase. The briefcase bore the tools of his trade: a carefully folded *Examiner* and a pair of brown felt slippers.

'I'm a martyr to me feet.'

He was standing now in his favourite position, the door behind him slightly ajar so that he could scan both ends of the corridor. The first fag of the day was already well under way, hanging from a pale, freckled hand.

'Noreen,' he said to a passing nurse, 'would you look at the child Connie sent up to us. I'd better send for Mamma.'

'Mamma', I discovered, was his code name for Reverend Mother, a tall, spare and serious lady who seemed to run on castors. She shunted me ahead of her into the gated lift and we ascended in an awkward silence to the top floor. The tour started there and spiralled back to the ground floor through the wards on each level. I noticed that the basement kitchen wasn't part of our itinerary.

My impressions were of long waxed corridors lined with portraits of the usual saintly suspects. High windows looked out on the terraced back gardens. The wards to the front of the building were spacious and bright, benefiting from the sun's passage across the city from Blackrock in the estuary to its red roost over the shoulder of Sunday's Well. White beds replicated each other down both sides of the wards. The nuns in charge shook hands briefly and fell into step as a guard of honour until we left their domain for the next ward. Mamma set a brisk pace but I saw men and women who smiled or nodded from beds or chairs, and some who hardly dented the bedclothes, their eyes locked on the faces of the young nurses who stroked their yellowed fingers. It took all of ten minutes to march me through my entire parish, and then at the door I was handed back to Pat, who would 'look after me'.

'Time to view the villa,' he said, smiling, when we were safely out on the steps. I paused by the railings, pretending to admire the view across the spiked spires of the city but guiltily gulping deep breaths of fresh air. No amount of disinfectant and air freshener can fully camouflage the smell of sickness and my stomach rolled dangerously. Pat, ever the diplomat, retied his perfectly tied laces until I was ready. Just then an apparition appeared around the gable-end and headed in our direction. She was a woman of indeterminate age, dressed in a nurse's uniform straight out of Gilbert and Sullivan.

'Pat, who's that?'

'That's Kathleen,' he said ominously.

'And what's that sample in front of her?' I asked, nodding towards a small hairy bundle that hoovered the ground before her at the end of a dog-lead.

'For the love and honour of God, Father dear, be careful. That mangy excuse for a dog is Dinky and he's the light of her life. For the sake of peace on earth, don't cross her.'

I was reared on terriers that earned their keep and our respect taking rabbits from the ditches of Nash's boreen and snapping rats in the small backyards off the lane. There was a small pink bow tied to the tuft of hair between this article's ears. It was all I could do to be civil.

'Lovely dog, ma'am.'

Kathleen seemed to inflate and glow. 'Dinky, say hello to the new priest.'

The sample and I regarded each other with mutual suspicion.

'Come on now, Dinky love, or we'll be late for our tea.'

Pat waited until she was well out of earshot.

'D'ye know,' he said, 'she was taking Dinky for his constitutional one evening and didn't she meet a fella walking a bitch of the same make. "D'ye know what, ma'am," says yer man, "maybe we could mate them."

'"What!" says Kathleen. "My dog was reared in a convent. He don't know nothing about them things."'

We passed a large statue of the Sacred Heart in the garden and it occurred to me that He was facing the wrong way, looking accusingly out over the docks with His back to the wards.

The villa was a felt-roofed flat tucked against the wall at the foot of the garden. We entered through a glass porch into a wide, carpeted living-room. I was transfixed by the open fireplace. Maynooth had never been warm enough and I think I got involved in dramatic productions because there was an open fire in the Green Room. Fuel for the fire posed a practical and a moral problem. The only turf available was neatly boxed outside the professors' doors. I've always thought that the soutane was a marvellous invention. Apart from giving ecclesiastical grace to the most ungainly of seminarians, it could also accommodate two briquettes in each pocket. Problem solved.

Off the long sitting-room were a kitchenette, bathroom and bedroom. To a fellow who had spent seven years in different single rooms, this was the Ritz.

'Pat, this is terrific.'

He looked out over the top of his glasses. ''Tis at the bottom of the garden up against a wall with a flat roof to catch the water. 'Tis a death trap.'

But even when my sisters sniffed suspiciously and an interesting green mould began to grow on my soutane, I could see no fault in it. This was home.

25

THE DAY

The old woman loved a love song:
'Sing "Sorrento"; course you know it
or "Sweet Mystery of Life".'
There's a song she'd sung by evening
Giving encore each new morning
In the hard-gloss hollow bedroom.
She was Callas, I Caruso
Till one night I said, 'Tomorrow,'
And she kissed my hands in parting.

The phone rang at 6.30 a.m.

'Good morning, Father. It's six-thirty and a lovely morning.' The night matron was properly formal despite the weather forecast. When we got to know each other better she'd say, 'Get up outta that! The holy nuns have a half a day's prayin' behind them already.'

The little sacristy was dark with mahogany, spicy and warm with incense and beeswax. On weekdays I flew solo and would dive into the vestments and sit for a while in the armchair, trying to come awake or at least gather my thoughts for mass. This was a slice of the day I grew to love, the time before anything started. It was a small circle of quiet away from the hustle and bustle, where the slow brown tick of the clock and the faint tap of rain on the roof combined to soothe me into stillness. I think it reminded me of the 'caboose' under the stairs at home, where I could curl up, alone and undisturbed. The bell shook me awake.

'In the name of the Father ...'

At Sunday mass I was shepherded by the Campbell brothers;

rangy redheads, buttoned into sawn-off soutanes, uncomfortably clean in white surplices. Dave, steady and wry, was the elder of the duo. Frank was designed by a committee in disagreement, each of his legs on a separate contract. Dave spent half the mass nudging me in the right direction and the other half anticipating Frank's disasters. While he was distracted one morning, Frank managed to miss the chalice and pour a whole cruet of wine up my sleeve. For a mad moment I was about to offer the other sleeve for the water. When he arrived with a fingerbowl and without the towel, I got a sweet revenge by drying my hands in his surplice. It nearly shocked him into coordination.

At the stroke of seven on weekdays I hit the altar at full throttle and was swept along through the Eucharistic mystery, buoyed up on the soprano responses of the sisters counterpointed by the bass rumble of the Christian brothers, who joined us each morning. At the end of mass I took the full ciborium and set out for the wards, one of the sisters walking ahead of me with a small warning bell and a lighted candle that pushed the shadows before us.

'The Body of Christ. Amen.'

Those who were able sat up in their beds, the women with shawls around their shoulders, their faces stretched from the face-cloth, composed and stiff. The men always reminded me of how Pop would receive communion. I remember his stillness when the priest approached and how he'd raise his head and give a little nod, as if to acknowledge a friend. He looked as vulnerable as a child when he put out his tongue for the wafer. Then he'd return to his seat, slowly and distractedly, as if he were carrying on a conversation with himself. I learned to read the nods and signals of the nurses who hovered in the shadows near the beds of those particularly low, and sometimes broke a host to place a tiny fragment on a dry, swollen tongue.

It often happened that someone was too weak to receive and I remembered something I had started to do instinctively while I was in the cathedral. Parents often brought small children with them to the rails and, to pre-empt a premature first holy communion, placed a hand over the child's mouth as they themselves received. I was often confronted by a parent with eyes shut and mouth open, and their gagged image and likeness glaring at me in indignation. So I began to put my hand on their heads briefly in blessing. This became my practice in my new parish among people whose sickness had already excluded them from so much.

Breakfast was served by Marie in the chaplain's dining-room. She staggered in under a tray that could have fed Collins Barracks.

'Marie, I'll never manage that.'

'You will, Father,' she said pleasantly.

Another legacy of Maynooth was a shrunken stomach.

'I won't, Marie.'

She evaporated in confusion, to be replaced by a sister from below, her sleeves rolled for combat, her face shiny with determination.

'Will you not ate your breakfast?'

'I couldn't manage it, sister, but I'd love an egg.'

'An egg. Sure you couldn't live on that.'

'Well, maybe a bit of toast with it. That would be grand.'

A plump chaplain was a source of pride. I was a great disappointment to them.

So here I was, twenty-five years old and I had never seen anyone die. I had managed to go through seven years of training without a single lecture on how to be a hospital chaplain. What to do? From the time I first learned to read, I found a world of answers and escape in books. There had to be a book somewhere that would tell me what to say and who to be. It was time to go to Egan's.

In Cork at that time there were shops and stores and Egan's was neither. It was an establishment. The two windows fronting on Patrick's Street were ambivalent in their dedication to God and Mammon. One side glittered with expensive silver plate and the other shone with chalices and cloth of gold. The lower floor was an Aladdin's cave of light-filled cabinets, groaning under the weight of potential wedding presents, trophies and silver salvers. The walls were studded with clocks that tocked in time to my footsteps on the polished floor. A broad staircase swept upwards and divided. Whichever route took your fancy, you fell under the benign gaze of Tom, a smooth, smiling Buddha, who had the soft, hushed voice of a librarian. The bookshop itself was a large high-ceilinged room, a treasure-trove of titles. Where else in Cork could you find a slim, erotic D.H. Lawrence cheek by jowl with the stolid Hans Küng? Where would you find P.G. Wodehouse, chirping lightly about the unflappable Jeeves, or Heinrich Böll describing someone as 'having the eyes of a cardinal who had lost the faith'? It was a place where time stood still, and I often had to run the Wellington Road to deliver a sweaty Benediction.

It was here, as I expected, that I found the answer to my prayers. Elisabeth Kubler-Ross was a Swiss GP who had a Pauline conversion to the care of the dying patient. Almost singlehand-edly she had dragged her profession out of the trance of tech-nology to consider the needs of those for whom 'no more could be done'. More important still, she had distilled all the answers to my questions into one slim volume. Dan, a former Glen hurler and therefore a member of the extended family, took my bundle at the register.

'How are you getting on above, boy?'

'Fine, Dan.'

He was always happier with round figures.

'We'll say a fiver.'

A visitor once asked Pop if I was fond of the books.

'Fond of them? He ates them, boy,' he answered proudly.

I devoured that book, underlining passages in biro and scrib-bling notes in the margins until I could recite some pages by heart. I was now the world's living expert on the stages of dying and could trip them off my tongue from denial to acceptance, like a child answering his catechism question and with about the same level of comprehension.

Ah, pride! I had forgotten the famous words of our ecclesiastical history professor in Maynooth. This man would often quote Dante in Italian as if we should know it and stare in mock horror at our blank expressions. One particular day he leant dolefully over the podium and declared, 'Look at them. All of them reading about life and none of them living it.'

We thought it was hilarious. The following morning I was to discover just how cruelly prophetic his words could be.

'Father, Sadie on the top floor wants to see you.'

I was suspicious of the suppressed smiles on the faces of the two nurses waiting at the door.

'We'll take you in to her, Father.'

There was a bump in the bed and no sign of Sadie.

'He's here now, love.'

The bump moved and Sadie's grey head rose like a periscope from the depths of the blankets. 'Ah, sweetheart,' she trilled in a high girlish voice.

I tried to ignore the giggles behind me and concentrate on Elisabeth Kubler-Ross. My mind was a complete blank. My Swiss guru was off eating Toblerone in some other dimension and I was marooned with Sadie.

'Will you do something for me, darling?' she cooed.

'Anything at all,' I answered manfully.

'Will you sing a song?'

Elisabeth Kubler-Ross came rushing back to me, chapter and verse, and there was not a single solitary reference to singing a song for the terminally ill. Even worse, I recalled that whenever I sang at home my father would laugh and say, 'Will you stand out at the front door so the neighbours will see we're not bating you.' At this stage the two helpful hussies were out in the corridor, hugging each other for support, breathless with laughter.

'What kind of song would you like, Sadie?' I said, stalling for time.

'A love song,' she said dramatically, 'always a love song.'

Most of my generation grew up giggling through the songs of

aunts and uncles at family parties. Subconsciously, I suppose, we must have learned the words and airs of hundreds of old songs. 'Ah, sweet mystery of life at last I've found you,' I began. I could hear one of them coughing outside.

May she choke, I thought savagely.

Sadie turned her head sideways on the pillow, her milky eyes questing away from the here and now in search of happier times.

'Now at last I know the secret of it all.'

She nodded sadly at that line then joined me in a high, cracked voice for the rest of the verse:

All the longing, seeking, striving, waiting, yearning,
The burning hope, the joy and idle tears that fall;
For 'tis love and love alone the world is seeking;
For 'tis love and love alone that can repay.

As we moved to the final line I sat beside her and her withered hand stole into mine:

Now the answer, 'tis the end and all of living
For it is love alone that rules for aye.

In the sudden silence she raised my hand gently to dry, feathery lips.

'Thank you,' she squeaked, and submerged again under the blankets.

As the days went by, I looked forward to the crazy concerts with Sadie. Many's the time I dragged reluctantly up the stairs, freighted with the worry of a child in school or a dark tale from the 'box' or just the emptiness of the flat, and found solace with Sadie. She never allowed any change in the programme. Theology, philosophy or any talk of death were strictly off limits – the song was all. Gradually I forgot all about the stages of dying and Sadie's progress towards acceptance, until one morning Pat called me into the cubicle on my way to the boiled egg.

'They want you for Sadie.'

'Sure I only anointed her lately.'

'She won't do, boy,' he said gently.

I took the stairs at a run, angry with myself for letting Sadie 'sell me a pup'. My job was to steer her through the stages of dying, get her habit on, hands crossed, have her pointed east and ready for take-off. Then I would have done my job; then I could mark my internal scorecard with a tick against Sadie's name, yet another one notched up for God.

This time her head didn't rise, so I knelt near her and shifted the blanket so she'd see my face. She came back from a distance to focus on me, as if I had called her.

'Ah, darling,' she said in a tired whisper, 'just in time for a song.'

There was one song I had studiously avoided during all our concerts. It was my father's song for his dead Maura, a pledge of love and loyalty he was true to forever. Yet now, without thinking, I began to sing, 'We are in love with you, my heart and I.' I was kneeling on the lino, holding her hand in mine, and when I finished she raised my hand to her lips as always.

'Goodbye darling,' she said, 'and thank you.'

The business of the day swept me away from her room and it was at the communion round early the next morning that I discovered her empty bed. I was rooted to the floor. The sister turned with the candle and came back to me. 'She left us during the night, Father,' she said, and went back to stand guard outside the door while the chaplain sat on Sadie's bed and scrubbed his face with the hem of his stole. Sadie had gone to better things, where she could have her pick of Gigli, Caruso or Mario Lanza to sing her love songs. And she had left me something precious. I realised my job was to accompany the dying on their own private pilgrimage and not to push them along some route of my own. There was no book and never would be one that could teach me what to say or do. The heart would do the right thing if I wasn't too afraid to let it.

The little bell tinkled from the corridor, calling me back.

26

BEING THERE

The pools that were her eyes
flowed ever fuller in her face
as life began to ebb.
The plumb-line of our talk
no longer snagged
on the trivial flotsam of our lives
but daily deepened
till the line was taut and spent,
and words refused to measure more.
So, taking off my shoes
I paddled in the shadows of her room
or schoolboy-skimmed the pebbles of my prayers
across her pain.
And, for my effort
she would ripple me a smile
that lapped around my heart
and splashed my eyes.
I watched her for a month or more
I watched her thrash the seine of binding sheets
until she rose majestic on the waves
and left me silent on the shore,
bereaved.

When I was a child, nuns were the people who chased us out of the convent garden as we waded through cabbages in search of a submerged ball. Later there was Sister Eucharia, my teacher in school, who hassled and hugged us with equal passion, so that we vied to be her pet. While I was in secondary school, a pal of mine decided she wanted to become a nun. She was a bright, life-loving girl with an infectious laugh, and I wondered if that life would change her. She turned out to be dafter than ever, a northside

Maria Von Trapp, who could never manage to 'walk, sister, walk'.

Maynooth admitted nuns to our lecture halls and they became so familiar as to be invisible. In the final year the custom was to get a photograph of everyone who had ever been part of the class and bequeath it to the college wall. Some fellas got a 'rush of blood to the head' and thought it inappropriate that the sisters should hang with the rest of us. At a noisy meeting they threatened to stay out of the frame if the nuns got in. The nuns smile down from the wall to this day. The objectors don't feature. We thought of ourselves as liberal young men of the new church, and yet old stereotypes die hard.

I remember I had a part in a college play and some of the lads took a bra from the costume hamper and snuck it into my laundry bag. The laundry went out once a week to the convent outside the village. As soon as the van left the gates the plotters revealed the deed. I was in a sweat, waiting for an outraged letter from the sister-in-charge to laundry number 254, or worse, an ominous nod from the dean. 'Mr Kenneally, an object of lady's apparel, etc.' When the laundry returned I found the contentious article neatly laundered and folded with all the other unmentionables. There was a short note pinned to the bag, signed by the sister-in-charge: 'We hope you'll both be very happy.'

And yet, when a nun came to die, I wasn't sure how I would relate to her.

'How are you, sister?'

'I'm afraid,' she said simply. I was so shocked that she laughed.

'Well, that makes two of us, sister. So, what will we do?'

'We'll see,' she said.

She made all the running herself. Some days we talked about something in the news and other days we talked about ourselves, swapping the kind of small childhood stories that people place in the foundation of what might become a friendship. Occasionally I brought her the gossip from the streets, stretching chords of contact to the world beyond the walls. As time passed I grew more comfortable with sitting in her silences, just keeping her company.

'D'ye know,' she said one day, 'you've never offered to pray with me?'

'No,' I said. 'I knew a chaplain once who didn't know what to say. He got more and more uneasy with the silence so he said to the man in the bed, "Will I pray with you?"'

'And what happened?'

'The man said, "Yes, if it helps you, Father."'

She began to laugh until the tears streamed down her cheeks. Then she coughed and fought for breath as blood appeared on her lips.

'Nurse, nurse!'

'No, no, I'm grand now.'

She took the tissue from me and dabbed her mouth.

'Would you like me to leave now?'

'No. I'd like you to pray with me.'

I'd been saying prayers since I could talk. I was most comfortable with the tried and trusted, and very wary of the scary ones in the ritual that were heavy on guilt, like the small print on a certificate for fire insurance. I had no book now and I was afraid. As a child I had prayed really hard that my Mam would come back and that Pop and Nan wouldn't die. She didn't and they did. My success rate was poor. But I knew she wasn't asking for an 'asking' prayer. We both knew that she would die, and soon. And so, with great trepidation, I stepped into unscripted waters, simply thanking God for being with us in the stories and the laughs and the silences. And then I was silent.

'Are you asleep?'

'No, but I think I can now.'

It was the last time we spoke. As she sank lower and her face took the colour of the bedsheets, the nurses were anxious that we should go through the rituals.

'Will you anoint her, Father?'

'No, I don't think she'd want that.'

They brought the candles and the crucifix anyway but I persuaded them that it would be better if I sat where she could see me when she woke. Occasionally she did wake and her eyes would fasten on me. I resisted the urge to take her hand, sensing that she was a very private person and that it would not be a comfort to her. But I broke our agreement not to ask God for something. I asked Him to let her die; she had suffered enough.

At some time on a spring afternoon, when the light threw lace patterns on the wall and the curtain swayed with the breeze from the open window, she stopped breathing.

27

MIRACLES

The countryman had put his trust
In the strong, wrist-hitch of harness,
Hup and heave of haybales
Plough-lined corduroy of an autumn field.
The cancer on his lip
Could not be burnt like gorse
Or blasted, like the tumours on his land.
With every passing day,
The weed moved deeper in the man
And parasitic, sapped the manhood from his eyes
It brought him to despise his patch of clay.
The head, bent low between the shoulder-shafts,
Bent lower into shadow every day.
'I'm God's obscenity,'
He seemed to say.
The city girls were ignorant of blight
That rotted all things growing in the ground
But, wise to deeper things, they nursed the heart
And when he looked them in the eye
A man looked back.
They gentled him to live a second spring
His eyes were full of blossom
When he died.

I didn't believe in miracles.

How could God save me and lose you, and how did He decide? The picture of the Almighty sticking a pin in the paper, like my aunts did for the Grand National, didn't appeal to me, any more than soliciting the help of some heavenly TD to put a word in the right ear. But miracles do happen in the everyday and we had one.

Tom came in an ambulance without a siren. There was no

rush; Tom was someone who couldn't be saved. He was a farmer who had ignored the lump on his lip until the mirror scared him into hospital. By then it was too late. They cut away a chunk of his lower face, swaddled him in bandages and sent him to us to die. As it happened, Tom had gone into remission, that limbo time when a cancer just stops developing. People stay in remission for different periods of time and it looked like Tom could stay there indefinitely. But he was suffering from a second illness, a kind of cancer of the soul, brought on by disgust at his own appearance. He hid his head on the way from the ambulance and, as soon as the bed was ready, he made a little tent of the blankets and crawled inside. At first I was never sure which end of him I was talking to. For my pains I got the odd grunt from the tent and gradually my talk petered out. I began to invent good excuses to visit other patients more often. This was always a great temptation. There was satisfaction in getting feedback from someone who wanted to talk and I succumbed to it. Now I only met him on the ritual rounds for communion or anointing. And then, the miracle happened.

Two 'young wans' from the Lower Road had a notion that they'd like to be nurses and were given summer jobs as aides on Tom's ward. They were as 'scattered' as their age entitled them to be and rarely out of trouble. But it was obvious to all that they had heart in abundance. However it happened, they were put in charge of Tom, looking after his small needs, and these included washing his face. I was at the door of the ward one day when they started with the facecloth. Tom kept his hand clenched firmly over the bottom half of his face and his eyes locked into the middle distance. The two teenagers talked easily about dances and fellas: who'd pay your way into a dance and who'd meet you inside.

'Yerra, that fella would buy you a bottle of orange at the dance and try and turn you into a cocktail-shaker on the way home.'

And all the time their hands moved gently with the cloth as if they were distractedly washing the jammy face of a well-loved child. He was looking from one to the other, amazed, I think, at the ordinary way they looked at him. Then, heartened by the warmth of their young hearts, his hand unclenched and left his face to rest easily on the bedclothes. Because two 'young wans' had given him back the gift of himself, he would never cover his face again.

As I stood in the doorway I began to realise that I had been intent on serving only half my parish. I had neglected the staff, especially the night staff, those women who came with sleepy eyes in the morning and the ones who worked below ground in the kitchen. I was a flat stone skimmed by a child across the surface of a pond. I could barely touch the patients' lives. These were the people who were with them all day, every day. It was time to ordain the staff.

I decided to start underground and work my way up.

We lived in a two-up, two-down house in Convent Place. It would be more accurate to say that we lived in one room. The 'front room' had the radio, the good table and the glass-case. It was for visitors and special occasions when we could sit before the fire in pyjamas making striped toast at the grate. We lived in the kitchen. The first time I ventured below ground to the hospital kitchen there was consternation.

'Was there something wrong with the breakfast? Did Marie forget a tray?'

'No, sister, I came down to have a cup of tea with yourselves on your break.'

Sisters Salome and Sabina were probably named by some novice mistress with a grudge, but they were hardworking and sensible women who surfaced for mass in the morning and submerged for the rest of the day in the steaming kitchen. What light there was in the kitchen emanated from themselves, because they made light of their lot and made much of the girls who worked with them. After the first fairly formal reception, they got used to me and stopped the vain search for a 'good' cup among the mugs in the cupboard. I noticed how they looked over my shoulder when I arrived, as if anxious that Mamma might be hovering behind me. Mamma, I was to learn, held the strong belief that all things had their proper place, including the chaplain. Occasionally, around a mouthful of Fig Roll, I painted pen pictures of the men and women in the beds above.

'John is low today but Suzy is a lot brighter.'

One day I surprised them by asking for their prayers. Most of the kitchen girls were from County Limerick and weren't shy about coming forward.

'Our prayers,' the redhead from Rathkeale laughed. 'Yerra, I prayed me oul' fella's greyhound would win the coursing and he's still runnin'. He says he's goin' to take him for a long walk out the country and run away from him.'

The two sisters exploded with laughter before their sense of decorum could kick in.

'Sure, Father, we don't get time to pray. 'Tis different for the nuns on the wards. They can be over and back all day to the chapel once they're covered.'

'Well,' I said, 'my Nan was always up to her elbows in flour and suds. She said she hadn't time to be sick; didn't she inherit the four of us when my mother died.'

'God rest her soul,' they chorused.

'Anyway, I'd say I learned more from my Nan about prayer than I did in seven years in Maynooth.'

This had a whiff of heresy about it and they were hooked.

'How's that, Father?'

'Well, everything she did was a prayer because she did it for the love of us, and I feel the benefit of her prayers to this day.'

'What will we pray for?'

'Pray for me,' I said, ''cos, to be honest with ye, there's days when I don't know what to do for the ones in the beds.'

They were aghast. How could a priest need prayers? But there were nights when I called on the power of the kitchen to see me through the watch with someone who was dying hard. They never failed me. I also believe they saved my life.

195

I preached a short sermon that particular Sunday, mindful of the journey before me. Fergus, my classmate, wanted me in Galway to help him pour water on his newest nephew. It would be a chance to renew our friendship and to experience that special affection parents have for a priest-son's friend. It was a perfect day, bright with promise, as I left the familiar closeness of Blackpool and blessed myself at the signpost for Whitechurch cemetery. Did that simple sign alert the dead? The Mallow road was only twenty miles long but it boasted over 108 bends. At one of them I struck the shoulder and felt the car go over. There was a huge grinding noise and then I heard the birds pick up their song uncertainly, as if disturbed at their Matins.

I was lying in a field with a perfect view of the mangled wreck that had been my car now beached upside-down beside me. Arms and legs moved; no pain. Standing, I tugged my shirt out of my trousers, and the windscreen, a shower of diamonds, fell around my feet. Two men stood on the ditch.

'Oh Jesus, 'tis a priest. Are you all right, Father?'

I saw ashen faces and felt eager hands.

'The top button is gone out of my shirt,' I said.

I was in someone's kitchen, sipping strong tea served by a fraught woman. Two children stared at me from solemn faces, the smaller one moustached with milk.

'Yes, I'm fine. I'm home now. Thanks very much.'

The two Samaritans drove off. I was in the kitchen.

'Father?'

'Have you any brandy, sister? I'm not hurt, but I'll go down now for a rest.'

'Yes, Father.'

The doctor arrived at the villa in a flurry of nuns. The visible evidence was sparse – two bruised knees from the steering wheel and a bruised shoulder from my exit through the door.

'Someone must have been praying for you, Father,' he said wryly, shaking his head. How could I explain that the prayers of two kitchen Sisters, combined with those transferred from a slow greyhound in Rathkeale, had plucked the chaplain from an early grave? The stethoscope might have moved from heart to head. And how could I admit it to myself and not be challenged at the core of my beliefs?

Their sisters in the dark were the night staff. Many were married women who tucked their children in and left their sleeping houses to watch the night in St Patrick's. I wandered up around midnight and found the door locked solid. The bell jangled unmercifully. Tentative footsteps sounded inside.

'Who is it?'

''Tis me, the chaplain.'

Bolts rattled and keys turned.

''Tis easier to get into Fort Knox,' I said pleasantly.

The night nurse looked uncertain. 'Were you sent for, Father?'

'No, nurse, I just want to spend some time with the night staff.'

Her expression suggested disapproval and she disappeared towards her office on the ground floor. I hared up the stairs, suspecting she would be on the phone to warn the troops. The long black soutane was a mistake. Halfway down the dim corridor a nurse sailed backwards from a ward, balancing a tray of medications.

'Goodnight, nurse.'

'Oh Jesus. Well God forgive you, Father, but you took the heart out of me.'

''Twas one way to get you down on your knees,' I said, as we hunted on all fours after rolling tablets.

'For God's sake, will you leave that black yoke off you when you come up or the girls will think the place is haunted.'

It was a sound lesson in appropriate liturgical dress.

Everything was different at night. All the hubbub of the day, the rattle of trolleys and the clatter of heels were gone. The low lights smudged the high ceilings with shadows while, here and there, a night-light lapped devotedly at a saint's plaster toes. The sleeping forms around me hushed my voice, smoothed and oiled my movements as I walked between the beds.

'Is that you, Father?'

''Tis, John. Can you not sleep?'

'No, I find the night very long.'

'Mary was in tonight?'

'She was. She never misses. 'Tis hard on her, Father.'

This was often the prelude to a conversation or revelation that rarely braved the light of day. But we were two castaways sitting on a raft-bed, adrift on a sleeping sea. For an hour or so I could step from raft to raft with a small gift of words to pay my passage, or simply sit and stroke a hand or cheek with a tenderness I was shy of showing by day.

'Is there anything that helps you during the night, John?'

'There is, Father. I do see that small light at the bottom of the ward, where the nurse sits. That gives me great heart, 'cos I know she's there, like.'

I took that message to the tea-circle in the alcove off the ward, to emphasise the influence they had if they could be open to what the dark might offer.

Tess moved seamlessly in and out of reality but tonight she was wide awake and shaking.

'What is it, Tess?'

'Oh, Father. I'm in dread of me life.'

'Of what, girl?'

'Father, if a man got up to that window there – ' She paused for dramatic effect' – and got in,' she added darkly.

'Tess, there are three floors under us and bars on all the windows. Any man who could climb in that window deserves whatever he can get.'

Her eyes were like saucers with shock.

'God, you're a terror,' she said happily and lay back to sleep.

My last call was always to the blind woman.

''Tis me.'

'I know your step.'

The skin of her face was stretched from questing after sounds, but her hands could see. I grew accustomed to the way she'd raise them up to read my face, finding and kneading the cleft between my eyes with rough affection, like Nan and Dad did whenever I was sick at night and scared. Her fingers drew the tension from my day so that I could face the bed, a little less afraid of all the phantoms I had gathered on my rounds.

'Mamma's on the prowl.' Pat was as cryptic as ever. 'Were you up to any blackguardin'?'

'No more than usual.'

He rolled his eyes theatrically.

'Storm force ten, batten down the hatches,' he said gaily, curling his long legs into the cubicle. I hadn't long to wait. I had just decapitated the boiled egg when the formal tap sounded on the door.

'Come in.'

'Good morning, Father.'

'Good morning, Mother.'

I turned the knob of the radio and Terry Wogan beat a hasty retreat. He was well out of it.

'Wasn't that a very interesting reading at mass this morning, Father?'

'Oh, which one was that, Mother?' I hedged, drawing a complete blank in my memory of either.

'The first one, from the Old Testament, about Noah. Wasn't it wonderful how he took two of every creature into the ark?'

'Yerra, that's only a myth, Mother.'

There was the kind of silence that had occurred in the kitchen at home the day I asked Mary Ann what had happened her nose.

'A myth, Mother. Ye know, a story to get across some truth or revelation to the listeners,' I added lamely.

''Tis the inspired word of God, Father,' she said with great deliberation.

Suddenly the boiled egg assumed massive importance as I

mined the yolk with a surgeon's precision.

'I understand you visit the wards at night, Father.'

The ferret was in the ditch now for certain. I laid the spoon aside and returned her gaze.

'I do, Mother.'

'Why?'

'To visit the patients who are awake and the night staff.'

'You didn't ask my permission.'

I was brought up to be that most peaceful and dangerous of creatures, the nice child. The nice child always says and does what is expected. The nice child goes to visit relatives and sits quietly for hours while they exclude him from the conversation. The nice child says 'Sorry' when he hasn't done anything wrong and smiles when he wants to scream.

'I don't actually need your permission, Mother.'

The breath hitched in my throat but I continued.

'Maybe I should have mentioned it to you first, out of good manners, but I didn't think of doing so and I apologise for that.'

She nodded slightly.

'Do you intend to continue visiting the wards at night?'

'Yes, I do. Whenever I'm able.'

She stood up. 'Good morning, Father.' The interview was over and I was trembling.

Pat's head snaked around the door before I could draw breath. 'Will I send for O'Connor's undertakers?'

'A bit soon for that, Pat,' I said wanly.

He sat on her empty chair as I got a cup and saucer from the press and put them before him, annoyed at the rattle.

'I'd say she took Machiavelli for her confirmation name. I don't trust her.'

Pat had the last word. 'And she doesn't trust you either, boy. No, don't be gettin' up on your high horse. Christy boy, you're young and you have all these new notions about the patients and the staff.'

'But, Pat …'

'Didn't I tell you to shut up and hear me out. If that woman stabs you it'll be in the front and then she'll offer you a cup of tea. Sure there's no understanding them. Anyway, 'twill be all the one to the worm.'

He was right. We had many battles, Mamma and I, and she never once sulked or carried a grudge. And years later when I walked into a hospice in Scotland where she was retired in exile and introduced her to my wife, she kissed me on the cheek. 'Ah, Christy,' she said, with a mischievous glint in her eye, 'as boyish as ever.' And I was glad to see her.

28

BACK TO SCHOOL

I was beginning to find my bearings without a map on a scrap of paper. I could navigate confidently from Camillus' through Patrick's to Anne's. I could even manage to operate the lift on my own and only very rarely make a grand exit from a ward into a brush cupboard. Like Alexander the Great, I was beginning to feel I had no more worlds to conquer. The blue envelope was leaning casually against the boiled egg and the sight of it brought me out in hives. Surely the bishop wasn't moving me just when I was getting the hang of things.

Chaplaincies like mine were sometimes seen by the higher powers as a handy base from which you could go out to work somewhere else. Once you had the mass behind you and a few anointings done, sure what would you be doing with the rest of your time? It was a bit like the old story of the parish priest who was asked to recount his day. 'Arrah,' he said, 'I say mass and a few prayers. I read the paper and have the breakfast. And then I slacken off a bit for the rest of the day.'

It was a shock to discover that himself was appointing me as chaplain to five of the secondary schools in the city.

On Monday morning I adjusted my GAA and northside prejudices to present myself at Presentation College on the Western Road. Brother Jerome, the principal, was larger than life and generous with the surplus. He was a glowing powerhouse of enthusiasm, radiating energy so that his cassock seemed to strain at the seams, and only the bellyband saved us all from an explosion. A priest I knew had said about him, 'You'd have to change your shirt after talking to that man.'

He whirled me through the introductions in the staffroom, then slapped me on the back. 'Go for gold, boy.' The staffroom flooded and ebbed with flying black togas at bell-marked intervals. Teachers rushed in for a cuppa, a mouthful of biscuit, a mound of copies, and then stormed off again. I was dizzy at the comings and goings, but the mid-morning break was an entertainment. Dan Donovan could have the place in roars as he moved like a chameleon from Shakespeare to what the huckster said in the Coal Quay.

'She decided to go upmarket from fish to lobsters and, of course, they were alive and racing around under the pram. She was down on her knees chasin' them when a Montenotte voice said, "Are they fresh?"'

'"Well," says she, "I'm not windin' em up."'

I remember Jim Corr, kindly and solicitous, making the introductions and nudging me quietly into the circles of conversation. We decided that the best use of my time was to preside at class masses, which were always held in the Sacred Heart Missionaries chapel at the head of the dyke. A young teacher called Hugh was charged with shepherding the group of reluctant Christians to the church without losing a few souls along the way to the wide open spaces of Fitzgerald's Park.

Some of the Sacred Heart Missionaries were around my own age, and one in particular was a dyed-in-the-wool devout support of St Finbarr's Hurling Club. All my crowd were rabid Glen Rovers followers. Uncle Joe had played with Ring and Jack Lynch in the banded jersey, and after him my brother Michael picked up the mantle and carried it with pride until he emigrated to America. Even I had managed to pick up senior and minor county medals with the club, more by accident than ability. Battle was joined, but in typical Cork fashion the 'slaggin'' and 'ball-hopping' were a camouflage for the genuine admiration and affection that existed between both camps. The Eucharistic Procession match was due, and it was usually a holocaust when these two were competitors. The bishop always threw in the ball to start the game and then had the good sense to sprint for the sideline out of the way.

'I suppose Connie will throw the ball to Jackie Daly, like he did last year? Ye have him well-trained.'

'He will, boy, but he'd better anoint Doolin first.'

In the hospital I could go for weeks on end without meeting another priest. This casual contact with a group of priests was very precious. One of their gifts was that they never took themselves too seriously. They told me one day of one of their members who liked to extend his influence to some of the city pubs on a Saturday night. He was wont to come home under the same influence, but when he boarded the bus he would announce in a loud voice that he wanted to be let off at the African Missions House. At the designated stop he would be assisted to the pavement by the conductor and bid all in the bus a warm goodnight. Then, having ruined the reputation of that innocent order, he would weave the half mile back along the road to his own.

Now that I was 'back to school' I began to learn valuable lessons from the teachers.

Eamonn Young came to teaching as an afterthought. He brought with him to Bishopstown School all the man-management savvy he had gleaned as an army commandant, and a passion for his subject that took him out of the army and into the Uni. I learned from Eamonn that even the laziest pupil can't resist a teacher in love with his subject.

The first-year class in Douglas school came to a class mass, perfectly tutored in the responses, which they roared back at me. I tried dropping my voice to tempt them into lowering theirs, but they roared even louder as if to encourage me. They had prepared their own prayers of petition and these were a lurid litany of requests.

'For me Nanny, 'cos she had her leg off. Eh, above the knee. Lord hear us.'

'Lord graciously hear us,' they thundered.

Brother Bede in Turner's Cross pulled out all the stops with themes and posters and readings they could pick from any source. He encouraged the lads to mine their own music for lyrics that were meaningful to their own lives. In short order we waded through the entire libretto of Jesus Christ Superstar. Jarlath, a retired and saintly Brother, always knelt at the back at these masses to show solidarity with the boys. The poor man had to endure endless readings from Jonathan Livingstone Seagull and The Little Prince but his martyrdom was highlighted when they struck into a song about Vincent Van Gogh and sang, 'How you suffered for your sanity'.

Mayfield was special. They were starting with a brand new school and wisely determined to build from the bottom up. John, the principal, was a smiling man who shrewdly built up the morale of the staff while he built his school. Apart from himself and Dan, the vice-principal, I was a senior statesman and the only religious in a group of young, vibrant teachers. Already a local cleric had sounded off from the pulpit about the setting up of 'a godless college', but the local parents placed their faith and their children in the new community school. Any clerical affectation was soon kicked out of me in five-a-side soccer tournaments. But my visa into acceptance was stamped definitively the day I opened the tin at the break. Sister Sabina fretted at the idea that I wouldn't be back for the lunch.

'You'll never last on a boiled egg.'

Every morning a tin appeared on the table and when I opened it in the staffroom the teachers gathered like bees to honey. It was full to the brim with sandwiches and Club Milks. They got a terrible death from the healthy appetites around me, and Sister was overjoyed at the empty tin. I believed that my first ministry was to the staff and became good friends with many of them. The normal awkwardness between males and females seemed to be cancelled out by the collar, but in its own way the very ease of the relationships marked me out as different.

Clare was from the southside but apart from that, as I often told her, she was all right.

'For a mongrel you're very saucy,' she'd retort. 'Wasn't your own father from the southside?'

Clare brought me home to a house in the lee of the South

Chapel, where I could drop anchor with her family and boyfriend and be ordinary. John and Marie brought me to the Opera House and came back to the flat for the night supper. In her innocence Marie asked me to do something on child development with her class. Fired with enthusiasm, I began to draw a womb on the board and a foetus floating in amniotic white chalk. The girls, who were always years ahead of the boys, concentrated on looking superior. The boys' jaws sagged on the desks. By the grace of God, the school inspector walked in the door. He must have wondered at how quiet the children were and why the teacher kept manoeuvring to block his view of the board. Sensibly, Marie never asked me to talk to them again.

The children were second-generation northsiders with all the subversive wit of their elders. One day I noticed a lad had brought his dog to school. The dog was a few steps above Dinky on the evolutionary ladder but a little to the left of any recognisable breed.

'What d'ya tink of me dog, Father?'

'He's, eh, very interesting, Mick. What did you call him?'

'He have no name.'

I launched into a lecture on how a dog had to have a name. How could he have any identity or dignity without a name?

'Watch him now, Father. Here, stupid.'

The little dog zoomed to his master, propelled by his stump of a tail. Who needed a formal name when you could be hailed in the community with 'sham' or 'bater' without ever losing your dignity?

I revelled in the energy of the place, helping Maurice with the musical and whirling the youngest ones on to the floor at the discos. After the all-boys schools, it was a culture shock to encounter a mixed group. I discovered that while the lads were going through early adolescence properly preoccupied with football, the girls were years ahead in terms of emotional development – twelve going on twenty-seven. Around that time we had an influx of 'refugees' from the north. Sharon was a 'wee' lass with enormous composure. She set her sights on the lankiest of the lads and decided that they were 'going steady'.

'Aren't you a bit young to be doing a steady line, Sharon?'

'Och, Father, sure I'm nearly thirteen so I am.'

Seamus was blissfully unaware of his romantic status. Like most of his group, he had all the coordination of a newborn foal. In his scheme of things, football was God and girls were a distraction. Sharon would not be sidetracked. I found Seamus pressed into a corner one day while Sharon blocked his escape with implacable determination. He gave me a beseeching look.

'Father, for the love of God, will you take her away outta that?'

Apart from cooling Sharon's ardour and saying class masses, I wondered what my real function was as their priest. Then I remembered something from my childhood that dispelled my worries. When we were very young my eldest sister Kay was going to dances with her friends from school. Sheila, Eily and Anne always came back to our kitchen for the post mortem. As soon as we heard their voices in the kitchen, we three younger ones would tiptoe in our pyjamas to the top of the stairs and huddle behind the banister, sitting on the cold lino risking piles, trying to muffle our laughter at the vivid expressions from below.

Sometimes Kay would check the stairs. 'Are ye up there?' Michael and I had to gag Bernie before she could answer, 'No, we're not.'

I remember one particular night someone mentioned that an older girl was getting engaged. As soon as the fella's name was mentioned, the others went into spasms of disbelief. 'What does she see in him?' they wondered. Years later I asked Kay if that couple had actually married.

'They did.'

'And how did he turn out?'

'Well, he turned out a marvellous husband. He hands up all his money and he's very good with the children.'

As I reflected on the story, I began to realise that the girl had seen whatever was best in that lad. Every time she spoke to him 'twas to the best in him and, of course, the best in him grew to fullness. I developed a motto from the story: 'Whatever you shine your light on will grow.' If I wanted to see cafflers, blackguards and problem children, there would be no shortage of candidates, but I would never see beyond the actions to the real child and never be an agent for growth for any child.

Like any child, I brought stories home from school. To the patients they were pictures from a lost world and I warmed myself to their delight. Often a hand would reach from under the covers to mine and a voice would ask, 'How's the young one you asked us to pray for, Father? Did she pass her exam?'

'She did, Mick.'

'Ah, thank God,' he'd say with a contented smile.

It worked the other way as well. The children often asked me about the hospital and the patients and would punctuate my stories with, 'Ah God help us!' or 'Sure, Gawdy love us.' But a young one, on the verge of tears, once entreated me, 'Ah, Father, don't be tellin' us them stories any more about the old people. Sure you'll draw a fit of depression down on top of us.'

I began to realise that many of them lived in the new housing estates that spread like spokes from the hub of the school. Most of their grandparents lived in the more settled areas, so it was un-likely that the children would see sickness at first hand. I won-dered how they'd respond to a real live sick person and made Jim Keating an offer he couldn't refuse.

'Jim, I'm saying mass on Thursday for the children in Mayfield. Would you come up and give me a hand?'

The same day, a group of his butties were holding court in the bedroom. Led by Colm, the taxi-driver, they were measuring him for the coffin. Very carefully they ran a twine down his length in the bed and matched it to the door.

'Keating, we'll never get you out that way. We'll have to move the jamb.'

Jim played his part to perfection.

'But lads, ye can't leave me here. I have a deposit paid on the plot in Curraghkippawn. Anyway, the neighbours will complain.'

There was much mock scratching of heads all round and then, inspiration.

'Keating,' says Colm, 'when you feel death comin' on ya, could you lean over a bit sideways like in the bed, so that when you stiffen up we can angle you out the door?'

We all laughed heartily at that. It was only through such outlandish rituals that we could cope with the thought of losing him.

The following Thursday he was gleaming in a white shirt, sitting ready in the wheelchair.

'What'll I say to them?'

'Don't worry, Jim,' I said. 'You'll know when the time comes.'

There was nearly a small riot when they saw the wheelchair, and eventually we had to have a draw for the driver. The classroom was festive with posters, the makeshift altar awash with flowers. Uncharitably I wondered which local garden was the unsuspecting donor. But as the woman from Blarney Street said to the post office mistress when she queried her sending a turkey by surface post to the son in Australia, 'Sure, 'tis the thought that counts.'

After the gospel I introduced him.

'Boys and girls, this is Mr Jim Keating. I grew up around the corner from him and, since I was a child, he has always been my great friend.'

Then I sat down. Jim started to speak in his gentle, earnest voice and they leant forward to listen. Without a shred of self-pity he told them about his sickness and how he tried every day to cope with it. He spoke of good neighbours who brought the *Examiner* in the morning and the *Echo* in the evening, and faithful friends who called in casually on the way home from work. It was a lesson in love that I didn't have the personal authority to teach, and, like the children, I sat humbly at the feet of a practising Christian. When he finished there was wild clapping and not a few tears. They crowded around to shake his hand and I winced at their hearty handshakes, knowing how much pain even the slightest pressure could produce. He showed no sign of it, smiling and nodding his head in benediction.

When I got him back to bed he was grey with exhaustion. I think he read the guilt in me.

'Sit down there, boy, for a minute.' He patted the bed beside him.

'I have plenty of time for rest, all right? That was a great privilege for me today and I won't forget you for it.'

He leaned forward and kissed me on the cheek.

'D'ye know what?' he said suddenly. 'I think I'll stand for pope.'

29

THE CHILD IS FATHER TO THE MAN

A span of three long winters, I have known,
November on November, and alone
Have walked among the phantoms etched in gloom,
My sky, the void above the light,
My world, the shadowed room.

And I have heard the secrets of the ones
Who throng about the threshold of the grave,
Who hang old hurts about the sapling-man
And sway his heart to shrive and salve and save.

And when, at last, their winter thawed to spring
Their mortal husk, soft-folded into clay
I stayed behind, a bird of bonded wing
My flock all light-wing wheeling
And away.

After a seven o'clock mass for the nuns on Sunday morning, I said another on the hill for the people who lived in the high houses that stepped in ragged formation from the barracks to the railway station. Theresa, a lean whippet of a woman, sold the papers from inside a wooden hut at the church gate.

'Lovely day, Father. Dere's to be a coalition government and 'tis full of doctors. You'll have to have a prescription to get a house.'

I got the *Press* and *Independent* every Sunday. Old habits die hard and I came from a crowd who bought both, despite their regular complaint: 'There's nothing in either of them.' Theresa just looked at me when I offered to pay, and I was casting about for some way to counter this when she said, 'Himself wants to be an altar boy.' I was at a loss to know how Theresa's husband could be exalted to that position, when she nodded meaningfully at the counter. The top of a small head loomed like a rising moon from behind a stack of papers and two pale eyes held me steady in their sights.

'Would you like to be an altar boy?'

The eyes blinked.

'Send him in next Sunday before mass, Theresa, and I'll sort him out.'

'Twas a done deal.

Himself arrived earlier than the others and I had time to get a good look at the rest of him. The round head was perfectly matched by a perfectly round body with legs and arms that looked as if they were stuck on as an afterthought.

'You're welcome,' I said. 'Put on the gear now, like a good boy.'

He blinked. He was a man of few words and had obviously used all of them. I tried every tack I knew to cajole a few words from him, to no avail. If there was ever a lull in the conversation, he planned to be in the thick of it.

Himself rolled out on to the altar like a roly-poly pope and presided from the bench while the others trotted about their business. For every yin there's a yang, and himself had an exact opposite in Michael. Michael's mouth ran like a tap in the sacristy and he just lowered the volume on the altar. One Sunday, while I was getting my sermon notes in order, Michael paused for breath and himself spoke. It had the same effect on us as the burning bush had on Moses. Even Michael suffered a complete stoppage with shock.

'Father,' himself said in a growly voice, pointing at Michael, 'I hates dat boy.' His eyes had the sort of tight expression I remembered seeing on the hurling pitch when plastic surgery was imminent.

'Ah no,' I said hastily. 'You might dislike him but you don't hate him.'

Himself was implacable. 'I hates him,' he said evenly. 'Dat boy is a disturber.' He was off like a Jack Russell terrier after a rabbit. The 'disturber' read the danger signals faster than me and was already climbing up on to the vesting bench for sanctuary.

'Get him off me,' he screamed.·

I had himself in a headlock, trying to keep my hand away from his teeth, and Michael was screaming from the bench, 'He bit me, Father. He bit me. I'll get the lockjaw', when the parish priest sailed in the door. Everyone turned to stone before the gorgon. Macbeth had always been my favourite Shakespearean play and this man had been my teacher:

> We are in blood
> Stepp'd in so far, that, should we wade no more,
> Returning were as tedious as go o'er.

he paraphrased, and turned tail on the confusion. The mass bell rang.

A very flushed and dishevelled procession emerged before the un-suspecting congregation. Every few minutes I stabbed the two gladiators with dagger looks to keep manners on them. When I lifted the veil of the chalice, I found that I had forgotten the paten in all the confusion.

'Psst.' Himself appeared at my elbow.

'Whass wrong?'

'I forgot the paten. Will you go in for it, please?'

'Whassa paten?'

'The round goldy thing for the top of the chalice.'

'Why didn'cha say so?'

He had not forgiven my intervention. A genuine Jack Russell must never be disturbed at the kill.

After mass I coursed him out to Theresa, intent on revoking his hunting licence.

'Isn't he dotey on the altar, Father? D'ye know what, I think he'd make a priest.'

One bad word from me and himself would be history. In the best northside tradition, Theresa would drive straight over him and reverse in case she missed a bit. Then she would dance on his corpse for 'making a show of her'.

'Actually, Theresa,' I said, 'I was thinking myself what a great bishop he'd make. He has all the right qualities.'

She glowed. Himself blinked one eye. We were friends.

Around this time I got friendly with Ronnie and the two Mauras. The three gangly teenage girls were regular visitors to the patients and I was touched by the way they leant in close to catch a fading voice. They seemed to gravitate naturally towards those who had only occasional visitors, and their mad laughter chased the silence for an hour and drew luminous smiles from the shadows. They started to drop into the flat for night supper before heading home.

'Have you any records, Father?'

'Yes. I have Gigli, Mario Lanza – and this one has a brilliant duet from *The Pearl Fishers* with Jussi Björling and Robert Merrill.'

They looked at each other as if I 'had a want in me'.

'Have you any modern ones, like?'

'Well, I have Barbra Streisand.'

'Ancient.'

We compromised on the Beatles. I got to write a sermon while the three ate all my night supper to *Sgt Pepper's Lonely Hearts Club Band*.

Ronnie was the natural leader of the trio.

'Would you come up and talk to the girls in our class?'

'About what?'

'Ah, ye know,' she said awkwardly, 'fellas and stuff.'

'Why don't ye bring them up to the flat on Friday night?'

They were elated. If wisdom is knowing how much you don't know, then for once I made a wise decision. A priest's family are always the first victims of his pastoral zeal. Kay, my eldest sister, was unflappable. She heard me out over a steaming plate of skirts and kidneys.

'Would you stop inhaling that and ate it before it goes cold. Friday night? Grand. Myself and Caleb will come up.'

On Friday night the flat was strewn with 'young wans' stretched in a comfortable semicircle on the carpet before the fire. After the introductions the silence was deafening.

'Christy, weren't you going to show Caleb the garden?'

'What? Oh right.'

Bemused, I went out with Caleb and the two of us ambled around the lawn.

'What's all that about, Caleb?'

'Sure they'd never talk while we were there,' he said easily.

An hour later we were dizzy from circling the garden. As soon as we came in the door, the talk stopped. After the night supper, the trio stayed behind to tidy the flat.

'How did it go?'

'Grand.'

The conversation was over. What words of wisdom did she give them, I wondered. Did she tell them how she knew for certain that she would marry Caleb? He came up to our house one night to collect her for a dance and she was up to her elbows in the sink, peeling spuds. With two younger brothers, a younger sister and a widower father, she always had a lot to do.

'Caleb, I can't go anywhere until the spuds are peeled for tomorrow's dinner. If you want to wait, the *Echo* is there on the table.'

He took off his coat and rolled up the sleeves of his best shirt.

'You go on up and get ready, Kay. I'll finish the potatoes.'

She knew at that moment that she had found her partner for life.

The flat became a sort of halfway house for the trio and the other youngsters who visited the wards. A 'goozah', in Cork, is an unwelcome third party on a date. My cousin Peter and his girlfriend Kay regularly brought ten goozahs on their dates. They were involved in a northside youth club and, every week, shepherded a gang of youngsters to visit the wards. Naturally, they came en bloc to the flat for the tea afterwards. I remember that one of them turned into a most unlikely angel to teach me a lasting lesson.

Cancer usually hides inside a person and rarely gets in the way of conversation. Jerry's lump loomed on the top of his head. I tried to ignore it but it was huge, and every time I looked at him my eyes were drawn to it. I made a special effort to look elsewhere, looking behind and away from him so that the poor man must have thought the room was haunted. And then Timmy joined the youth club. Timmy was a collection of ankles, elbows, acne and neuroses. He was at that awful age when even a mother's love can be strained. On his very first visit to the wards, like a pigeon homing to a loft, Timmy headed for Jerry.

'What happened your head?'

'I have a bit of a lump, boy.'

And that was the first time in months that Jerry was spoken to as a normal human being.

My Nan often said that some people were 'all eyes and no sight'. In this case it was a perfect description of her grandson, but Timmy's experience converted me. Wouldn't it be wonderful if even very young children could have easy access to the patients? Wasn't it bad enough for a terminally ill man to be losing his life without losing touch with his family as well? And why should we presume that because they were old or dying, they had lost their grá for children?

I had it all worked out.

Mamma was a brick wall.

'No. You couldn't have children seeing cancer.'

'But, Mother, children are the only ones who don't see cancer.'

'No.'

We needed a miracle to melt her opposition.

It was May, and the children of the parish made their first holy communion.

I was drafted in to help with the first confessions. The girls sang their sins with something approaching pride, and the boys trembled on the brink of involuntary liquidation. The sun smiling on their big day lured them to blossom on our lawn for photographs. Moving among the parents, I happened to glance up at the front of the building. I was transfixed. Every window framed a face. There were men and women up there who rarely bothered to leave the bed, and yet on this special day the beauty and joy of young voices called them from their shadows.

I found her in a circle of tiny brides.

'Mother, will you look up there.'

She looked for the longest moment.

'I suppose you'll give me no peace anyway,' she smiled, and our doors swung open to the angels.

And there were doors of comfort open to me also.

The families on the hill encouraged me to call. After a hectic day, I could kick my cares away playing soccer with the O'Connells in the lane. I could be pleasantly humiliated at Scrabble by Nuala or tied in theological knots by her daughter. Elaine was a member of a running club and full of missionary zeal to spread their painful gospel.

'Will you come for a run?'

We drove out to the Powder Mills in Ballincollig and started with exercises. When I was completely exhausted she said, 'Right, that's the warm-up done, now we'll run.'

Pride is a terrible thing. I rushed to keep up with her long, graceful stride. By the time we started on the second lap, I was beyond agony. I had hit 'the wall' so many times it was beginning to hit me back.

'How did the Church move so far from the simplicity of the apostles?' she asked.

I dropped to my knees, gasping like a mullet strawkhauled on the North Gate Bridge.

'Are you hyperventilating?'

'No, I'm dying. Listen, Elaine ...' I managed, when my breathing had settled down to the merely asthmatic. 'I can run or I can talk theology, but not together. And another thing, could we run together? If I'm behind you, they'll think I'm running after you, and if I'm in front of you, you'll get a bad name.'

She kept that pact for another lap before she laughed, 'If St Paul had done a bit of running, the readings on Sunday would be a lot shorter,' and she was off again like a greyhound.

On Sundays, when the three masses and Benediction were over, I could go to my cousin Nora's. She lived in a small, warm house, angled on a hill within sight and smell of Murphy's brewery.

'Go up to Willie's bed. I'll call you for the tea.'

It was enough to watch the telly, anonymous among my own, until the phone rang again to call me back. Nora sprinkled me with holy water at the door, patting my overcoat against the cold. I always glanced in the mirror at the brewery corner, to catch a final glimpse of the small woman, limned in light, her hand up-raised in blessing, a talisman against the dark.

It began to dawn on me that I was adopted. Ronnie, the Mauras and the youth club came and went at will, but the Campbells had squatters' rights. Frank and Dave, my two foxy altar boys, had foxy sisters and brothers who wandered easily in and out of the flat. The three youngsters, Dave, Frank and Dorothy, ate all my biscuits, and the older ones balanced their depredations with homemade apple tarts. They were happy to watch the telly, sailing on the mat before the fire, while I read in the armchair, and they would let themselves out across the hill when I was called to the wards.

Seven years in the company of one's peers is no preparation for the reality of children. The *Echo* announced that Hamlet would be on the telly, with Laurence Olivier agonising around Elsinore. I got the jobs finished early, the telly and teapot warmed, the arm-chair angled for a night with the bard. Shakespeare was 'big' in the northside thanks to Fr O'Flynn and the Loft Drama Group. Not everyone was enamoured of Fr O'Flynn's obsession. Two elderly ladies were stationed one day in Mulcahy's fresh meat shop in Shandon Street, conferring on the 'seed, breed and generation' of everyone who passed the window. Just then Fr O'Flynn hove into view, in what P.G. Wodehouse would have described as a 'dignified procession of one'.

'Moll,' said one, 'would you look at Fr O'Flynn, and he tryin' to walk like Shakespeare.'

The productions in the Opera House were usually lavish and well-acted, before an audience of Leaving Cert boys and girls who were much more interested in the dramatic hormonal tension among themselves. The director always managed to iron the spiky accents of Cork into a passably level tone, until the night the messenger missed his cue during a production of Macbeth. There was a long dramatic pause and then the hapless fellow rushed on-stage to announce, 'De Queen, me Lord, is dead', in an accent that had all the grace notes of Blarney Street.

The production on the telly was the genuine article and I was ready for a feast of culture when the doorbell rang. Three foxy heads bobbed expectantly in the porch.

'Come in quick. The tea is in the pot and the Club Milks are in the tin. Hush now, let ye.'

They grouped on the mat before the fire.

'Who's he, Father?'

'That's Hamlet, Prince of Denmark.'

'Who's yer wan?'

'That's his mother, Gertrude. She married his uncle when he killed his father.'

'Jay,' they chorused, exhaling crumbs on the carpet.

'And who's yer woman?'

'Oh, for the love of God, that's Ophelia. She's doing a line with Hamlet but she'll go mad and drown herself.'

'I wouldn't blame her,' Frank said with feeling, watching Olivier talking to a skull. The philistines were out in force to-night. I turned it off.

'Will we play cards?'

Sometimes their Mam and Dad would come to hunt them home and stay for tea.

'Are they driving you mad, Father?'

'No, but ye can drop over the children's allowance book.'

Almost imperceptibly, they widened the warmth of their family circle to include the priest. Like a grandparent, I could always ruin them and hand them back, but without their laughter the flat contracted and grew cold. I quizzed my motives for keeping an open door for all who came to call, and admitted before God that I was selfish. I had grown to love their company and was frightened to find that I felt less and alone without them. The books were some solace but the groaning shelves bore testimony to time spent alone. With the turn of a switch I could have Gigli or Streisand for company, but when the needle lifted from the last track the silence seemed deeper than before. Many's the night I sat the fire out, watching the last spark until it grew too tired to glow. This was the lot of the priest, I thought, to be available to all and belong to none.

'You must pray.'

The voices of spiritual directors echoed from the seminary. I opened up this pain as prayer, spreading it out in the dark before God. But God seemed to have followed the laughter to sit 'where two or three were gathered', and warm himself to their companionship. And who could blame Him?

30

ALL FALL DOWN

And there were silent evenings,
Sitting sightless with a book
The heart-eye, parsing through
A Braille of scarcely dented beds.
When pressure of their hands
Would set my hand-heel
Grinding in my eye
And all the reasons why
Just swept around the steady stone
Of their blind pain
And mine.

The Kerryman declared that he was God.

'How do you know?' the neighbours enquired cautiously. 'Well,' said he, 'whenever I say my prayers, I feel I'm talking to myself.'

Sometimes the boundaries between who you are and what you do become blurred. A priest can be seduced into thinking of himself as pivotal to the work and begin to fill the spaces with it to keep them clear of doubt. He can run so fast that he outpaces thought and falls finally into bed, convinced by his exhaustion that he has 'run the race and won the prize'. That man was me.

The work became my painkiller and my pride. Rushing to and fro gave me the illusion of achievement. Time was hot money; it would burn holes in my hands if I held it fast, and when 'twas spent there was always more that could be borrowed from the night before and the morning after. But there is no sweet music from a string too tightly wound. Time with one patient became time taken from another, and unconsciously I developed a measurement of needs and pains. There was a hostel connected to the hospital by a short corridor. It was a place where elderly ladies could recuperate after an illness or retire to if they wished.

John died slow and hard late in the night and his death-rattle was still echoing in my head when the call came from the hostel in the morning.

'One of the ladies would like to see you.'

The short connecting corridor was a decompression chamber between one world and another. The building was beautifully appointed, many of the residents kept their own furniture, and the room I entered was heavy with mahogany. The lady was gentle and welcoming.

'D'you know, Father,' she said, 'I can't get any good out of that geranium.'

Mentally, I held up the yardstick of John and his killing cancer against this woman and her wilting plant. It was no contest. I thought, wouldn't I love to have your worries. I had forgotten my Nan's wisdom that 'everyone's pain is their own'. But personal pain consumes the available energy as fire devours air; it can cause the heart to contract in contemplation of itself. This was the dark I had feared since childhood and I carried it now inside me in the broad light of day.

It's a fortunate priest who is never 'the priest' to his own. When I rushed into Kay's for a fast cuppa en route to somewhere else, she looked up from the sink.

'God help us,' she said tartly, 'but here's a watch wearing a man.'

My younger sister only saw her brother when he needed a haircut. When Michael woke me with calls from New York, his usual good humour foundered in the shallows of my silences. I took my darkness to my father and fidgeted on the oilcloth until he said, 'Wouldn't you take it a bit easy, boy? You have the weight of the world on you.' Defensively, I listed the litany of needs and night-calls, until he raised his hand in defeat. 'You'll be damn-all good to them dead.'

The spirit works in mysterious ways. I didn't die heroically, like Damien of Molokai. I just slipped the cartilage in my knee.

It happened first in Maynooth. Fifteen of us were attempting plastic surgery on fifteen of them. In the seminary this passed for hurling. I slipped and fell and couldn't rise, noticing with a sort of detached curiosity that my knee was cocked at an interesting angle. The surgeon in the Mater banged it enthusiastically with his fist and announced to his nodding entourage that I was 'an interesting meniscectomy'. The radio played the 'Hallelujah Chorus' as I was trolleyed to theatre, and before I went to sleep the man in green asked me to indicate the knee for the op.

Our college doctor was known to the students as Game Ball. This was his optimistic response to almost all ailments presented, except mine. 'You'll never hurl again,' he said cheerfully. 'Take up golf.' The young physio in the Mater would have been ejected from the SS for being too rough, but she had me back walking in no time. 'Motivation is everything,' she'd say as I sweated under the weights. I had the greatest motivation in the world. I couldn't wait to get away from her before she killed me altogether. In four weeks I had swapped the crutches for the hurley and was scourging a sodden sliotar on my own, willing the leg back to par. But Game Ball proved a prophet of sorts. The game that should have saved me was my downfall.

While I was in St Patrick's, Michael's second son was due into the world and I rushed across the Atlantic to christen him. Ivan wisely stayed in the womb until I was well over the Atlantic on my way back, but I did play one round of golf before leaving. We teed off in Mosholu Park and when I swung there was an old familiar pop and my leg was on a separate contract again. On my return to Ireland the nuns hurried me to the Orthopaedic Hospital in Cork. For the first few days after the op I fretted from inactivity. The nurse in charge of the ward was a formidable lady. She had a look that could wilt a young nurse at fifty yards and a voice that could clear visitors like smoke in a draught. 'There was a great barmaid lost in you,' I told her when I got to know her better.

'D'you know who make the worst patients?' she asked.

'Would it be doctors?'

'No. And they're bad enough, God knows. No, the worst in the world are missionaries.'

'Why so?'

'Well, they spend all their time fretting to be back on the missions baptising black babies, and because they can't they make life miserable for the craythurs here who must look after them.'

Point taken.

'I heard you were plastered?'

Pat was as chirpy as ever.

'How are things in the hospital, Pat?'

'Marvellous altogether. Mamma got the loan of a Dominican and he's anointing everyone. I'd say he's in dread of her.'

So the place hadn't ground to a halt after all.

Early the following morning a hush spread in the corridor outside and it was no surprise when the bishop walked in. I was reading a novel called *The Kapillan of Malta* and felt a vague sense of relief that there was a picture of a priest on the cover. As we swapped small talk I began to rehearse my script. This was a God-given chance to tell him that the day couldn't be stretched to take in my list of duties. As I drew breath he asked, 'Does anyone visit Glasheen School?'

'I don't know,' I stammered.

'Would you add that to your list.' He paused at the door and smiled. 'I'll pray for you,' he said calmly and was gone.

As soon as his footsteps faded I couldn't hold it in any longer. Two young nurses rushed into the room. 'What's wrong with you, Father?' But I was laughing hysterically and couldn't answer them. Gradually the madness died down and I wiped my eyes on the blankets.

'Can we do anything for you, Father?'

'Ye can. Would ye ever wash my hair? I haven't been able to shower since I came in and I feel like Murphy's pup.'

I started laughing again and they backed out of the room. I

was remembering one of my Uncle Christy's stories about Dinnie and the jennet. Dinny was a character from 'long 'go' who kept a jennet in the house. He was also noted for his meanness.

'D'ye know,' Uncle Christy would say drolly, 'just when Dinny had the jennet trained to live on nothin', didn't he die!' I wished I had told the bishop that story.

They came back with a basin and shampoo and set about the head. It was the first time in a long time that I felt relaxed and the first time that I had let anyone minister to me.

The remaining days were blissful. Nurse brought a small table, and a collection of crocks on crutches staggered in for mass. I discovered the children's ward one day by accident as I backed through double doors on the crutches. Two rows of miniature convicts peeped at me from behind the bars of high-sided cots. A balloon dithered forlornly on the floor in the middle of the passageway.

'Man,' a tiny boy called from his cell. 'Man, will you get my balloon?'

For what other purpose would a man spend seven years in a seminary? It was my finest hour. Balancing on the good leg, I extended the crutches and gripped the balloon between the rubber tips. Then, with the bad leg stuck out backwards for ballast, I raised the balloon and dropped it in the cot. Nureyev couldn't have done it better and I was half disappointed at the lack of applause, but they were goggle-eyed with admiration. Then a shower of balloons sailed out of every cot in the ward. I beat a hasty retreat.

My room began to resemble the front window of Nosey Keefe's shop with all the fruit brought by the visitors. I decided to share my bounty and made regular pilgrimages to the cots with oranges and grapes. This corporal work of mercy was brought to an abrupt end when a flushed nurse laid down the law. 'Would you stay out of the children's ward. We're changing nappies by the new time.'

All too soon it was time to go back.

31

ENTRANCES AND EXITS

We were walking on a high-ditched boreen west of the city. I was striding as I remember my father doing when we were children, leaning into the road as if to outpace his pain and wear it down. We children would stop to admire a feather-galleon on a pool and race to catch him up, irritated at his unrelenting pace. Now I was the pacemaker. Con, a retired scoutmaster, erect and precise, prodded the road suspiciously with his stick. The Doc flapped along beside him, a black-sailed schooner in a fitful wind, tacking wildly to the sudden gusts of argument. They were going through the comfortable ritual of reminiscing about scout camps in the past that were one step away from typhus in terms of hygiene but were peopled with incredible characters.

'D'you remember the donkey, Con?'

'Will I ever forget?'

I could have whistled this one. The scouts were camped in Tom Deane's field beside a stream that fell from the high fortress of Cahirconree and emptied into Tralee Bay. After an uneventful week the local garda meandered in on his bicycle and, after exchanging the formalities of weather and football, announced that there was a dead donkey upstream. 'He must be there a week,' he said easily, and politely refused the cup of tea before sidepedalling off again, his duty done. This was the stream the camp drew water from to wash, drink and cook.

'You never saw such gawking in all your life.'

The Doc stopped in the middle of the boreen to catch his breath before taking up the narrative. One of the scout leaders shanghaied a troop and borrowed a rope to deal with the dead donkey. The same man was known to have a delicate stomach but as they neared the spot he gathered his courage and rallied the troops.

'Now, lads, just remember ye're scouts and must act like scouts.'

'Oh sir, looka de donkey in the water. He's manky.'

'Gawk,' went the leader.

Eventually the young fellas waded out to the carcass and lashed the rope to a hind leg. Just as the leader was surfacing for air, the lads heaved and the back leg of the donkey parted company with the rest of him.

'Gawk.'

Con and the Doc were now convulsed in the middle of the road, while I marked time with impatience.

'Are we walking or what?'

Doc levelled his stick at me. 'Con,' he thundered, 'that young pup thinks he's the Curé of Ars.'

'And he died roaring,' Con replied blithely.

'He did not, ye bleddy pagan,' the Doc spluttered, 'but that ordained eejit will die young on us.'

There was no let-up. Back in Con's kitchen the Doc worried at me like a terrier. 'Listen, boy, our Divine Lord and Saviour had sense enough to take a rest. Wouldn't you get involved in something?' He picked up the *Cork Examiner*, the Corkman's Bible, and flung it across the table. 'Read that,' he commanded, stabbing an ad on the inside page. The Everyman Theatre Group were looking for people to audition. 'Didn't you do some of that blackguardin' in Maynooth?'

'What d'ya think, Con?' I asked doubtfully.

'Eat the rasher,' he replied diplomatically. 'You're like a pull-through for a rifle.'

John O'Shea loomed large in the shadows of the theatre.

'And your name?'

'Christy Kenneally.'

His eyes dipped down to the collar and back to my face.

'Right eh, Christy. Maybe you'd read the underlined passage for me. Good. Can you do a Dublin accent? Fine. I'd like you to take a part in the play. We're doing *The Plough and the Stars*.'

We were all amateurs except Laurie. She was brought all the way from Dublin to play one of the female leads and we were a bit in awe of her. Over the weeks she melted our reserve with a repertoire of theatre stories. Somehow she was the only one who didn't know what I did for a living. We were waiting our cue one night at rehearsals when she asked me.

'I'm a priest.'

'Ah, go to God!'

'I am.'

'And I thought you had a thing for wearing black.'

'If you two are finished with that particular scene, you might like to join our play.'

'Sorry, John.'

Laurie stayed in a flat during rehearsals and commuted home to Dublin at weekends. She became a regular visitor to my flat and regaled the young ones with lurid tales from the stage. I knew that many of the patients would remember her from *Tolka Row* on the telly and asked if she'd like to visit the women's ward. As we neared the door she paused and closed her eyes. Then she straightened up, took a deep breath and sailed across the threshold like a queen.

She was recognised instantly from the soap opera and soon she was surrounded and bombarded with questions.

'Did he really marry her? Declare to God and she was no oil paintin'.'

'And what about yourself, girl?'

'Ah, you were much too good for that waster anyway.'

I watched her flash among them like an exotic bird from a strange land, and marvelled at the ease with which her aura kept reality at bay for just a precious while.

The cast grew accustomed to seeing me change out of a soutane and into a volunteer's uniform, and the performances played without a hitch to packed houses until the chaise longue collapsed. The scene demanded that I fight with Nora, my wife, and then lead her tenderly to the chaise longue to make up. I lay back and took her hand, ready to draw her to my manly breast and sing 'Nora'.

When the leg snapped I was thrown backwards with my feet in the air. The audience gasped. Miraculously I was still aboard the furniture when the dust settled, but at a much more interesting angle. The 'wife's' eyes were out on stalks.

'I thought you got Fluther to fix that thing?' I said accusingly.

'Well,' she answered in a fit of inspiration, 'he didn't.'

I drew her to me and began to sing, 'When I first said I loved only you, Nora'. By now she had moved from shock to hysteria and as she muffled her mad giggles in my shirt her head banged time on my chest.

'How did you get that lovely quaver into your voice?' someone asked afterwards.

News spread to the Green Room and the cast were congregated in the wings at the end of the scene to congratulate the happy couple. Mick McCarthy, a neighbour's child from the northside, was among them.

'Doubt'ya, boy,' he smiled. 'Maybe you'd try O'Casey's lines tomorrow night?'

But my nights were numbered.

Even Pat was subdued.

'Himself down below phoned while you were out. He wants you to call down at seven sharp tomorrow night. I dunno were you wise to go into that bloody play at all.'

Then he brightened.

'By the way, was that bit with the sofa part of the play?'

I didn't bother to reply; he had cast his shadow on me. 'Himself down below' was a formidable ecclesiastic. By geographical accident I was within the boundaries of his jurisdiction. Even worse, when I called one of the lads for counsel he exhaled loudly on the phone before remarking in a cagey whisper, 'There's two divils in this diocese, boy, and he's both of them.'

At seven sharp I was ushered into 'the presence' by a silent, self-effacing housekeeper. My grandfather would have described the man within as 'a butty little man', but he wore a coloured bellyband and exuded an aura of easy power. He was seated at the far end of his desk when I entered, and motioned me to the chair on the other side.

'I believe you are active, Father?'

He smiled, but the smile never reached his eyes.

'I am.'

'Well, I'm sure you're aware that up to recently, priests were not even permitted in theatre audiences?'

I did know that, and I also knew that they sat in the wings to obey the rule until it died of shame in 1969. I said nothing.

'We are not men who seek the limelight or admiratio,' he continued smoothly.

Someone once asked a fella in Blackpool if it was true that all the Glen hurlers were fiery by nature.

'Ah no, boy,' he replied, 'dey all have long fuses but dey burns awful fast.'

I sat on my hands.

'You will of course desist from this pursuit, Father, and there will be no need for the matter to go further.'

Self-preservation is a very strong instinct but I said it anyway. 'I made a commitment to these people to see this current production through. I must fulfil that commitment.'

We locked eyes for a few moments in silence.

'Very well,' he said finally. 'Good evening, Father.'

I found my own way to the door.

Striding up the hill, I began to laugh out loud. Passers-by nodded deferentially, then looked away in embarrassment at the sight of a young cleric under the influence. But I was intoxicated by an old memory that had bubbled up to life. We were at a scout camp in Kerry, two weeks of damp tents and optional food. The scoutmaster was a jovial fella, a bit older than me. The camp had only a nodding acquaintance with hygiene, but once the latrines were dug well away from the tents and liberally blessed with Jeyes Fluid, God was in His Heaven and all was well with the world. This idyllic existence continued until the day the commissioner hove into view. As soon as the car bumped into the field, the bush telegraph beat out the alarm and we strove to put some order on the chaos. It was a wasted exercise.

He sniffed delicately at pots that were scrubbed with gravel from the river and still carried a cargo of sediment, roughage for the next meal. Ropes were loose, pegs were missing and half the young fellas unconsciously offended him by reversing the two-fingered salute. Word went out that we were to gather in a large ridge-tent for evaluation. We found ourselves ringside seats at what turned out to be our scoutmaster's autopsy. The commissioner chanted tonelessly through a long list of infringements, peppering his tirade with 'never in all my years' and 'a disgrace to the organisation'. The only one who seemed unabashed was the scoutmaster. He stood before the fusillade like a shell-shocked soldier, a vacant half-smile hovering on his face. At last, the damage done, 'the wrath of God' departed.

In the mortified silence, the scoutmaster roused himself from his stupor and remarked, 'Yerra, don't mind him, lads. He have worms.'

It wasn't exactly a philosophy for life, but the memory helped to straighten my back and lift my spirits that evening.

An old Cork cynic was known to say, 'God never closes a door but He catches your fingers in it.' But as the stage-door closed another door opened. Aine McEvoy phoned from RTE. Would I do the *Thought for the Day* on radio? I met her in Dublin and she scanned the scripts. 'They're good,' she said slowly, 'but there's something missing. Do you know any sick person?'

'Sure I know loads of them.'

'Yes, but do you know one in particular who listens to the radio?'

I told her about listening to the pope's blessing with Jim Keating.

'Isn't that for the City and the World?' he asked.

''Tis Jim.'

'Sure 'tis for no one really.'

'He's right about that,' she said, 'and that's what's wrong with your scripts; they're for no one in particular. Now, I'd like to meet this northside philosopher.'

They hit it off immediately. He made her laugh at his condition and she told him her story. Years before she had fallen under the shadow of TB. The doctors held out no hope to her parents and they decided to send her to Lourdes. They saw her off on a stretcher at the railway station, certain that she would come back in a coffin. When she did return they didn't recognise the smiling girl who walked down the platform to meet them.

She decided we would broadcast mass from the hospital and we went into overdrive to prepare. Our little choir worked themselves 'into oil' and when the great day dawned hundreds of people joined our congregation on air. It had a remarkable effect on the patients. Some dressed up for the occasion, despite the fact that they could not be seen, and the responses were prompt and hearty. A nurse summed up their feelings when she said, 'Sure it put us on the map.' This was a hospital that cured nobody. These were nurses that would never see a patient go home and these were patients who had heard their death sentence in the phrase, 'There is no more we can do for you.' Today they were reaching out to broadcast a message of ordinary heroism and extraordinary love. If they could never go again to the country, then for one special and memorable hour the country came to them.

But I was haunted by the faces at the windows. On the threshold of sleep I would see them mutely looking through the reflection of the world outside. They came to us to die, but what did they do in the meantime? They sat quietly in the wards or made the short pilgrimage to the day room to sit around the walls while the sun moved the shadows across the carpet until it was time for bed again. The visitors were sparks that brightened up the gloom all too briefly and then were gone. The patients went nowhere.

Nurse sighed tiredly into the chair. She plucked a pin two-handed from her cap, shaking out her hair

'Will you have tea?' I asked.

'No thanks, I'll be away home to my bed in a minute.'

'How are your lads?'

'They're there,' she replied philosophically, 'but Paddy is driving us mad.'

Paddy had arrived in the silent ambulance a month before. A spare, quiet man, he lapsed deeper and deeper into silence as the days wore by.

'We can't get a cheep out of him at all, and when we do 'tis only about his cancer. The girls are beginning to avoid him, and who could blame them? Anyway, maybe you can do something,' she said doubtfully.

Having a chat with Paddy was like ladling soup with a fork.

'Grand day, Paddy.'

Nod.

'Will the Glen do on Sunday, d'ye think?'

Shrug.

'Herself was in last night?'

'Yes.'

Sing ye choirs of angels! Paddy actually said something. Now, keep him talking.

'How's she keeping?'

Shrug.

A radio was playing somewhere down the corridor and as we sat in awkward silence two beautiful female voices coiled around each other to spin a sound that stretched across the spaces. They seemed to draw other voices from the shadows, as if the walls themselves wanted to give witness to the men and women who had once come here to die, and whose heroism would never be known. It lifted Paddy from the chair and turned him to the window where the fading day revealed the image of the man he once had been. His hand moved tentatively to touch the glass in a gesture of longing or farewell. His eyes were silver pools. As the voices soared and pulsed a final time and spiralled down to silence, he turned from the window, his face suffused with a rare glow.

'*Lakmé*,' he said, in a tone that tugged my heart.

The following day I met a friend in Patrick's Street. The same fella was known locally as a 'chancer'. A chancer, in Cork, is neither a fraud nor a liar; he is someone who takes creative liberties with the truth. 'Twas said about this fella that if he fell from a fourth-floor window he'd land in someone else's shoes. He also 'found' things. To be fair, he balanced his larcenous nature with a generous heart, after the style of Robin Hood. When he saw me coming he amputated himself from the corner at Woolworths, bobbing and weaving to avoid imaginary bullets.

'C'mere, how are things above?'

'Not bad at all.'

'Good man. Listen, I have something here you might use.'

He plucked an envelope from inside his coat, his eyes constantly roving over my shoulder, and then he was gone. I flipped the top of the envelope and discovered three tickets for the Cork Opera House.

'Nurse, would you like to go to the Opera House?'

She gave me a level look.

'Oh, and we'd be taking Paddy,' I added hastily.

Paddy, very properly, sat between the two of us in the theatre, silent as ever. In the rush to arrange the outing it never occurred to me to check the programme. As the curtain rose my heart sank. 'Twas far from the ballet I was reared. northsiders loved opera and, as an old neighbour remarked, 'Drama, girl, sure we're never short of that at home.' But ballet ran a poor second to hurling, pigeons, bowling and dogs. I prayed that Paddy would like the music anyway and wondered was it significant that he kept his cap firmly in place for the entire performance.

Nurse came to the breakfast table after mass to tell the story. She said that Paddy had walked into the day room that morning and announced, 'I was at de bally last night in d'Opera House.'

'What was it like?' they asked when they had recovered from the shock of Paddy's maiden speech.

''Twas de divil altogether,' he declared happily. 'Dere was young wans with half nothin' on 'em hoppin' around and fellas wearin' less dan a hanky hoppin' after 'em, and catchin' up with 'em.' Paddy had decided that the meantime might be worth taking more notice of after all.

They have a phrase in Cork to describe someone who is good company. They say, 'Sure he'd take you out of yourself.' Eily was one of those. Many of our patients got so much attention paid to their sickness that they were tempted to make it their life's work to the exclusion of everything else. There was no fear of Eily doing that. She was a small, shapeless woman with straight grey hair and City Hall glasses. She was also a most defiantly alive human being and she drove the nun in charge to distraction. In Sister's order of creation, nurses did and patients were done to. A nurse who slowed down to chat was suspect. As for a nurse who might sit on the side of the bed, well, sister didn't have a vocabulary sulphuric enough to deal with that sacrilege. The joke did the rounds that one particular nurse always took a hypodermic syringe with her when she went to visit the patients. As she sat on the bed she'd confide, 'If yer woman comes, you're getting a jab of this.'

As a patient Eily broke the mould and sister's heart. She insisted on helping with the wash-up or carrying trays to other patients and was thick-skinned enough to ignore looks or sarcastic remarks. She was also an insatiable magpie, hoarding pieces of material from all quarters to make soft toys. Her bed was her warehouse and workshop. The mattress was so high from stored contraband that I asked her if she got nosebleeds during the night. The very first time I was introduced, she said shyly, 'You don't know me, boy, but I know you and all belonging to you.'

'How so, Eily?'

'Sure I'm from Gerald Griffin Street and wasn't I in school with your mother Maura, the light of Heaven to her.'

She had a captive audience from that moment as she wove coloured threads in and out of my fading memories of Maura. Eily went to see me in the play and greeted the cast afterwards like the queen mother. Sometimes I linked her down to the flat for her supper and one day I plucked up the courage to ask her if she would come with me to my mother's grave.

It was spring and the ditches along the road to Whitechurch were flickering with wrens and spattered with primroses. 'Pull in there, boy,' she commanded and we plucked handfuls of the delicate blooms to place with our prayers before the headstone. We were easy with the silence on the way back and I was startled when she said, 'D'ye know, I still have me home. Would you like to see it?'

Eily's home had all the look and smell of desertion and decay. The houses on either side, like two good neighbours, did their best to shoulder it upright but it was dying of emptiness. I watched her carefully as she picked her way around the rubble from room to room. She stopped here and there and touched the walls with a tenderness we reserve for old faces which have become precious in their fragility.

'I dunno will I ever come back here,' she whispered. 'The nuns want me to sell up but this is my home and so long as I have it …' Her voice trailed off wistfully and two enormous tears loomed behind her glasses.

'Will we say a prayer for our dead, Eily?'

'We will, boy,' she answered strongly, giving her nose a vigorous wipe.

'For Maura, your mother, and all my own.'

The house seemed to sag when she stepped back over the threshold. She turned at the door of the car to look back. It was a look of such love that I thought, she will bury the lot of us because she has something to live for. And at that moment I envied her that sad old house.

32

LETTING GO

October coughed a few times in the chimney as, outside, a few last hardy leaves flushed hectic red. The change before death. Cork buried itself in a brown smoke-shawl; the city spires loomed, marooned, glinting coolly in a low-slung light. Beyond the wall, tyres pressed dead leaves to patterned mush as children, shapeless in coats and scarves, leant into the wind, tacking reluctantly to school.

Our world contracted. The pallid garden grass was lichen-low; the fingers of bare trees beseeched the sky. Squalls swept the paths of autumn's store. The wind died in the dark; frost formed and silvered up the steps to weep beneath the threshold of the door. And then November came, the dying of the year.

The climate in the wards remained the same but there are also seasons of the heart, and in this dark, cold time so many hearts let go. The phone beside my bed became a thing of dread, waiting to shrill at 4 a.m. when life is at its lowest ebb, to drag me up and out, to hold the man whose chest rose up and down and up and down and stopped.

'Saints of God, come to his aid.'

Norma saw the curtains close and heard the prayer murmur from within. She fled the ward. She had a man and children, three good reasons to defy her death. Her refuge was a wheelchair parked against the corridor wall, and there she kept her vigil, listening for the tread that had to come, but not today. Sweet loving Saviour Jesus, not today.

We sat there, side by side like conscripts bloodied from the line, pulled back to rest awhile. I was too tired for small talk, contented just to keep her company, watching as the last light of day ebbed from the windows and another night began.

'Do you ever get browned off, Father?'

'Sometimes.'

The silence stretched.

'Arrah, Jesus,' she said suddenly, 'we're not dead yet. Come on and I'll give you a race.'

Chair to chair, hub to hub, Messala and Ben Hur, we tensed for off.

'Ready, steady, go.'

We strained and slapped the rims and flashed along the lino, laughter flaring like a ribbon in our wake, and crashed together in a wreck beyond the nurse's station, wheezing for air. And there beyond the pane, squat and small, was the mortuary.

'I suppose 'tis out there for me, Father?'

Somewhere in the race, we had crossed the bounds of priest and patient.

'Is there something I can do?'

'The kids are very small. Mike is a good man and I know they'll want for nothing. Maybe they'll forget?'

Her eyes beseeched the only answer I could give.

'No, Norma, they won't forget. My own mother died when I was five. I miss her to this day.'

She nodded and tried to smile. Slowly she sat upright in the chair and smoothed her dressing-gown.

''Tis time to go back inside.'

For three endless weeks I broke the Body of Christ into smaller and smaller pieces as they held her upright to receive. The morning came when nurse just shook her head inside the door. Mike sat, awkward in his big overcoat, his open face creased with waiting. As I bent to touch her cheek she tugged her eyes open.

'Am I dying, boy?'

'Yes, Norma. Mike is here now and he'll stay with you.' She took our hands and turned to face her husband.

'Will you say the prayers, Father?'

The stilted words were ashes in my mouth. I faltered to a halt, laid down the book and prayed. 'This is a good woman, Lord. She has been a good wife and mother, loved by her own, and by those of us who have come to know her. She has suffered enough. We give her into your peace. Grant her rest now and let her go.'

Mike stretched across the bed and squeezed my arm. 'Thanks, Father.'

This was his place now; it was time for me to leave.

'I'll be below if you want me.'

The frost crunched like pebbles on the path. I felt cold to the bone, hollow and empty. Cork lay below me, asleep beneath the fog, a haze of yellow light rising from the silent docks.

Inside the flat I fumbled for the bottle in the press and drank to melt the lump of ice that lodged inside my chest. As the level dropped, the shadow-places filled with faces, faces leached of colour, luminous with the final flare of life. Faces that were white peaks and dark hollows. And the eyes, always the eyes, fearful or amazed, until they turned inside, untethering the soul. I tried to weave these phantoms into prayer; a prayer that often stumbled into some old comfort tune my father used to quell the demons of the dark:

> So tooreloo reloora loora lie bye,
> In your Daddy's arms you're creeping
> And soon you will be sleeping
> Toreloora loora loora loora lie.

A moment's panic as I realised that cracked and quavering voice was mine. I bit down hard upon my fist, fearing that the shakes would let me loose and I might howl and batter hard on Heaven's door and never ever stop.

33

IGNATIUS

A 'wilder' in his day, they said.
Could toe to hand the hard-fought ball
Or tacking through a reef of shoulders
Drop-kick home, to spume their wild applause.
All ebbed to dim reflection
In the body that betrayed him,
Took his legs and predeceased him,
Made his sky a patch of ceiling.
This Brother taught Melchisedech to dance
To watch the blossoms bud between the tombs
And when my steps moved surer to the tune
I heard him laughing.

There was an odd camaraderie among those who dealt in death, a rough and covert kindness that helped us take the strain. Like the Masons, we had our secret signs: a nod across the empty bed, a china cup of tea, conjured from among cracked mugs, a soft 'God keep you' at the closing of a late-night door. The undertakers assumed their rightful place among our group. Vested in sombre black, they moved through rituals as reverently as any priest, ambassadors between the living and the dead, ever watchful for the smallest deed that might assuage the pain. The O'Connors were an integral part of northside life and death, held in wry esteem by generations of potential customers. The older folk engaged in the sort of banter people use as a defence against the inevitable day.

'Hello, Mr O'Connor.'

'Hello, ma'am. How are you?'

'I'm grand, thank God. You needn't measure me at all yet.'

They measured, boxed and buried someone for all of us and were known to lose the bill when times were hard or someone hadn't 'chick nor child'. These mild-mannered men had an avuncular affection for the young priest. I remember one of them taking me for a stroll in the cemetery one wet day after a burial.

'Don't take me up wrong now, Father,' he said gently, 'but have you an overcoat?'

'I have,' I said defensively, 'but the oul' anorak is warmer.'

'Well now, that's true, but everyone else wears an overcoat for funerals. 'Tis more respectful, like.'

The petrol strike grounded my car and I took the bus to school. Riding upstairs, looking into back yards or steering the bus with the metal bar at the front had always been pleasures of my childhood.

'Hello, Christy boy.'

Fonsy, a great Glen hurler in his day, swayed up between the seats, his conductor's purse swinging on his hip like a gunslinger's holster. He plonked his feet on the floor and parked his bottom on the rail.

''Tis seldom enough we get one of ye,' he smiled.

'How much do I owe you, Fonsy?'

'Go away and have sense. Tell your father I was asking for him.'

I sat in dread of an inspector until we reached my stop and the bus exhaled me onto the pavement. I resolved to walk from then on but I couldn't walk to funerals. Mr O'Connor anticipated my problem. 'Go in the hearse with the lads.'

It was a funeral with a difference. Bertie was eighty years old and an orphan. At least he had none of his own that we could trace when he died as quietly and anonymously as he had lived. The graveyard was outside Mallow, a twisting twenty miles away from Cork, and I sat between the driver and his helper in the silver hearse. Conscious of Bertie lying in state behind, we were a bit subdued on the way out, steering the small talk into the safe waters of sport. The graveyard itself was a jungle of briars and tumbled stones. Apart from the officials, the two nuns from St Patrick's were the only mourners. There was a few bob somewhere in Bertie's family tree and he was to be interred in a vault. We had a moment of confusion as the undertaker searched for the entrance.

'Hello,' cried a voice from a nearby headstone, and a character emerged like Lazarus to the light. He was lanky and lean, a greyhound of a man with long legs in outsize wellies and a cap on his head that looked welded.

'De dead arose and appeared to many,' the driver whispered out of the side of his mouth. Undertakers, I discovered, were practised ventriloquists, capable of keeping up a ribald sub-commentary on the most sacred of occasions.

'Are ye lookin' for the door?' the apparition enquired. 'Tis down here,' he shouted and disappeared into a hole. Sure enough there was a small metal door set into the base of the vault wall. Hinges screeched with rust and indignation as our new-found guide forced entry. Eventually the cap emerged from the gloom. 'Dere's no room,' he declared.

'Well, we can't take him home,' one of the undertakers said blandly and jumped down to investigate. After much heaving and shoving, Bertie's ancestors were rearranged in their eternal slumber to make space for their descendant. 'Lave her down to me now,' said our friend, and the coffin was lowered by ropes until he fielded the front end to his chest. The lads upped the rear and pushed. Yer man backed into the vault. When the undertakers had climbed out, they dusted their knees and clasped their hands across their stomachs in readiness for prayer.

'I can't get out,' the voice called tremulously from the tomb. Mr O'Connor had another funeral waiting in Cork. With a flourish, he swept the sheet of plastic grass over the hole in the ground and anchored it with wreaths.

'We'll have the decade of the Rosary now, Father,' he said piously.

Glory be to God, I thought, we're burying a live man. I started the prayers as steadily as I was able. After the first Our Father, I noticed I was on a solo run, as the others coughed into handkerchiefs or leant on each other, laughing silently. At the end of the decade I had four half-moon dents in my palm from digging in my nails to avoid joining them.

The hearse rocked on its springs with high spirits as we sped home to Cork.

'Is this a Rolls, lads?'

''Tis, Father.'

'God, 'tis very quiet.'

'You could do a ton and hear nothing in this, Father.'

There was a straight stretch coming up and, to prove their point, they put the pedal to the floor. The Rolls responded with the exuberance of a pure-bred stallion, normally forced to trot between the traces.

'Lads, aisy on a small bit. What about the guards? We might get a summons.'

'Yerra, we'll say we're on a sick call,' they laughed, and the needle crept higher.

The summons that did come was one I had to answer. Ignatius was a Presentation Brother, bound to the bed by paralysis. He had a quick tongue, a sharp eye and legions of visitors. As well as his brothers of the cloth who tiptoed awkwardly to the wards in regular pilgrimage, he had a line of lay people who came for his counsel. It was as if the paralysis had released him from the inhibitions that curtail the rest of us. Ignatius had served his time in the silence of Melleray before joining the Brothers and when he said something it was because he had something to say. More than one pilgrim got such a straight talking to that it 'cured his cough'. I had no dispensation from his candour; Ignatius took no hostages.

My downfall was determined when I took the high moral ground on gossip. More than once I had a tearful nurse salting the breakfast boiled egg with a sorry tale of 'someone said'. Any institution can fall prey to loose talk and I undertook to use the power of my office to nip it in the bud.

That Sunday morning I closed the gospel and let them sit a moment in silence. I ran my finger slowly along the front of the pulpit, raised my finger to my lips and puffed.

'My dear friends,' I said solemnly, 'it would be easier for me to recover every grain of that dust than it would be for you to recover an unkind word spoken of another.'

The effect was a little spoiled by the fact that no pulpit in a nuns' chapel has ever known a single speck of dust. But they were dumbstruck and I was up and running, warming to my theme. Afterwards, still humming with righteousness, I was summoned by Ignatius.

'Fine sermon, Father,' he said gently. 'But you forgot who you were talking to.' I looked around the ward at souls who were carrying heavy burdens, and realised that my fine words had done nothing to lighten their load. It was an opportunity missed and I felt ashamed.

'Right, Brother,' I said meekly.

'Light a fag for me,' he said firmly and I knew I was forgiven. I lit the cigarette and placed it between his lips, holding the ashtray like an acolyte until the ash drooped like a diviner's rod.

'What do you think of the Jesuits?' he asked suddenly.

'A Jesuit is a man who can eat just one Tayto crisp,' I said lightly, kicking for touch.

'I had one of them here yesterday,' he continued, 'and he told me that Pope John XXIII would be in purgatory for a million years for calling the council.'

Like most priests of my generation, I had a vague affection for the fat little pope who was elected as a caretaker pontiff and then set about spring-cleaning the Church from spire to crypt.

'I don't agree, Brother.'

He stopped mid-drag on the fag, the smoke crinkling his eyes. I wondered if I had strayed outside the bounds of loyalty to the caste.

'And tell me now, Father,' he said seriously, 'would the likes of me end up in purgatory?'

This was a familiar theme. Many of the older people were so afraid of punishment in the next life that it overshadowed the little bit of life that remained to them here.

'Why would that happen, Brother?'

'Maybe I was a bit of a 'wilder' when I was young.'

'Maybe you were. Maybe we all were – and still are. But my father didn't love his saucy caffler any the less for it. And what sort of father would deny his child for being human? Didn't God love our humanity enough to send His son to bless it. No, Brother, there's too much talk about fault and not half enough about love.'

'You're preaching again,' he said, laughing, and added seriously, 'Were you a late vocation?'

'No, Brother, I was early, much too early I think. I got the notion at fifteen and held it. I often wonder would I be a better man and priest if I had waited.'

'"Might have" is a waste of time, boy,' he said firmly. 'I should know. But you're right about love. I see it here all about me in the nurses and the nuns and these other craythurs. I might have run too fast to ever see it if I had legs. You let the fag go out!'

Ignatius became my spiritual sparring partner, jabbing me back to earth whenever I left it. When I preached on daffodils coming up through concrete and talked of hope and the indomitable spirit for growth that God had planted in all of us, he reminded me of the patch of ceiling that was his horizon from dawn to dusk.

'Bring God's love out of the plaster, boy,' he challenged.

I tapped his wisdom as often as I tapped the ash from his cigarette, watching it glow between us like a sanctuary lamp.

I was kicking a ball with children in Mayfield when the call came. The candles were already burning and the oils laid ready. Around his bed the nurses who had turned him like a child knelt on the cold floor, many in tears. As soon as we finished the prayers, he sighed softly and his soul left him. For a moment I had a blurred vision of a young Brother holding his soutane with one hand while he lashed a football against a gable-end. Then I was sitting in the tiny chapel gallery wondering at the blood that poured from my nose to join the tears pooling in my lap.

34

CHRISTMAS

People rarely died at Christmas. An air of expectation seemed to permeate the wards and lighten heavy hearts. Throughout the hospital the transformation started early. Holy pictures sprouted holly as bewildered plaster saints anchored the sagging bunting. Plastic Santa faces bloomed on every door and Pat was obliged to limbo under the massive tree to get in or out of his cubbyhole. Catching him on all fours with tinsel in his teeth, I joked, 'Mecca is the other way.'

But he was already hip-deep in presents and ignored me. Families never forgot the courteous and kindly man who met them at the door of a place they held in dread.

Some people hate the hustle and bustle of Christmas. 'Sure 'tis only the one day' was a familiar refrain. One weary woman toiling up Shandon Street on Christmas Eve, laden down with bounty she could ill afford, was heard to remark, 'Tank God he didn't have a brudder.'

To us it was a time of escape from the round of death and dying. Just as some of our people lived beyond their expected span for a daughter's wedding or to hold a first grandchild, so too would they revive in preparation for the coming of the Christchild. It was a time when we could release the child in all of us, and the hospital buzzed with renewed energy. Every softhearted fella within a three-mile radius who could play the accordion, and more who couldn't, wound up gigging on the wards. Carol singers trooped the corridors to sing outside the doors, their young and rosy faces reflected in tired eyes, cracked and quavering voices joining in their chorus.

This was my third Christmas and my third time calling on Bríd to come and sing for us. She was a most talented singer who performed during the year in Bunratty Castle for the tourist brigade from the States. It was her affliction to be my cousin. This year, like every other, she answered the call and leant on her father, my uncle Joe, to transport herself and the harp to the hospital. As I lugged the harp from ward to ward, I often prayed fervently that she would be converted to the flute.

Bríd brought magic with her. I remember a lady who was on the Brompton Cocktail, a concoction of drugs designed to quell chronic pain. Sometimes it worked and sometimes it didn't. A patient in acute pain has little room in her for anyone or anything else. Her every waking hour is spent shoring up her energy against the next wracking wave of pain and then the next one after that. The nurses were doing their best to bring Lily some small comfort as Bríd set up the harp, and as her fingers stroked the strings to life, the delicate notes soothed the ward to silence.

'Fill, fill, a rún-o,' she sang. The old and plaintive air rose and fell and surged across the lined faces, a wave of beauty washing smooth their cares. It filled the eyes of young and old alike, and stilled. Then Lily whispered, 'Nurse, would you move a little, dear. I want to see that young wan.'

That sea-change travelled with the harp from room to room, leaving a blessed solace in its wake, until we came to Nora.

A month or more before, Nora had given up the fight and lapsed into a listless, almost catatonic state. We had tired of calling her from her private world and contented ourselves with stroking her hand or cheek as we would a calm, daydreaming child. Bríd settled herself on the stool, stilled her mind and leant into the harp: 'Mellow the moonlight to shine is beginning ...'

And again the small knot of people around the bed were loosened and lost to the soft hypnotic spinning of the wheel. As the last delicate notes trickled off and died, Nora spoke.

'Darling,' she asked in amazement, 'how did you know that this was my favourite song?'

She was back from the dead.

The excitement built to a climax for Christmas Eve and midnight mass. In most of the city churches midnight mass had moved back to nine o'clock. This was to avoid disruption from craythurs who had drunk 'not wisely but too well'. Sadly, the manger was becoming sanitised of earthy rough and tumble into ritual respectability. Because of our tiny chapel, we were reduced to the painful practice of handing out tickets. But at least we could be sure that those who had been part of our family throughout the year could sit at the table with us on this special night. The families on the hill trooped through the gate to kneel among the wheelchairs or line the walls. The children perched attentively on the altar steps until the little chapel seemed to swell and fill with warmth.

Sitting in the sacristy I could hear the expectant hum as the clock ticked towards midnight, and was wondering what few words I could say that would move through the microphone to the speakers in the wards and carry some measure of solace. Even the altar boys were subdued, as if they sensed the magic of the hour. Then, in a rustle of white vestments, we went out to greet the Child. It was usually a challenge to rescue the ritual from the dullness of overuse, but on this night I found the words startling and sweet and echoed back with strength in the responses. A senior nurse brought all her years of caring to the reading from Isaiah, moving with unpolished authority through promises of better times to come. The simplicity of the gospel story stilled us all to silence. This is not a night for preaching. The Word is best left undiluted by more words. I contented myself with giving the Christchild into their care, knowing that He would be in good and loving hands. We moved together through the mystery of the Eucharistic Prayer to the Consecration and a trembling of bells. And then they came to claim the Child with outstretched hands and swollen tongues, supported by a daughter, nurse or son.

And afterwards we sat, as friends sit after meals, easy in each other's company, and Bríd sang 'O Holy Night'. For a long time after the last notes had faded, I was afraid to speak and certain that they would be unable to respond. Then I roused myself to bless and let them go. My father and sisters went for tea with the other visitors and I went to the wards.

'We were in Heaven,' Nora said simply, holding the hands of her boy and girl.

Like every other meal, I had the Christmas dinner on my own. It was the way of things then. Throughout the day I watched cars come and go, and children dance to the door, laden with bright boxes. In the evening I saw the last ones leave the pool of light before the door, and watched it close again against another year. The visitors are the true heroes of our story, I thought. The quiet, faithful ones who take the bus and climb the steps in trepidation day after day to sit with Mam or Dad and then retrace their well-worn path across a city innocent of their pain. I see them now as steady stars, glowing in the dark around the beds. I see the twins who came, light-footed out from school to race the stairs and do their 'eck' on either side of Daddy's bed. I see a daughter 'mother' her mother, crooning to her to take a tiny sip as she nestles in the cradle of her arm. I see the three fine sons whose mother had survived the *Lusitania*, keeping loving vigil on the shore as she made ready for her final voyage. In time we'd gather in the mortuary and watch them shoulder Mammy home. Perhaps they'd call once more, a final pilgrimage to collect that small, sad bag of clothes.

The bunting was coiled in the biscuit tin to sleep another year. Winter counted up its toll of empty beds and ceded us to spring. Leaves, young and eager, stretched from tree to tree to shield us from the summer's glare. I had been three years in this place, as unaware of passing time as a boy who hovers with his kite is lost to the spinning of the world beneath his feet.

The priest was a spare, balding man with intense dark eyes barely contained behind his black-rimmed specs. He had a relative in the beds above and concelebrated mass with me each morning. As we folded our vestments on the bench, he told me he worked in the Catholic Communications Centre in Dublin and was on the lookout for his successor.

'You write a bit, Christy, don't you?'

'I do, Pat, but mostly for my own amazement.'

'You did the Thought for the Day on radio?'

'I did.'

'Yes, well, we'll see.'

In the business of the everyday it became a pebble in the shoe, a niggling thought and not much more. The bishop was his usual mixture of warmth and formality.

'I had a request from the Catholic Communications Centre. They want you to work there. Would you go?'

'Do you want me to?'

'I do.'

'Then I'll go.'

There was no other answer. I knew the score. None of us could stake our claim on anyone or any place. This was the cutting edge of priesthood; I could not expect exemption from the blade.

Mamma was quieter than usual. Unexpectedly she accepted the offer of tea and passed no remark on the untouched breakfast before me. We chatted with forced brightness about the new job and how different it would be. I couldn't sustain it and we fell silent again. She placed her cup and saucer on the table and stretched her hand to mine across the cloth. 'We'll miss you, Christy,' she said softly, and left the room.

Pat was like a mother hen, clucking busily in and out of the flat. 'Are you sure you have everything? The key, did you leave the key? Ah sure, I have it here in me pocket. I'm getting bothered.'

He tugged the last box of books into the porch. Now there was no more to be done and we had to face each other.

'My bladder was always too close to my eyes,' he said and held me very tightly. 'You'll come back and see us, boy, some time?'

I couldn't answer him. We could never have our time again and both of us knew that. Another priest would come and grow to love them, and two would be a crowd. My last memory is of looking back over my shoulder at the hospice that had been my home and life for three years and at the statue of the Sacred Heart in the garden. Still pointing at His broken heart and still looking the wrong way.

For three short years
I trod the winepress of their pain
Until I could no longer tell
Whose blood I wore upon my feet.
Their reaching out
Surprised my hidden self to love
To touch, caress and hold
To walk the water
Of a thousand tears
Or sit quite still
In their dark silence
Simply being awake.
The little music I could make
They savoured, stored
And measured back
A hundredfold to me.
And though I banged the Temple door
And flung my 'Why?' before His face
The morning brought me
Humble to the mill
That ground the kernel of their spirits fine
And there was in the wine
The blood their hearts had wept
While mine had slept.
And though I raised them up
With arms of lead
And leaden-tongued
Pronounced the words of life
I glimpsed a gleam of glory there
To spark and flare
Like fire on my clay,
That glazed my dross to shine
For yet another day.

Also available from
Mercier Press

LIFE AFTER LOSS
Helping the Bereaved

Christy Kenneally

What do you say after you've said 'Sorry for your trouble'?

This is not a book for the bereaved but for those of us
(all of us) who are unsure how to act and what to say when faced
with friends, family, loved ones, colleagues and acquaintances
who are bereaved.

Life After Loss was written for what Kenneally calls 'the second
circle' who are dealing with the bereavement of others.

Drawing on twenty years of lecturing, training and broadcasting
on the subject of bereavement, Kenneally has put together a
book strong on human interest, anecdote and even humour.
It is written in tribute to the countless people who told him
their own stories of bereavement.

ISBN 1-85635-243-9

PASSING THROUGH
Declan Hassett

Declan Hassett concludes his three-part memoir with this enchanting look back over the haunts and people of his youth; his varied career as a journalist in an emerging Ireland, his heroes from stage and field, and his hopes and dreams for the future of a country he loves so dearly.

Passing Through is a captivating read, a guided tour through the life of an original romantic in the town he loves so well.

ISBN 1-85635-446-6

BURIED MEMORIES
David Marcus

'*In my beginning was my end*, that encapsulated the story of my first volume of autobiography, so logically it was from there that any second one should take off: *In my end is my beginning*.'

Buried Memories is Marcus' second volume of autobiography, a unique and fascinating work which moves seamlessly between the fictional life of Cork's last Jew, Aaron Cohen, and memories from Marcus himself.

ISBN 1-86023-157-8